Practical Network Scanning

Capture network vulnerabilities using standard tools such as Nmap and Nessus

Ajay Singh Chauhan

BIRMINGHAM - MUMBAI

Practical Network Scanning

Commissioning Editor: Gebin George
Acquisition Editor: Shrilekha Inani
Content Development Editor: Ronn Kurien
Technical Editor: Manish Shanbhag
Language Support Editor: Storm Mann
Project Coordinator: Judie Jose
Proofreader: Safis Editing
Indexer: Mariammal Chettiyar
Graphics: Tom Scaria
Production Coordinator: Nilesh Mohite

First published: May 2018

Production reference: 1220518

Published by Packt Publishing Ltd.
Livery Place
35 Livery Street
Birmingham
B3 2PB, UK.

ISBN 978-1-78883-923-5

www.packtpub.com

mapt.io

Mapt is an online digital library that gives you full access to over 5,000 books and videos, as well as industry leading tools to help you plan your personal development and advance your career. For more information, please visit our website.

Why subscribe?

- Spend less time learning and more time coding with practical eBooks and Videos from over 4,000 industry professionals
- Improve your learning with Skill Plans built especially for you
- Get a free eBook or video every month
- Mapt is fully searchable
- Copy and paste, print, and bookmark content

PacktPub.com

Did you know that Packt offers eBook versions of every book published, with PDF and ePub files available? You can upgrade to the eBook version at www.PacktPub.com and as a print book customer, you are entitled to a discount on the eBook copy. Get in touch with us at service@packtpub.com for more details.

At www.PacktPub.com, you can also read a collection of free technical articles, sign up for a range of free newsletters, and receive exclusive discounts and offers on Packt books and eBooks.

About the author

Ajay Singh Chauhan is an experienced network and security architect, and he has been working extensively in the IT industry for 15 years. During his career, he has had varied responsibilities, ranging from looking after an entire IT infrastructure to providing network operations, implementation, and network design solutions.

Ajay works almost exclusively with large-scale cloud data center multivendor technologies. He contributes to the Cisco blogging platform by providing IT professionals with troubleshooting tips and tricks.

About the reviewer

Kuldeep Vilas Sonar is a cyber security expert with almost 8 years' comprehensive experience in various vertical fields of cyber security. His domain expertise is mainly in cybercrime investigations, vulnerability assessment, and penetration testing. He holds a master's degree in computer applications and several industry-recognized certifications, including CCNA, CCNA Security, CEH, IoT Security Essentials, and Cyber Security for IoT. He has delivered training and consultation for organizations in India, the U.S., and Singapore.

I would like to express my sincere gratitude to the many people who have been extremely helpful in technically reviewing this book. Special thanks to my teacher and inspiration Prof. Hemant Patil. I am always thankful to my mother, Ranjana; father, Vilas, wife, Sandhya; lovely son Ninad; and the rest of my family and friends, who always supported and encouraged me in spite of all the time it took me away from them.

Packt is searching for authors like you

If you're interested in becoming an author for Packt, please visit `authors.packtpub.com` and apply today. We have worked with thousands of developers and tech professionals, just like you, to help them share their insight with the global tech community. You can make a general application, apply for a specific hot topic that we are recruiting an author for, or submit your own idea.

Table of Contents

Preface

Network scanning is the process of building an inventory of IT infrastructure assets by identifying an active host on a network. Similar methods can be used by an attacker or network administrator to assess security. This procedure plays a vital role in risk assessment programs and the preparation of a security plan for your organization. *Practical Network Scanning* starts with the concept of network scanning and how organizations can benefit from it. Then, going forward, we delve into the different steps involved in scanning, such as service detection, firewall detection, TCP/IP port detection, and OS detection. We also implement these concepts using a few of the most prominent tools on the market, such as Nessus and Nmap. In the concluding chapters, we prepare a complete vulnerability assessment plan for your organization. By the end of this book, you will have hands-on experience of performing network scanning using different tools and in choosing the best tools of your system.

Who this book is for

If you are a network and security professional who is responsible for securing an organization's network infrastructure, then this book is for you.

What this book covers

`Chapter 1`, *Fundamental Security Concepts*, explains the necessity for network security and covers a step-by-step approach to keep in mind for securing a network. You will also learn how to identify the need for security and the factors involved in network security.

`Chapter 2`, *Secure Network Design*, explains the security threats that exist in modern networks and how to design a secure network by keeping them in mind. It also explains network segmentation, defining a network boundary, and the importance of encryption, things to consider, and the benefits of implementing security on different network layers.

`Chapter 3`, *Server-Level Security*, gives us a basic understanding of protecting a server's infrastructure, including aspects such as hardening the server, the use of various authentication methods, password policies, and protection against viruses and malware.

`Chapter 4`, *Cloud Security Design*, explains the security aspects that you will need to keep in mind before migrating your critical data information to the cloud.

`Chapter 5`, *Application Security Design*, explains how to identify the common risks involved in designing and launching an application. You will also learn common safeguard methods from a user's point of view to surf an application in a secure way.

`Chapter 6`, *Threat Detection and Response*, explains various aspects of security IT infrastructure, from monitoring to responding to incidents and diverting attackers.

`Chapter 7`, *Vulnerability Assessment*, explains the vulnerability assessment methodology and generating reports based on assessment metrics for scoring.

`Chapter 8`, *Remote OS Detection*, explains methods for detecting a target's operating system with an Nmap application.

`Chapter 9`, *Public Key Infrastructure – SSL*, explains PKI and the implementation steps for securing an application using SSL.

`Chapter 10`, *Firewall Placement and Detection Techniques*, explains the aspects of designing a firewall to build secure network. It also explains the techniques and tools to detect firewall.

`Chapter 11`, *VPN and WAN Encryption*, explains how to design and secure a WAN infrastructure.

`Chapter 12`, *Summary and Scope of Security Technologies*, explains security trends and possible future security technologies.

To get the most out of this book

To understand the content of this book, it is recommended that you have basic knowledge of computer networks. If you are certified with CCNA network and security, that will be a good foundation for you to advance your knowledge about computer networks by reading this book.

As you know, it does not make sense to learn about computer networks without doing any practical work. Therefore, it is suggested that you practice TCP/IP, IP Packet Flow, Basic network design and setting up a LAN with at least a Cisco switch and router. Download emulators and simulators such as PuTTY and Tera Term, Packet Tracer and GNS3, Wireshark, Nmap, Nessus. All of the download links are included in the book.

Download the color images

We also provide a PDF file that has color images of the screenshots/diagrams used in this book. You can download it from `https://www.packtpub.com/sites/default/files/downloads/PracticalNetworkScanning_ColorImages.pdf`.

Conventions used

There are a number of text conventions used throughout this book.

`CodeInText`: Indicates code words in text, database table names, folder names, filenames, file extensions, pathnames, dummy URLs, user input, and Twitter handles. Here is an example: "For Linux, `sudo iptables -L` lists your current rules in `iptables`."

Any command-line input or output is written as follows:

```
netstat -antp | grep "LISTEN"
```

Bold: Indicates a new term, an important word, or words that you see onscreen. For example, words in menus or dialog boxes appear in the text like this. Here is an example:

Most of us share our personal information on many web portals by clicking **I Agree** or **I Accept the Terms and Conditions**

Warnings or important notes appear like this.

Tips and tricks appear like this.

Get in touch

Feedback from our readers is always welcome.

General feedback: Email `feedback@packtpub.com` and mention the book title in the subject of your message. If you have questions about any aspect of this book, please email us at `questions@packtpub.com`.

Errata: Although we have taken every care to ensure the accuracy of our content, mistakes do happen. If you have found a mistake in this book, we would be grateful if you would report this to us. Please visit `www.packtpub.com/submit-errata`, selecting your book, clicking on the Errata Submission Form link, and entering the details.

Piracy: If you come across any illegal copies of our works in any form on the Internet, we would be grateful if you would provide us with the location address or website name. Please contact us at copyright@packtpub.com with a link to the material.

If you are interested in becoming an author: If there is a topic that you have expertise in and you are interested in either writing or contributing to a book, please visit `authors.packtpub.com`.

Reviews

Please leave a review. Once you have read and used this book, why not leave a review on the site that you purchased it from? Potential readers can then see and use your unbiased opinion to make purchase decisions, we at Packt can understand what you think about our products, and our authors can see your feedback on their book. Thank you!

For more information about Packt, please visit `packtpub.com`.

1
Fundamental Security Concepts

In an ever-evolving world of technology, security and data privacy are of paramount importance. This chapter will address some of the basic concepts of IT infrastructure security. In order to secure a system, the key task is to identify and classify the information assets and define a security framework.

This chapter will cover what security means to network and system administrators. It will also explore how to build a secure network, incorporating the security principles defined in your framework.

Let's get started with network infrastructure security. We will cover the following topics in this chapter:

- Why security?
- Building blocks of information security
- Computer security
- Network security
- Internet security
- Security issues, threats, and attacks

Why security?

As the internet grows and technology evolves for modern computer networks, network security has become one of the most crucial factors for everyone. This includes everyone from end users and **small and medium-sized businesses** (**SMBs**) to cloud service providers.

Due to a growing volume of network attacks, network security should be a priority when designing network architecture. To understand the importance of this, imagine what could happen if there was a network integrity breach at a bank, stock exchange, or other financial database.

The importance of network security is not just limited to the IT industry. It is also important within industries such as health care. Health records contain some of the most valuable information available, including Social Security numbers, home addresses, and patient health histories. If this data is accessed by unauthorized persons, it can be stolen or sold to the black market.

Security awareness is important for everybody and not just the IT department. If you work with internet enabled devices, it's your responsibility too. However, you can only control information security once you know how to secure it.

No one can get into your system until something is compromised. Similarly, if your door is locked from the outside, nobody can enter your house unless they gain access to a duplicate key or have a similar key built by getting physical access to the lock. A few examples of how a system might be compromised are as follows:

- A targeted email could be sent to random users with an attachment (Drive by Download). If a user opened that attachment, their system would be compromised.
- An email is received which poses as a domain such as banking and asks you to change your password through a provided link. Once you do this, your username and password can be stolen.
- If a small typo is made when typing a website address into a browser, a similar page may open (**Phishing**) which is not genuine, and your credentials can be stolen.
- Features provided by websites for resetting forgotten passwords can also be very risky. Let's say somebody knows my email ID and attempts to access my account by selecting a **forgotten password** option. If the security question asks for my date of birth, this can easily be found on my resume.
- A password for an Excel file can easily be broken by a brute-force attack.
- The most widespread types of ransomware encrypt all or some of the data on your PC, and then ask for a large payment (the ransom) in order to restore access to your data.

- During DNS hijacking, an online attacker will override your computer's TCP/IP settings so that the DNS translation gets altered. For example, typing in `abc.com` will translate it into this IP: `140.166.226.26`. However, a DNS hijacker will alter the translation so that `abc.com` will now send you the IP address of a different website.
- Denial of Service network attacks disrupt the normal volume of traffic sent to targeted services with excessive amounts of traffic. This can be damaging in various ways. One example could be if a company has a Friday sale, and a competitor launches an attack on them in order to shut their services down and consequently increase their own sales.

According to research by British insurance company Lloyd's, *the damage from hacks cost businesses $400 billion a year.*

To further explore the cost of cybercrimes, visit the following webpage: `https://www.forbes.com/sites/stevemorgan/2016/01/17/cyber-crime-costs-projected-to-reach-2-trillion-by-2019/#612db25c3a91`.

The market research firm Gartner estimates that global spending on cybersecurity is somewhere around $96 billion in 2018. By 2020, companies around the world are expected to spend around $170 billion—a growth rate of nearly ten percent in the next five years.

Building blocks of information security

Your data can be easily separated into the following three categories. This is especially important to know in order to determine the value of your data before planning for security:

- **Low Business Impact** (**LBI**): If LBI data is disclosed, limited information loss could occur. Examples of this kind of data include name, gender, and/or the country of residence.
- **Moderate Business Impact** (**MBI**): If MBI data is disclosed, disastrous information loss could occur, which directly damages the reputation of an organization. Examples of MBI data include first and last name, email ID, mailing address, and phone number.
- **High Business Impact** (**HBI**): If HBI data is disclosed, serious information loss could occur. Access and permission must be controlled and limited to a need-to-know basis. Examples of HBI data include government IDs, credit card information, medical health records, passwords, and real-time location.

Proper security control measures are required to ensure tight security. The following flowchart helps us to understand the security process:

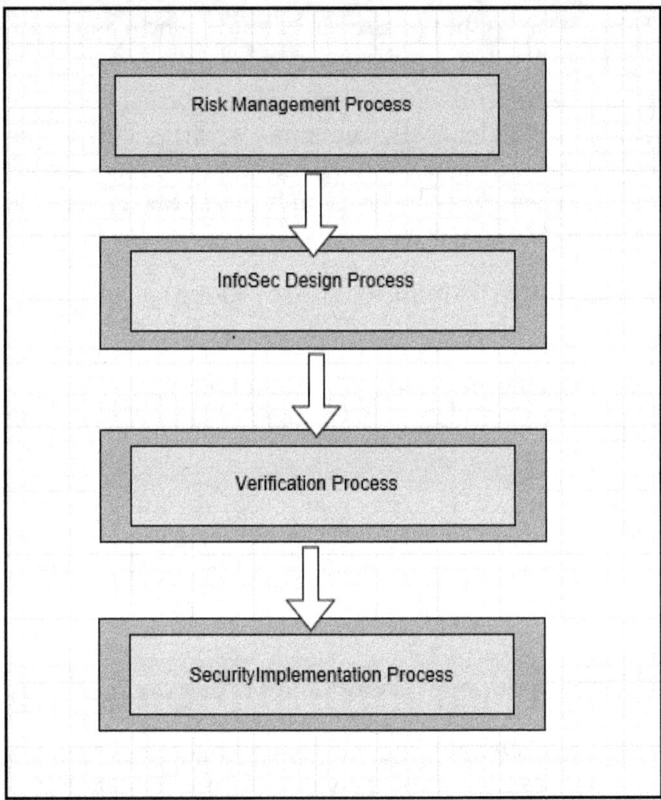

- **Risk Management Process**: This is particularly important when designing a secure network. Risk management analysis must be done in advance as this aids designing secure infrastructure. Steps should include risk identification, risk analysis, risk ranking, and mitigation plans. For example, an ISP link can be a public or private **Wide Area Network** (**WAN**) connection. Data transfer between two sites over public infrastructure can be secured by implementing VPNs. Data transfer between two sites over private links can be future encrypted by link device. The purpose and funding of connection must be identified, and a proper risk assessment must be carried out before installing or activating any links.

- **InfoSec Design Process**: Perimeter boundaries must be defined and documented. For example, connecting to WAN internet or connecting to another location over WAN must be defined. When I say *boundaries*, we should always take a layered approach. There is no ideal situation to ensure 100% security, but by implementing security on every layer, you can ensure tight security. A layered security method encompasses both technological and non-technological safety measures.
  For example, perimeter security can be protected by firewalls. Infrastructure details, such as server type and services running on the system, must be identified. Software and operating system bugs should be documented. IP space and security zones should be defined. System admin access should be controlled by security groups.

- **Verification process**: The purpose of the verification process for each extranet/intranet connection is to generate all audit evidence documented in the compliance procedures of the security design. This will have information about users, remote IP, and tasks performed by them. Network scanning, penetration testing, and scorecard reporting provide an in-depth view of infrastructure security.
  A periodic audit is always required in order to know if there is unexpected activity. Firewall logs, TCP/IP headers from load balancers on IIS, and two-factor authentications are examples of a verification process.

- **Security implementation process**: At this stage you should have the following items ready to be implemented:
    - Security policies—password policies and access control
    - Disaster recovery plan
    - Backup and recovery plan
    - WAN recovery plan
    - Network security zones
    - Database security
    - IIS or web security
    - Data and asset classification
    - Data encryption
    - Resource control for application users
    - Operating system security
    - Incident management and response
    - Change management and version control

Computer security

Computer security is not all about end user computing, it also includes server/application infrastructure. For any data transfer between server and client, both ends should be secure. Even the communication channel should be secure enough to avoid data theft.

We know that professionals understand network security, but how about end users? We can force users to implement security strategies, but is that enough? For better security, awareness is key. Security issues are constantly being found with the software we use every day, including common and reliable programs such as Windows, Internet Explorer, and Adobe's PDF Reader. It is therefore very important that we take some simple steps towards becoming more secure.

People often think of computer security as something technical and complicated, but that is not strictly the case. In the following, we will explore the most basic and important things you should do in order to make yourself safer online:

- Use antivirus and antimalware and know which links are safe to click in emails
- Be careful about programs you download and run; don't trust your pop-up notifications
- On the server level, encryption chips can be used just to avoid physical theft of hardware

Most computer facilities continue to protect their physical assets far better than their data, even when the value of the data is several times greater than the value of the hardware.

Since awareness is especially important, we should also consider how much awareness we have within the organization. This can simply be achieved by sending a few emails that look genuine and getting the statistics of how many users opened such an email. Activities can be tracked in terms of number. For example, the statistics can be viewed for how many users shared their password and how many downloaded an attachment.

Network security

With today's complex network architecture and constantly growing networks, protecting data and maintaining confidentiality play a very important role. Complex networks consist of network traffic flowing between enterprise networks, data center networks and, of course, the cloud as well. A secure network helps us to protect against data loss, cyber-attacks and unauthorized access, thus providing a better user experience. Network security technologies equip multiple platforms with the ability to deal with the exact protection requirements.

Firewalls

A firewall is a network security appliance that accepts or rejects traffic flow based on configured rules and preconfigured policies. Placement of a firewall totally depends on the network architecture, which includes protection for network perimeters, subnets, and zones. Perimeter firewalls are always placed on a network's edge to filter packets entering the network. Perimeter firewalls are the first layer of security, and if malicious traffic has managed to bypass, host-based firewalls provide another layer of protection by allowing or denying packets coming into the end host device. This is called the multilayer security approach. Multiple firewalls can be set up to design a highly secure environment.

Firewalls are often deployed in other parts of the network to provide proper segmentation and data protection within enterprise infrastructure, on access layers and also in data centers.

Firewalls can be further classified as the following:

- Simple packet filtering
- Application proxy
- Stateful inspection firewalls
- Next-Generation Firewall

A traditional firewall provides functions such as **Packet Address Translation** (**PAT**), **Network Address Translation** (**NAT**), and **Virtual Private Network** (**VPN**). The basic characteristic of a traditional firewall is that it works according to the rules. For example, a user from subnet (`10.10.10.0/24`) wants to access Google DNS `8.8.8.8` on a UDP port `53`.

A typical firewall rule will look like this:

Source IP	Destination IP	Protocol	Port	Action
`10.10.10.0/24`	`8.8.8.8/32`	UDP	`53`	Permit

However, Next-Generation Firewall works based on application and user-aware policies. Application-level control allows you to set policies depending on the user and the application.

For example, you can block **peer-to-peer** (**P2P**) downloads completely or disable Facebook chat without even blocking Facebook.

We will discuss firewalls in detail in upcoming chapters. The following diagram reflects zones and connectivity, which shows how firewall zones connect to multiple businesses:

- **Demilitarized zone (DMZ)**: Internet-facing applications are located in DMZ. Other services on other zones remain inaccessible to the internet. The most common services placed in DMZ include email services, FTP servers, and web servers.
- **Inside zone**: The inside zone is known as the trusted zone to users. Applications in that area are considered highly secure. In the trusted area, security is maintained by denying all traffic from less trusted zones in any given firewall by default.
- **Cloud and internet zone**: Let's not focus on naming these. They are standard segments we see on an enterprise network. These zones are considered to be below security zones.

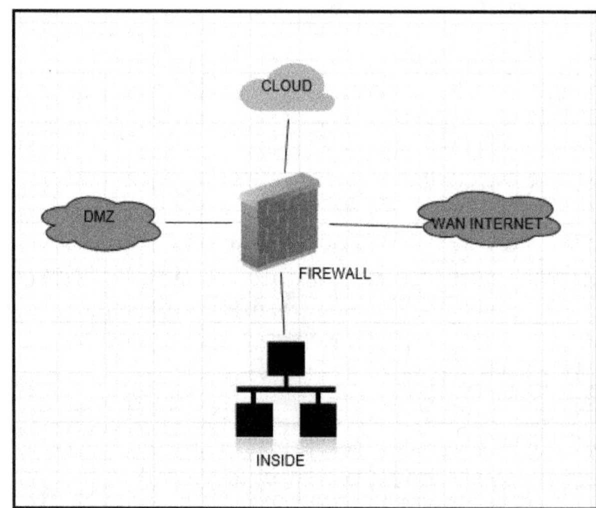

Intrusion detection systems / intrusion prevention systems

There is a high chance that attacks may enter a network. **Intrusion prevention system** (**IPS**) / **Intrusion detection system** (**IDS**) is a proactive measure to detect and identify suspicious or undesirable activities that indicate intrusion. In IDS, deployment can be online or offline, and the basic idea is to redirect traffic you wish to monitor. There are multiple methods like switch port SPAN or fiber optic TAP solution, which can be used to redirect traffic. Pattern matching is used to detect known attacks by their signature and anomalies. Based on the activity, monitoring alerts can be set up to notify the network administrator.

As the following diagram shows, SPAN port is configured on a switch in order to redirect traffic to the IDS sensor. An actual SPAN port creates a copy of data flowing for a specific interface and redirects it to another port on the switch:

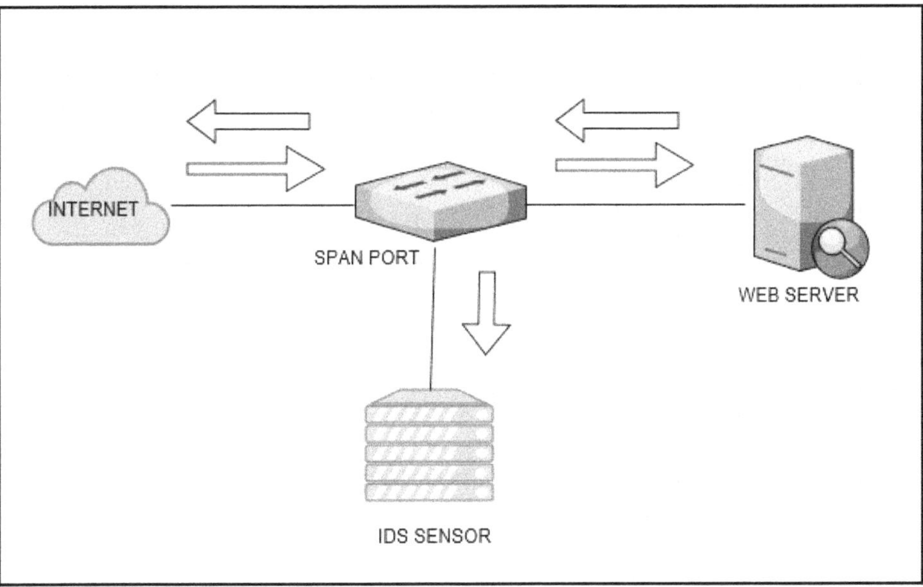

IPS offers proactive detection and prevention against unwanted network traffic. In an inline placement of IPS, all the traffic will travel via IPS devices. Based on the rules, actions can then be taken. When a signature is detected on an IPS device it can be used for resetting, blocking, and denying connections, as well as logging, monitoring, and alarming. A system admin can also define a policy-based approach with defined policy violation rules and actions to keep in mind when well-known signatures are released. Actions should be defined by the system admin.

The following diagram shows a topology for inline setup of IPS. All the traffic travels through IPS devices for traffic inspection. This is a bit different to doing a port SPAN, since all data goes through an IPS box. Consequently, you should be aware of what type of data has to be inspected:

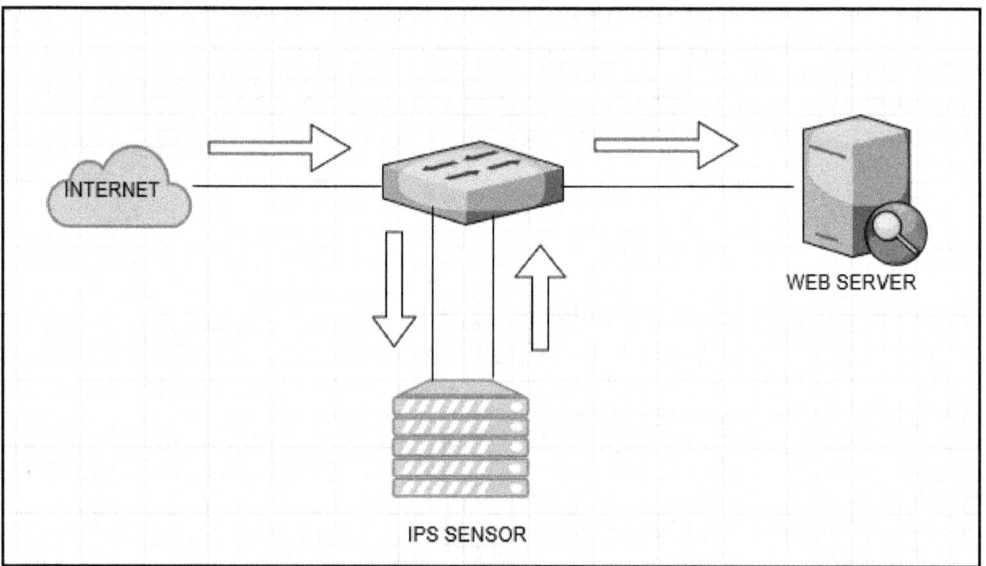

There are a number of different attack types that can be prevented using an IPS, including:

- Denial of Service
- Distributed Denial of Service
- Exploits
- Worms
- Viruses

Multitier topology

Multitier topology gives you flexibility to segment resources based on role and access policies. In a typical three-layer application, architecture that has web, app, and DB servers can be distributed based on location. Since web/app zone is something always exposed to end users, **Demilitarized Zone** (**DMZ**) IP space is always public. Subnet and database servers should not be directly accessible, hence why we should always allocate private IP space from RFC 1918.

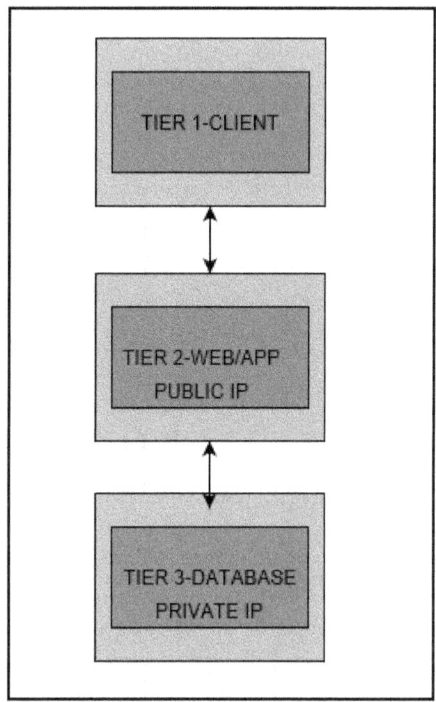

This offers gradual access to control, based on IPs and resource locations. When designing a network, you can introduce a multi-layer firewall approach. In a multiple layer design approach, the basic idea is to isolate resources from each other, considering the fact that if one layer is compromised then others are not impacted.

Cross-premises IPsec tunneling provides you with a way to establish secure connections between two networks and multiple on-premises sites, or other virtual networks in Azure/AWS. This can secure data transfer by encrypting your data via the IPsec encryption using the IPsec framework. Virtual networks in AWS are called VPC and, in Azure, VNET.

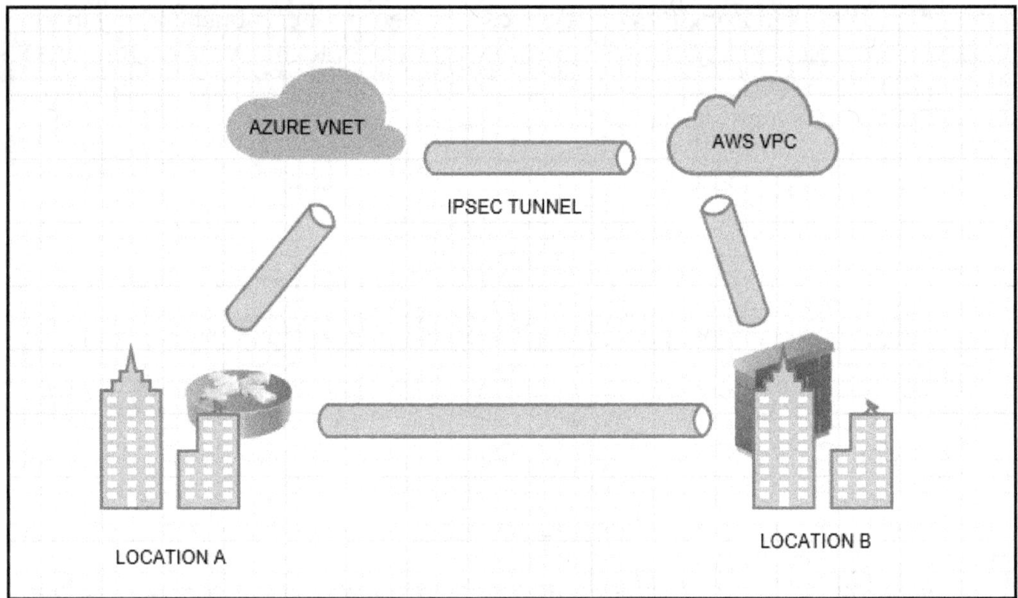

Distributed Denial of Service: A **Denial-of-Service** (**DoS**) attack or **Distributed Denial-of-Service** (**DDoS**) attack is an attempt to make a network resource out of service to its targeted users.

The real-world target would be online services such as e-commerce and the gaming industry, preventing the shop from doing any business by making front resources unavailable for end users. Just think about a situation during big billion-day sales hours if someone launches a DDOS attack and makes your e-commerce portal shut down.

The two most basic types of DDoS attacks are as follows:

- **WAN attacks**: WAN DDoS attacks utilize available bandwidth on physical links with a high volume of packets with bigger payloads, or a high volume of packets with smaller payloads. Bigger payload network resources such as router or firewalls will process packets and consume all the bandwidth. With smaller payload network resources like routers, firewalls will try to process all the packets. However, due to limited CPU, cycle hardware resources won't be able to process genuine packets from end users and can fail under the load.

  For example, let's assume you have a 10 Mbps WAN link and during attack BW, utilization is just 5 Mbps. However, a number of small packets can reach one million packets per second. In this case, assume that your network gear has no CPU cycle to process all tiny packets

  Another example would be if someone launched a DDOS attack using a large ICMP packet. This can choke your bandwidth and leave no space for the rest of the application.

  The most common form of bandwidth attack is a packet-flooding attack, in which a large number of legitimate TCP, **User Datagram Protocol** (**UDP**), or **Internet Control Message Protocol** (**ICMP**) packets are directed to a targeted or aimed destination. Such attacks become more difficult to detect if attackers use techniques such as spoofing source addresses.

- **Application attacks**: These DDoS attacks use the expected behavior of protocols such as TCP and HTTP. Application attacks are disruptive but small and silent in nature and extremely hard to detect since they use expected behavior. Application-layer attacks are easy to generate and require fewer packets with a small payload to achieve out of services for targeted applications. Application attacks are focused on web-application layers. For a small HTTP request, the actual server has to execute a lot of resources on the web server to fetch the content or resources. Every such server resource will have limited CPU and memory and can be easily targeted. In this example, I am not considering cloud-based web applications, where you have elasticity features enabled and with growth in the number of requests, server resources are automatically created to accommodate such requests.

Let us understand more about this with the help of an example:

- **HTTP Floods**: These are simple attacks in nature that try to access the same web page again and again in an automated fashion. They typically use the same range of IP addresses. Based on the trend, as this is being originated from the same source, the source pool can be blocked to mitigate attacks.
- **Randomized HTTP Floods**: These are complex attacks that use a large pool of IP addresses from multiple locations and randomize the URLs. Since these kind of attacks originate from multiple locations, it is not easy to block the source IP. However, the rate limit can be fixed on server resources.

To simplify, DDoS is a form of attack where multiple compromised networks/hosts are used to target a single system. This is like a zombie attack and it is very tough to identify genuine users. Once infected, the internet-connected devices become part of a botnet army, driving malicious traffic toward a given target.

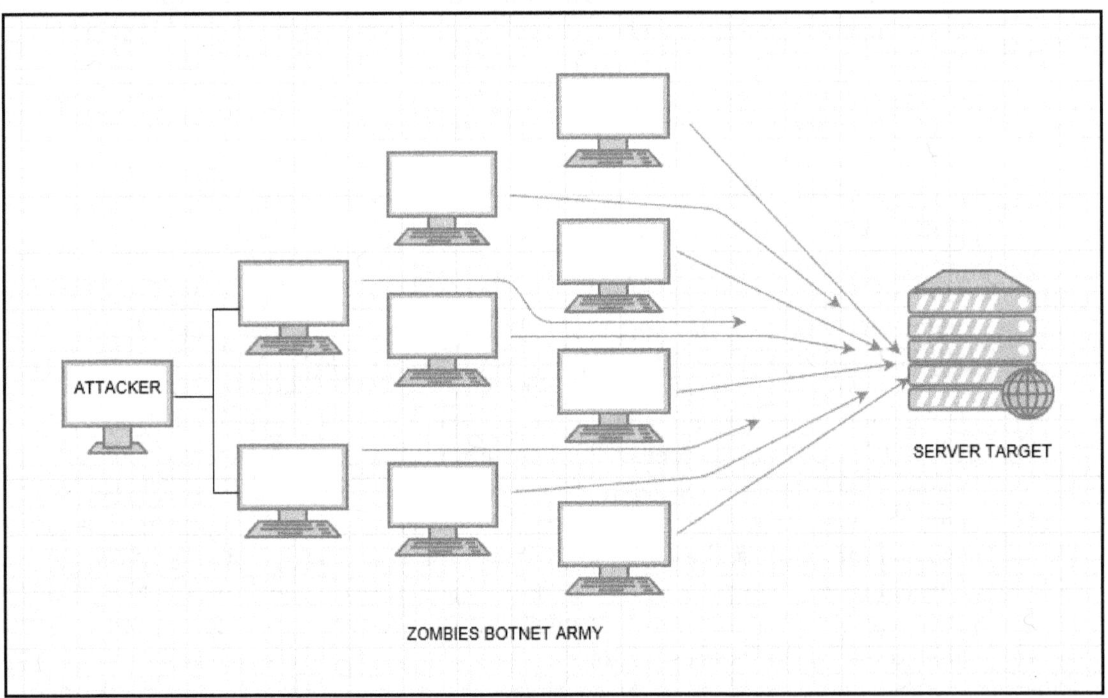

Internet security

These are the basic things you need to understand when you are working with online systems. When working with them day to day, we expose ourselves to risks.

Let's jump into the basic components of internet security.

Password

Since we own internet enabled devices, we are responsible for our own security. So, let's begin with our passwords. As users, we must choose a strong password. Alternatively, organizations should encourage users to choose one.

Password analysis shows that quite a common password used by users is `123456` and other similar, simple patterns. Most users choose the same password across multiple platforms. If a server or database is compromised by hackers, it would be easy to crack passwords such as this.

Few common web portals contain personal information. However, if an employee is required to create a username consisting of their first and last name or employee ID, and this is combined with a simple default password such as `abcX123`, then their information is easy to guess.

System upgrade and updates

The WannaCry ransomware attack was a worldwide cyberattack in May 2017 triggered by the WannaCry ransomware crypto worm. This attack targeted computers running the Microsoft Windows operating system by encrypting data and demanding ransom payments in the Bitcoin cryptocurrency. Such infection happens because people are running outdated software and attackers exploit this. This is not limited to PCs but also to mobile devices and other internet enabled devices.

Phishing

Phishing is a form of online fraud where you receive an email that looks similar to a trusted source. The message may ask you to validate, confirm, or update your account information by logging into fake websites. Targets are contacted via telephone, email, and text message, which are used to extract credit card details and passwords.

This is my own email box, which contains a message stating that I am supposed to get 13,17422 INR, and I need to update my details. While the attacker is using money as a temptation tool, it is important to think instead about your IT return. Is this type of mail really to be expected from the IT department? You can easily guess that this is not a genuine domain just by looking at the email header. Following the instructions of this message can consequently have disastrous consequences:

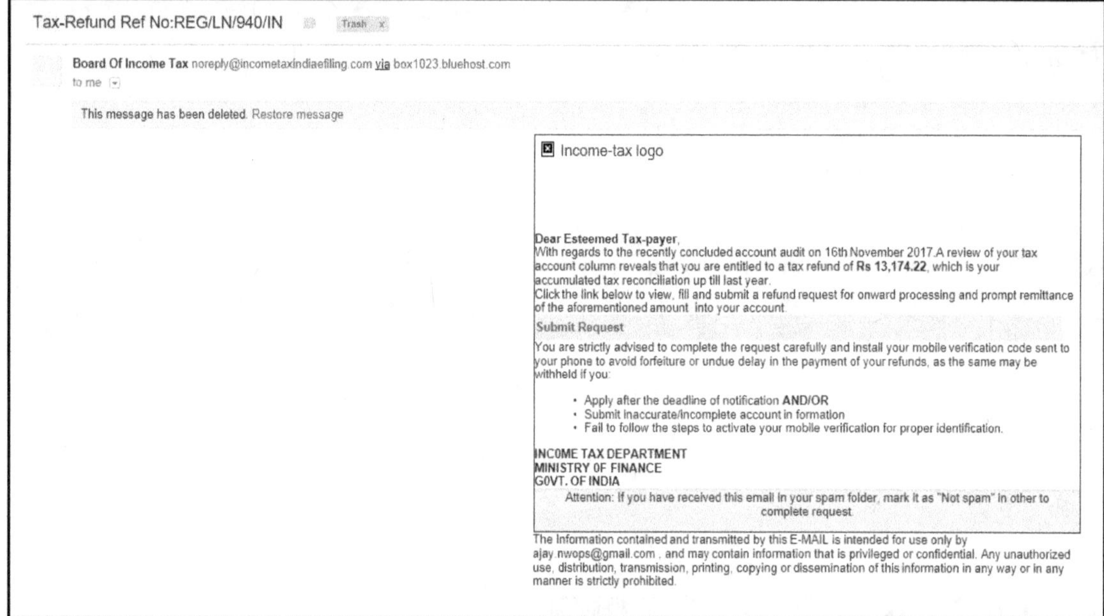
Tax-Refund Ref No:REG/LN/940/IN Trash x

Board Of Income Tax noreply@incometaxindiaefiling.com via box1023.bluehost.com
to me

This message has been deleted. Restore message

Income-tax logo

Dear Esteemed Tax-payer,
With regards to the recently concluded account audit on 16th November 2017.A review of your tax account column reveals that you are entitled to a tax refund of **Rs 13,174.22**, which is your accumulated tax reconciliation up till last year.
Click the link below to view, fill and submit a refund request for onward processing and prompt remittance of the aforementioned amount into your account.

Submit Request

You are strictly advised to complete the request carefully and install your mobile verification code sent to your phone to avoid forfeiture or undue delay in the payment of your refunds, as the same may be withheld if you:

- Apply after the deadline of notification **AND/OR**
- Submit inaccurate/incomplete account in formation
- Fail to follow the steps to activate your mobile verification for proper identification.

INCOME TAX DEPARTMENT
MINISTRY OF FINANCE
GOVT. OF INDIA

Attention: If you have received this email in your spam folder, mark it as "Not spam" in other to complete request.

The Information contained and transmitted by this E-MAIL is intended for use only by ajay.nwops@gmail.com , and may contain information that is privileged or confidential. Any unauthorized use, distribution, transmission, printing, copying or dissemination of this information in any way or in any manner is strictly prohibited.

Beware of phishing phone calls

Attackers might call you on the phone and offer to solve your computer problems by selling you a software license or by obtaining your personal information in order to update your details in a backend system.

Once they've gained your trust, cybercriminals might ask for your username and password or ask you to go to a website to install software that will let them access your computer in order to fix it. Once you do this, your computer and your personal information is hijacked.

In the same way, a banking fraud can take place. This includes cybercriminals calling you and trying to persuade you to share your credit card and banking details.

Some signs of phishing phone calls include:

- You have been specially selected for any offering
- You have won money in a lottery
- You have income tax refund
- Someone asking about credit card CVV and other details to update a banking database

Phishing protection

Phishing attack protection requires steps to be taken by both users and enterprises. For users, awareness is the key. A spoofed message often contains some mistakes that expose its true identity. These can include spelling mistakes or changes to domain names, as seen in the earlier URL example. Users should also stop and think about why they're even receiving such an email or phone call.

You should report such emails to authorities so that appropriate actions can be taken.

Security issues, threats, and attacks

Every day we use our computers and phones to connect to the internet, open emails, do online transactions, check our social media, create files, take photos of our friends, family or favorite places.

IoT security risk

The next big thing, which is going to play a big role in our life, is going to be **Internet of Thing** (**IoT**). Everything will be connected to the internet—fans, tube lights, refrigerators, doors, cars, even in medical terms, our heart—could be connected to an IoT sensor. This list will be long. Think about the situation if a person's heart rate controlled by an IoT sensor is hacked.

One of the most prominent IoT security issues is the problem with individuals using the same login credentials for everything.

Computer security risk

Computer security risks are events that may damage or steal data or allow unauthorized access to a computer without notifying the user. Your computer is all about operating systems and applications, the majority of such attacks come along with malicious applications, or bad software, in other words. It is commonly believed that all damages are only done by computer viruses, but in reality there are several types of bad software. Features such as back door, dialer, spyware, virus and worm, key logger, adware, and many more can result in a computer security risk.

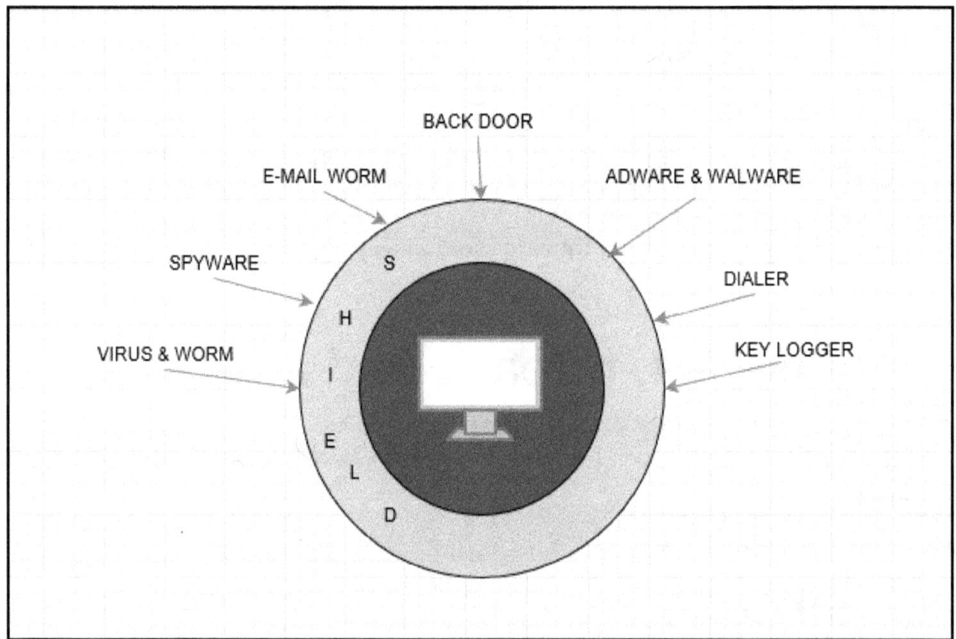

Security Risk-Border Gateway Protocol

In the networking world, imagine a situation where attackers plug their cable into your network, establish a **Border Gateway Protocol** (**BGP**) session, and sniff all the data going into the wire. This is not limited to sniffing your information, but you can cause a lot of trouble for others.

For example:

- **YouTube blockage by PTA**:
    - **Scenario**: Pakistan telecom was connected to the global internet via PCCW telecom
    - **Problem**: PCCW did not validate a prefix advertised by Pakistan telecom and there was no built-in mechanism in the BGP protocol to authenticate information
    - **Impact**: DoS to customers, traffic redirection, prefix hijacking, and AS hijacking
- On 24 February 2008, **Pakistan Telecom Authority** (**PTA**) began to advertise a specific prefix of YouTube. PTA intended to block access to YouTube in Pakistan and advertised the specific prefix `208.65.153.0/24`. This was part of the prefix used by YouTube `208.65.152.0/22-208.65.155.255`. The intention was that YouTube's traffic would be forwarded to Null0 interface and, consequently, YouTube would get blocked within Pakistan. However, the same route was advertised to upstream ISP (PCCW AS number `3491`). PCCW presented this information to other peers as well. YouTube then initiated a more specific prefix (`208.65.153.128/25`) to recover traffic.

- **MAN in the Middle (MITM)**: This is another example. Think about a situation in which someone from your organization can do the sniffing inside your network by configuring SPAN for switch where all finance employees are connected. All username and password information can be extracted if they are not using a secure way to access the finance portal. This is the reason I say there should be HTTPS for everything. Even hackers can gain access to sniff data, but they cannot decode encrypted data from the system. All these types of hacking come under MITM where attackers have access to data wire or are able to divert traffic.

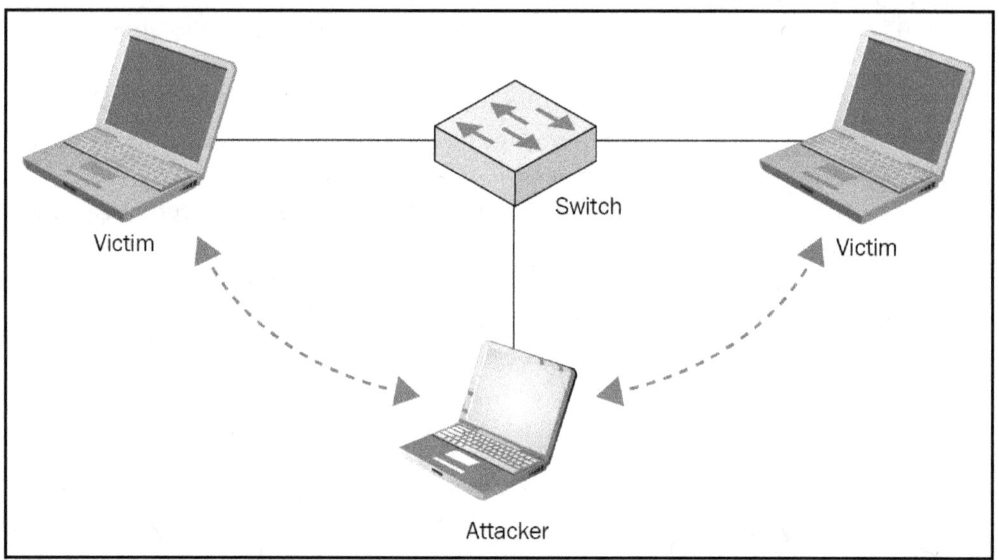

- **Address Resolution Protocol** (**ARP**): Spoofing can be a similar kind of attack. For local area network-address resolution protocol, it is required to know the computer identity on **Local Area Network** (**LAN**). Let's assume you are internet gateway configured in your LAN and all the internet traffic travels via that device. The attacker can do the ARP-spoofing and advertise a new system as an internet gateway. Now all the traffic for internet goes through the attacker's system, and they can sniff your data. There are many tools available on the market for spoofing, which do nothing but change the MAC address of your machine.

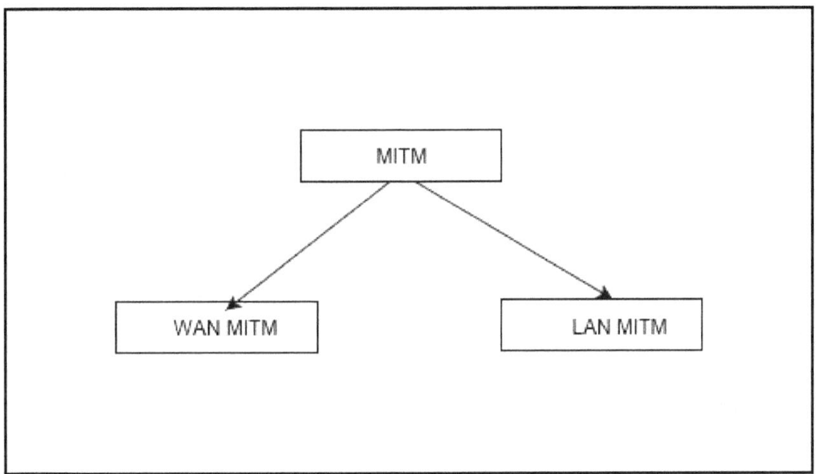

MITM attacks can be further divided into two categories: WAN and LAN.

Security and threats

In a growing connected world, security threats are constantly evolving to find new ways to steal or damage data. For any organization and any individual who has an internet enabled system, it becomes very important to protect that information. Malicious or ignorant human activity are major threats to computers. Malicious action always has a goal to achieve and a specific target to be attacked.

Attackers generally have motives or goals. These motives and goals usually abide by the following formula:

Motive + Method + Vulnerabilities = Attack:

As the following diagram shows, security threats are driven either by humans or natural disasters. Threats driven by humans can be further categorized into external or internal threats, or can be put down to user ignorance. We will discuss each of these in detail:

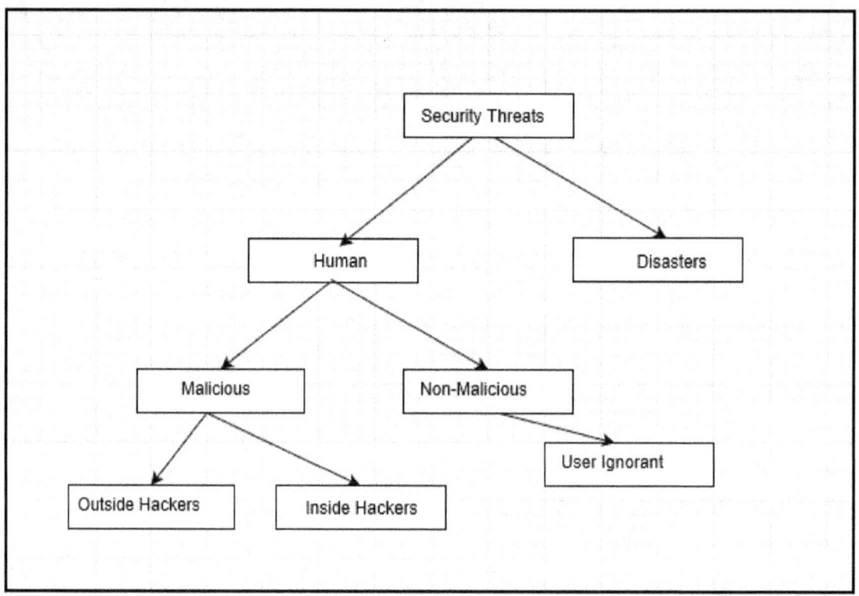

Natural disasters

A natural disaster is a major adverse event resulting from the natural processes of the earth. Examples include floods, hurricanes, tornadoes, volcanic eruptions, earthquakes, tsunamis, and other geologic processes. Nobody can prevent nature from taking its course. Such events can cause severe damage to computer systems. Information can be lost, downtime or loss of productivity can occur, and damage to hardware can disrupt other essential services. Few safeguards can be implemented against natural disasters. The best approach is to have disaster recovery plans and **Business Continuity Plans** (**BCP**) in place.

Human threats

Human threats consist of inside attackers or outside attackers. Insiders can be employees, vendors, or contractors with privileged access to systems. They can also be organizations and outside attacks by non-employees or groups of individuals just looking to harm and disrupt an organization due to a motive or aim.

The most dangerous form of attackers are usually insiders, because they have access to the system and know security measures that are already in place. Insider attacks can be malicious or negligent and can also be accidental.

All companies in this world have to deal with employee work force reduction and expansion. Consequently, controlling and changing the permission on system assets is a very important action item. Lack of process and failure to remove access to sensitive assets for employees who no longer have a business requirement increase an asset's exposure to unauthorized access. This can be a common cause of insider attacks, which is often overlooked.

Since there is usually a trust between employee and employer, most employees are not out to harm them. However, there's no way to ensure that this is the case with all employees, so the best practice is to be cautious and take the appropriate measures to prevent inside threat.

Here is one classic example:

A company's important application was operated by the personal credentials of an employee who had been working there for many years. However, one day the company laid that employee off. The next day, the IS department deleted his credentials. The application then stopped working. An issue like this can cause major damage to a system, and it will definitely take time to identify and fix the problem.

Human security threats can be something as simple as a person opening an attachment loaded with malicious script or malware that opens the system's back door and allows outsiders to extract information. The worst-case scenario often isn't a hacker breaching internal systems, but an employee that loses his smartphone or has his laptop stolen. The best defense lies in securing the data, not just the devices. This means encrypting at the file-level, so confidential information is protected even it is stolen.

Security vulnerabilities

A malicious attacker uses a method to find the resources of a target, finds known vulnerabilities of targeted resources, and then exploits vulnerabilities in order to achieve a goal. Vulnerabilities are weaknesses, misconfigurations or loopholes in security that an attacker exploits in order to gain access to the network or resources on the network.

Security vulnerabilities are not limited to web, SQL DB, or operating systems. The same approach goes for any infrastructure networking gears.

These are the three main categories:

- Technology weaknesses
- Configuration weaknesses
- Security policy weaknesses

Technology weaknesses

These include TCP/IP protocol weaknesses, operating system weaknesses, software weaknesses running on operating systems and network equipment weaknesses.

TCP/IP is a protocol suite, which is used to transfer data through networks. The most important part of the suite is IP, which is the user identity on a network. The main protocols associated are:

- **Transmission Control Protocol** (TCP)
- **User Datagram Protocol** (UDP)
- **Internet Control Message Protocol** (ICMP)

TCP ports numbers identify an application. For example:

- Port `21`: FTP
- Port `23`: Telnet
- Port `80`: HTTP
- Port `443`: HTTPS

TCP/IP was meant to provide a reliable connection between two hosts but does not provide any inbuilt security functions, such as encryption or authentication. Protocols like HTTP, FTP, TFTP, and TELNET are insecure since all the information is in clear text.

A SYN flood is a form of DoS attack in which an attacker sends a succession of SYN requests to a targeted victim in an attempt to utilize all available server resources to make the system unavailable to legitimate traffic.

This is normal behavior for TCP three-way handshake. The SYN packet is sent by a user who is then acknowledged by the server and, finally, by ACK.

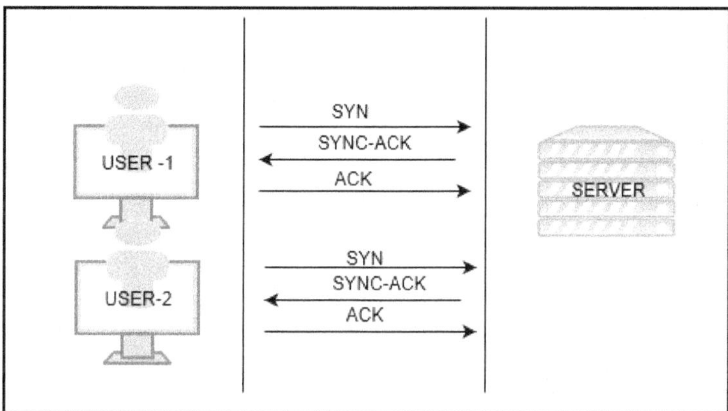

In the case of SYN, flood systems are unavailable to process SYN packets. Attackers in green send a series of SYN packets and get ACK as well. Meanwhile, attackers consume all server resources, hence real users in violet do not even get SYN-ACK.

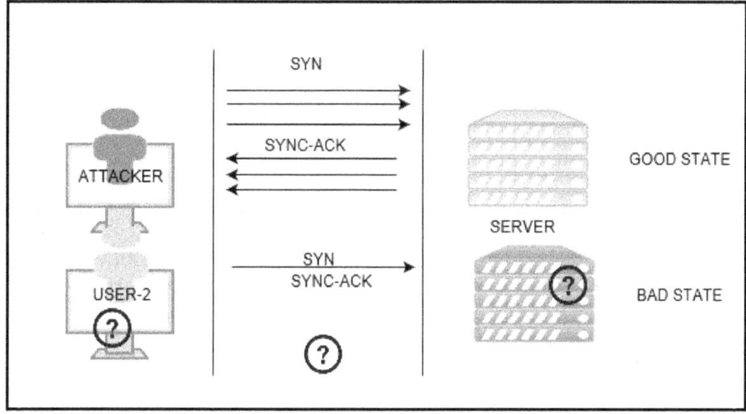

The UNIX, Linux, Macintosh, Windows, and OS/2 operating systems all have security problems. Security updates and bug fixes are released by these companies from time to time.

Network equipment such as routers, firewalls, optical equipment, and switches have security weaknesses that must be recognized and protected.

In upcoming chapters, we will discuss these kind of attacks in detail, looking at how to deal with them in a live network.

Configuration weaknesses

As a network/system administrator, we should know what configuration weaknesses are and what the corrective measures are for their computing and network devices.

User account information might be transmitted in clear text across the network, exposing usernames and passwords to an intruder. For example, if you manage your devices over Telnet, your username and password can be sniffed. The same thing is also applicable when you manage devices using GUI on HTTP.

Misconfigurations of the devices can cause significant network equipment security problems and open doors for unauthorized access. For example, misconfigured access lists, routing protocols, or SNMP community strings can open large security holes. Misconfigured encryption, lack of encryption, or low encryption ciphers for remote-access controls can also cause significant security issues.

Authentication and authorization is a major concern. If you are interested in knowing who is doing what on a piece of network equipment or system, then you might want to centralize authentication with a single authentication platform by accounting logs enabled to perform an audit regularly.

To reduce the threats to your network, the best option is to disable any unused services on all your networking devices and computing system. For instance, if you have a web server, you should disable FTP, SMTP, and other services. Another example would be if you are managing your devices with SSH, you can disable Telnet, HTTP, and FTP running on the same box.

You should only run the applications that are necessary on a device. All unnecessary applications and services should be disabled, to minimize exposure to the outside world.

Security policy weaknesses

Security policy weaknesses can create unforeseen security threats. The network infrastructure can pose security risks to itself if the system administrator does not follow the security policy, and best practices being used in the industry. Every organization must have a security policy and that should be enforced to all users/admin/infrastructure. Security weaknesses emerge when there is no clear-cut or written baseline security policy document.

Always follow a baseline for all infrastructure gears and networks for compliance with the policy. Systems should be in place to verify non-compliance devices. For example, if you have millions of devices in a network, it's very hard to check if all of them are matching compliances or not. However, a system like HPNA and other tools can scan a baseline set of configuration for all devices and reports can be generated.

Single password verification: There are three basic methods for authentication:

- Username and password
- One-time password
- Certificates

In the first methods, passwords are basically user defined, and certificates are computer generated and based on keys. Brute-force attacks can easily crack passwords; passwords are easy to forget and are often reused on multiple services or applications. These passwords are like symmetric keys and are stored somewhere within the service. It is the duty of the service provider to protect your password. However, on the news we also often hear that password databases are hacked and millions of passwords are leaked. The third method is based on keys and strong algorithms, but even they are not 100% foolproof as private keys can be stolen as well.

Two-factor authentication (**2FA**), often referred to as two-step verification, is a security process in which the user provides password information by combing two methods to verify that users are who they say they are. Two-factor authentication provides an additional layer of security by keeping half of the part of a password static in nature and the rest of the part dynamic, constantly changing after a given interval. This makes it harder for attackers to gain access to a person's devices and online accounts; knowing the victim's password alone is not enough to pass the authentication check, because a combined password is dynamic in nature and has an expiry associated with it. Two-factor authentication has long been used to control access to sensitive systems and data, and online services are increasingly introducing 2FA to prevent their users' data from being accessed by hackers who have sniffed or stolen a password.

Best practices are being followed by companies like Google. Even if you change your smartphone or browsers you get notified immediately. Companies follow methods of smart card authentication along with phone authentication in order to validate the identity of users. The banking sector distributed RSA tokens for 2FA.

Using unencrypted or weak encryption for a website

Protocols such as Telnet, HTTP, or FTP opens doors for MITM attacks. The main reason behind that is that these protocols do not offer end-to-end encryption. File transfer protocol is used for data transfer between two hosts, and every time you need to enter usernames and passwords, which are in clear text, and it is very easy for attackers to sniff credentials and data being transferred. To protect information from attackers, we should not use any protocol that does not support encryption. For example, for management purposes, we should use SSH instead of Telnet on any device. All websites must offer HTTPS, and instead of FTP data transfer should be done using SCP or SFTP. In particular, historically insecure services such as Telnet, FTP, SNMP, POP, and IMAP must be replaced by their encrypted equivalents.

SSL SHA1, an extremely popular hashing function, is on the way out. Strictly speaking, this development is not new. The first signs of weaknesses in SHA1 appeared almost 10 years ago. In 2012, some calculations showed that breaking SHA1 is becoming feasible for those who can afford it. In November 2013, Microsoft announced that they wouldn't be accepting SHA1 certificates *after* 2016.

Protect Domain Controller: Eliminates use of LM and NTLM (v1) in favor of NTLMv2 or Kerberos. Kerberos is a token-based system. Refresh time is so fast that even if someone hacked your session, you would get new tokens as refresh time makes it more reliable.

In the same way, you should float guidelines for the secure management of assets. All the servers and assets should be managed by domain controller security groups. Using interactive logon with a service account can cause major damage too, hence interactive logon for service accounts should be disabled. The reason behind this is that if a system is compromised, attackers can gain access to the domain controller as well.

Connect to unsecured Wi-Fi network access: Connecting through a public Wi-Fi network or hotspot can compromise your computer/mobile security and put your information at risk. Whether you are on your computer or your mobile device, it's relatively easy for hackers to access the information you type and send over an unsecured Wi-Fi network, including your login and password information.

Users need to be educated on how to use Wi-Fi with their computer devices. Here are some important tips that every company employee should know:

- If possible, make sure that you connect to secure networks only
- Use strong passwords for all your online accounts and change them often
- Use VPN for accessing corporate resources

Summary

So far, we discussed why infrastructure is an absolute requirement for today's internet world and what this means for system admins and internet users. We also learned how to build secure IT infrastructure and policy frameworks to protect information.

One of the major weaknesses in information security today is the human element. The everyday behavior of employees and end users represents one of the greatest risks to organizations and customers. IT technology is evolving faster than ever before. We are seeing new security controls, policies, and best practices put in place within organizations, but every day security breaches continue to take place. Nobody is 100% protected from small to large organizations. It only takes a simple mistake from an uneducated end user to leave a back door open in your information security. Organizations need to be aware of the people they work with, within the organization and outside as well. Developing adequate training and security frameworks for employee and end users becomes very important for protecting systems, especially considering the fact that it's not just technology which plays an important role, but also its users. I again repeat: if you have internet enabled devices, it is also your responsibility to secure them.

In 2017, Ransomware such as WannaCry, NotPetya, and Bad Rabbit have demonstrated the dangers of this threat and the potential impact on almost any industry. In 2018, it is predicted that IOT will be a big target for attackers in upcoming years, as well as Cloud infrastructures, **Artificial Intelligence** (**AI**), and of course the rise of mobile attackers increases daily.

In our next chapter we will discuss how to design secure infrastructure, keeping common risk factors in mind. This starts with placement of firewall and DDoS protection techniques.

Here is a famous quote to keep in mind:

> *"If you spend more on coffee than on IT security, you will be hacked. What's more, you deserve to be hacked"*
> *—Richard Clarke*

Questions

1. What are the different types of firewalls?
    1. Simple packet filtering
    2. Application proxy
    3. Stateful inspection firewalls
    4. Next-Generation firewalls
    5. All of above
2. What kind of attacks can be prevented using IDS/IPS?
    1. Denial of Service
    2. Distributed Denial of Service
    3. Exploits
    4. Worms
    5. Viruses

3. Which of the following pieces of information can be found in the IP header?
    1. Source and destination address of the IP packet
    2. Source and destination port of the IP packet
    3. Sequence number of the IP packet
    4. Both (1) and (2) only.
4. What is the standard port number used for requesting HTTPs?
    1. 80
    2. 53
    3. 443
    4. 25
5. Which of the following is not considered an external threat to a network?
    1. Human ignorance
    2. Virus
    3. Hackers
    4. Malware

Further reading

Visit the following link for more information:

- `https://www.sans.org/security-resources/policies`

2
Secure Network Design

In the previous chapter you learned about the basic concept of infrastructure security and built a strong foundation for the different areas required to understand the need for information security based on current security threats that exist in cyber space.

The internet has grown dramatically and has reached a stage where everyone must be connected in order to exchange information. Imagine that billions of people with internet enabled devices are directly connected to the internet, and some sort of unsecured network becomes a target for cyber criminals.

In this chapter, we describe how to secure a network and look at the significance of network security. In a layered fashion, we will also discuss methods and approaches to building a secure network based on business aims.

The following topics will be covered in this chapter:

- Access control
- Network management and security design
- Hardening your TCP/IP stack
- DoS and DDoS attacks
- IP spoofing
- Ping sweeps and port scans
- DNS vulnerabilities
- Two-factor authentication

Access control

As an application or network owner, we should know who or what is accessing our network resources. If we do not know or do not keep track of our activity and instead just assume what is happening on the network, we cannot guarantee data security and the safety of end-users.

We need to start with the basics of security. This begins with understanding what's on our network.

Asset classification and physical security

The most basic (but often most overlooked) element of network security involves keeping hardware protected from theft or physical intrusion.

As mentioned earlier, the first thing we need to classify is our assets. Once data classification is identified, network servers, network switches and other core network components should be protected in well-guarded facilities. Cages and racks should be locked and permission should be granted based on requirements with proper approval and proper security guidelines.

Authentication, authorization, and accounting

Authentication, authorization, and accounting (**AAA**) is a function for centrally and securely controlling access to IT infrastructure resources. This is achieved by enforcing policies and providing audit functionality by keeping track of activities performed on a given device. In simple terms, authentication can refer to identifying a user with a username and password. The AAA server matches user's authentication credentials against credentials setup and stored in a back-end database. The authorization process validates whether the user has the authority to do a specified task or not. This can include accessing or executing any command on a given resource. The final piece in the AAA function is accounting, which records all the activity on resources consumed by a user during access.

AAA functions are always offered by an exclusive centralized AAA server, a software program that performs all these functions. A current standard by which network access servers interface with the AAA server is the **Remote Authentication Dial-In User Service** (**RADIUS**) or **Terminal Access Controller Access Control System** (**TACACS**) protocols.

TACACS can be further connected to domain controller security groups, which gives elevated security access. You will have to create two security groups on domain controller, for example, *RO* and *RW*. After one or two human security approvals, your user account will be automatically added to the *RW* group. This provides a way to dynamically request administrative (admin) access to production machines. After the specified time, the account will be removed from there automatically.

Network management and security design

For managing network and networking assets, there must always be a centralized secure management utility subnet for services such as DNS, DHCP, NTP, AAA, and network management. By defining boundaries, it becomes much easier to troubleshoot problems with the services when they are in known locations with a few well-known access paths and methods.

Network segmentation

Most of us focus on front door security and threats coming from the outside world by putting some sort of firewall on the perimeter. In reality, relying upon perimeter security alone does not protect your network and information data. Doing this is like putting money into a bank which depends on one armed guard.

The concept of *segmentation* is based on ancient history, when Roman empires formed and fought units based on the ethnic and geographic identity of captured warriors. The idea was very simple: groups of warriors were formed on the basis of their similar backgrounds so that they could bond with each other and ultimately become better fighting units.

Resource consolidation, virtualization and network consolidation can be beneficial when focusing on infrastructure security. The consolidation of network infrastructure with improved security has been a crucial part of the segmentation strategy. A legacy model of distributed applications and services with complex designs are now migrating to shared physical infrastructure or cloud networks that require separation to maintain strong isolation. Similarly, networks have gone through abrupt changes over the past few years with the introduction of virtualization, **Software Defined Network** (**SDN**), containers, wireless connectivity, hosting services, Data Center infrastructure and the **Internet of Things** (**IoT**). Network separation can be achieved by implementing Layer-2 technologies such as VLANs, Layer-3 technologies such as **virtual routing and forwarding** (**VRF**) for routing separation, and zone based firewalls for segment separation.

In today's cyber security environment, you have to assume that you are not 100% immune to these threats and something malicious might already be on a network. Using a multi-layer approach, network segmentation makes it more difficult for an attacker to launch an attack throughout your entire network. It also adds an additional layer of deterrent for insiders because you can isolate valuable data and resources from insider attacks.

From a network design point of view, networks with limited segmentation, a high number of users and various applications typically experience access control issues. Every user group has access to pretty much every application in the enterprise network. All departments can connect to all other resources on a network, as shown in the following diagram:

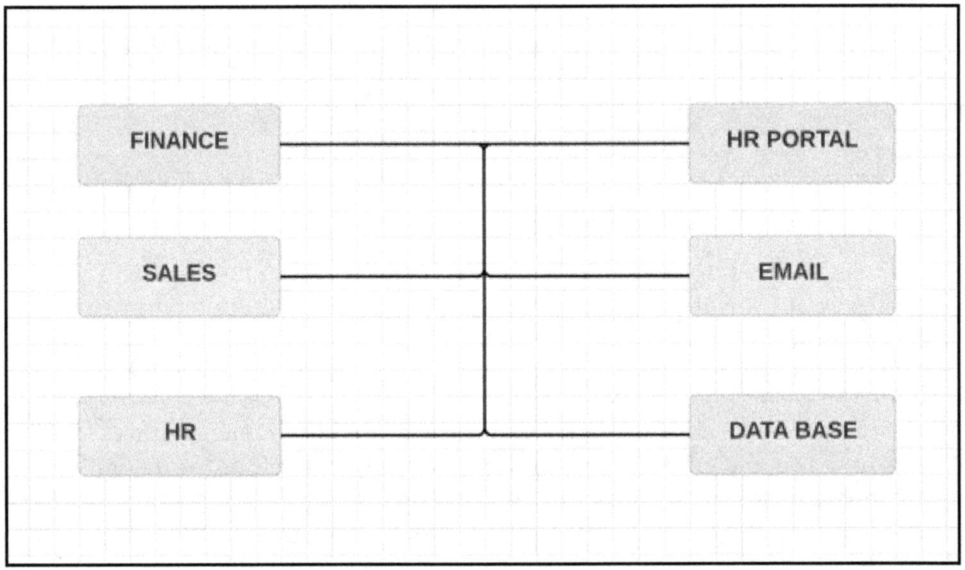

Segmentation strategy steps

Segmentation design and strategy should be based on the critical asset value or resource, not simply on network boundaries-based isolation. This design strategy should start as a high level network design which segregates the various zones through traditional network boundaries such as DMZ, data center, virtual cloud and campus network. It then consistently drills into each zone to provide isolation between the applications within it:

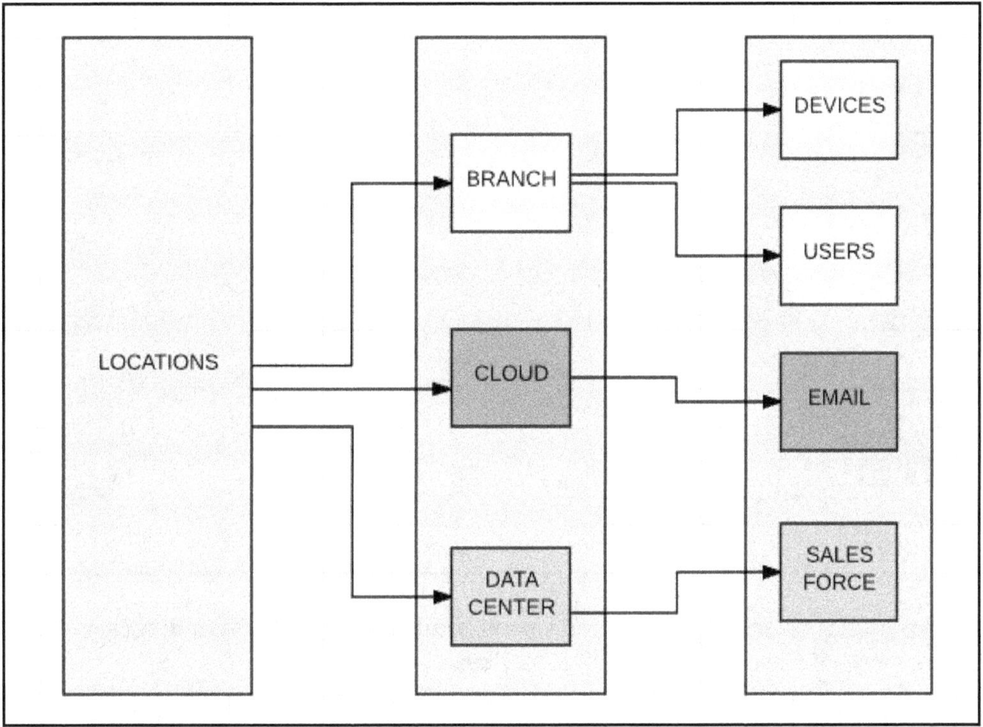

Virtual LAN (VLAN): A flat local area network segment forms a single broadcast domain. This means that if a user broadcasts information on a LAN, the broadcast will be heard by all other users on the same LAN. To limit the broadcast and to separate users and applications, the LAN segment can be divided into logical segments called **VLAN** while still sharing the same common wired physical network. In the following diagram, you can refer to the first VLAN as VLAN_1, which is dedicated to the finance team; VLAN_2 is dedicated to HR and VLAN_3 to payroll. All VLANs share the same physical media but are logically separated in order to limit broadcast:

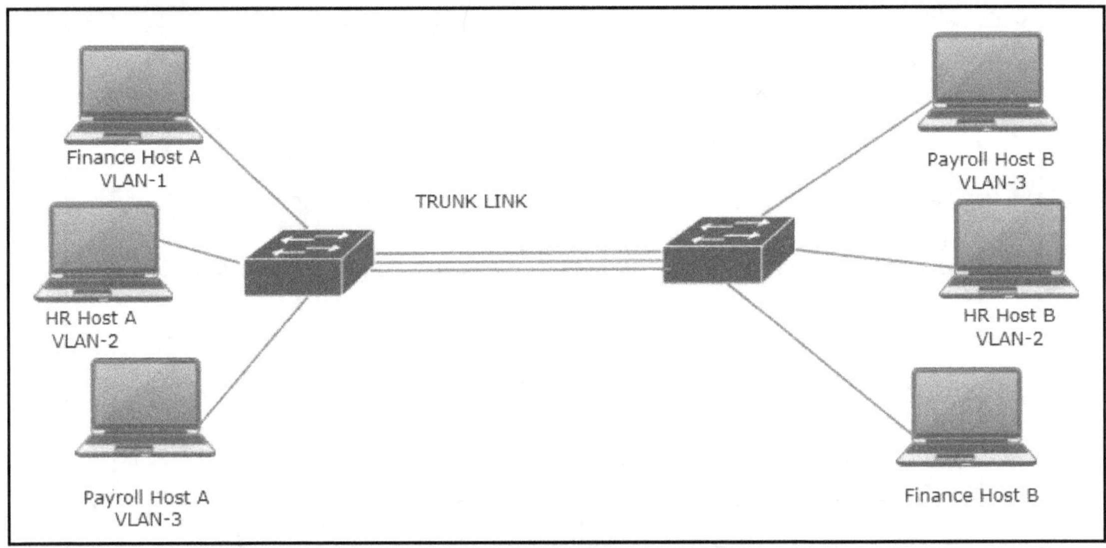

In the following diagram, each color represents a different VLAN. This diagram demonstrates what the connection will look like:

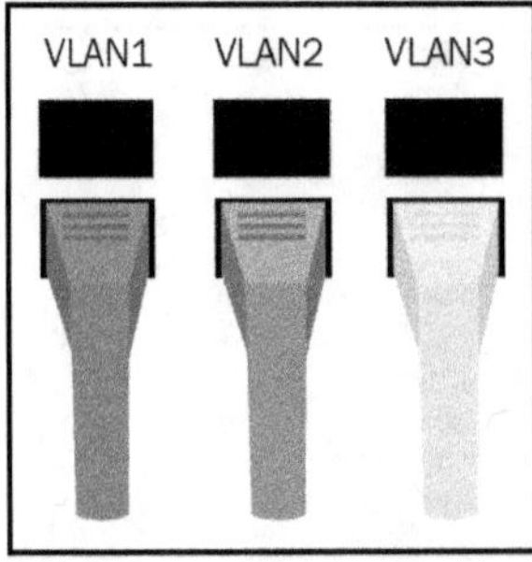

The red cable represents VLAN1, the violet cable represents VLAN2 and the yellow cable represents VLAN3.

Virtual Routing and Forwarding (VRF): Virtualization is a technique which has the great advantage of hiding the physical characteristics of computer resources shared with multiple operating systems. An end user interacts with those resources without even knowing the common shared resources. VRF is a technique for **Internet Protocol** (**IP**) network routers that allows multiple instances of a routing table to exist in a router and work simultaneously. VRF also increases network security, which is the reason why these VRF resources cannot talk to each other unless they talk via a separate Layer-3 device. The main advantage of VRF is that they can have overlapping IP addresses without having any conflict. For example, in an MPLS network, multiple customers are using the same IP range and service provider resources are shared. VRF provides the flexibility to use the same IP space for multiple customers and security as well. As shown in the following diagram, there are four VRFs and all are using the same IP range on the same router:

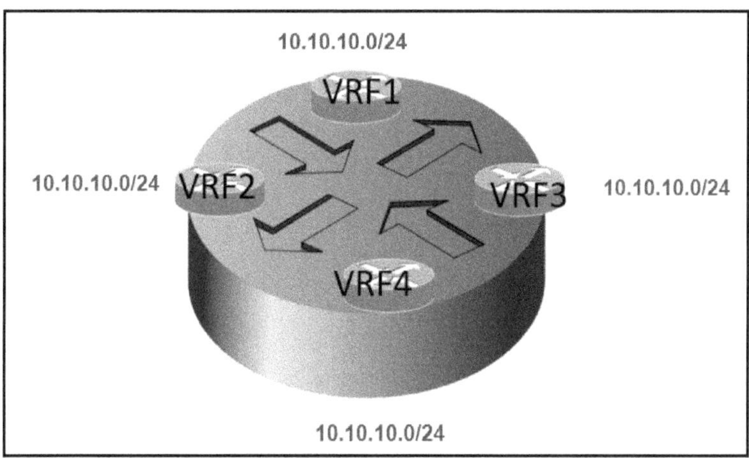

Network protection consideration and design

LAN protection revolves around Layer-2 protection on OSI models. All layers of TCP/IP have got its own security threats and vulnerabilities. A firewall is one very simple way to protect a LAN, but this only protects traffic which is coming from outside. Layer-2 attacks are sources from *inside* a LAN.

It is difficult for an outsider to achieve a Layer-2 attack, but never underestimate the power of insiders. Insiders can do more damage than outsiders by launching malicious attacks from inside the network. The proactive deterrence for this would be to keep track of your logs and setup your IDS to detect such attacks!

Before going deeper into this topic, let's get an understanding of how network switches work.

Let us examine a topology in a VLAN segment: A, B & C are three hosts which are connected to three different ports on a single switch. When host A sends data to host B through port `Fastethernet0/1`, the switch learns that host A is located on port `Fastethernet0/1` and records mapping into the **Content-Addressable Memory** (**CAM**). If host B does not initiate a connection and does not send even a single packet, then the switch is not able to locate host B and will therefore flood the packet originated by A to all VLAN ports. Learning by flood is the basic behavior of the switch which is carried out to discover hosts on a network:

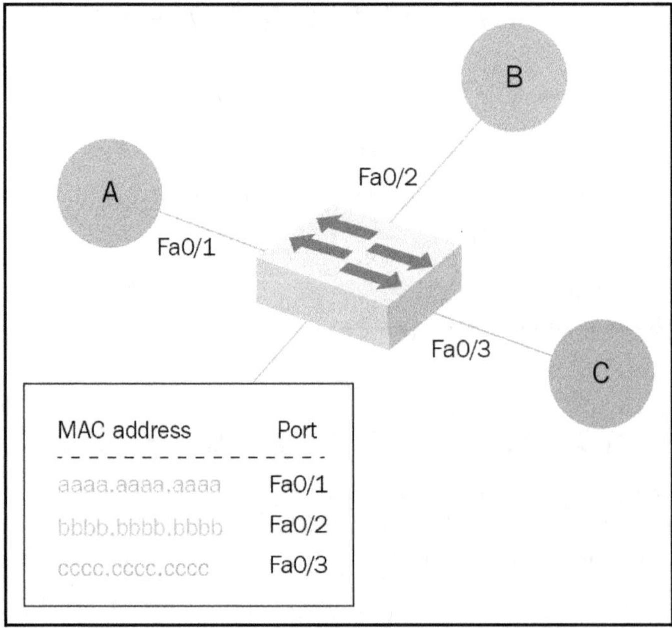

Here are the known major Layer-2 attacks:

- **CAM OVERFLOW / MAC FLOODING**: Switches store MAC addresses in a CAM table. Memory size varies according to each model and capacity, but memory size is limited. It is very possible to flood the network switch with fictitious MAC address data. The switch, not knowing how to handle the excess data, falls into a trap and starts acting as a HUB. After the attack, you can use a program like Wireshark or any other generic sniffer to listen to all the traffic on the network, because the switch will be forwarding data out of all other ports. Macof is a member of the `dsniff` suit tool set and is mainly used to flood the switch on a local network with MAC addresses. Macof generates thousands of packets per second, and each packet is sent random source and destination IP addresses. A source and destination MAC address is also different for each Ethernet frame.
- **CAM Flow Protection and Defensive Measures**: Port security features can be used to protect a network against this kind of attack, which limits the number of MAC addresses on an interface. Cisco is built into the IOS, and this allows you to shut the port down if the switch receives more than a certain number of MAC addresses on one port.

Nexus 3064 switch can hold 128k entries. Total MAC addresses learned by this switch can be viewed using this command:

```
             # show mac address-table count
MAC Entries for all vlans:
Dynamic Address Count: 2119
Static Address (User-defined) Count: 0
Multicast MAC Address Count: 0
Total MAC Addresses in Use: 2119

Total PVLAN Clone MAC Address Count: 0
             #
Ready
```

Cisco IOS switch 2960 can hold 8k entries:

```
                          #show mac address-table count

Mac Entries for Vlan 201:
---------------------------
Dynamic Address Count  : 141
Static  Address Count  : 0
Total Mac Addresses    : 141

Mac Entries for Vlan 301:
---------------------------
Dynamic Address Count  : 21
Static  Address Count  : 0
Total Mac Addresses    : 21

Total Mac Address Space Available: 7877

                          #
```

As soon as you launch the `macof` attack, available addresses become zero and the switch starts acting as a HUB.

You can limit the number of MAC addresses learned on this switch interface and define the violation action. Keep in mind that this is a simple step to secure the user port, but in the case of data center environments where virtualization is used, more MAC addresses are expected to be learned on the same switch port:

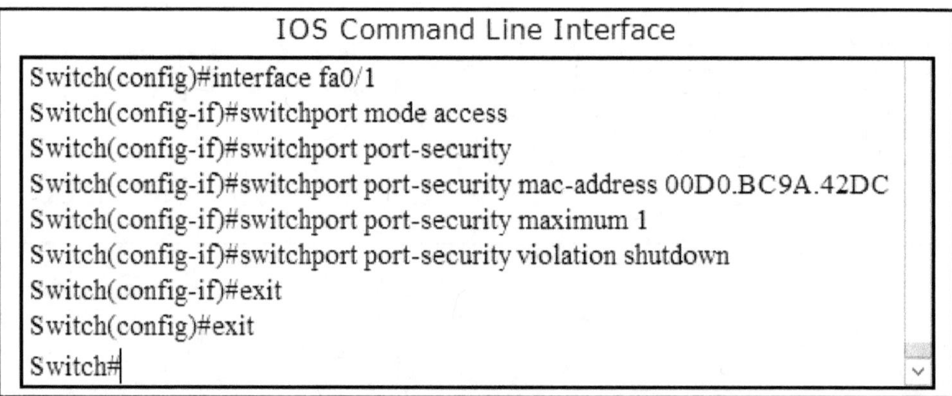

IOS Command Line Interface

```
Switch(config)#interface fa0/1
Switch(config-if)#switchport mode access
Switch(config-if)#switchport port-security
Switch(config-if)#switchport port-security mac-address 00D0.BC9A.42DC
Switch(config-if)#switchport port-security maximum 1
Switch(config-if)#switchport port-security violation shutdown
Switch(config-if)#exit
Switch(config)#exit
Switch#
```

This is a virtual environment and multiple MACs are being learned on the same interface. This is not an attack but you can still limit the number of MACs in accordance with the design guide:

```
        # sh mac address-table dynamic interface ethernet 1/1
Legend:
        * - primary entry, G - Gateway MAC, (R) - Routed MAC, O - Overlay MAC
        age - seconds since first seen,+ - primary entry using vPC Peer-Link
   VLAN     MAC Address      Type      age     Secure NTFY   Ports/SWID.SSID.LID
---------+-----------------+--------+---------+------+----+------------------
* 201      0015.5d0b.f0e8    dynamic   1251400    F     F  Eth1/1
* 214      0015.5d0b.f0e6    dynamic   1251400    F     F  Eth1/1
* 217      0015.5d0b.f082    dynamic   628840     F     F  Eth1/1
* 217      0015.5d0b.f0c1    dynamic   628820     F     F  Eth1/1
* 217      0015.5d0b.f0c9    dynamic   628840     F     F  Eth1/1
* 217      0015.5d0b.f0ec    dynamic   628840     F     F  Eth1/1
* 217      0015.5d0b.f0ef    dynamic   628840     F     F  Eth1/1
* 500      0015.5d0b.f0e9    dynamic   1251400    F     F  Eth1/1
* 500      0015.5d0b.f0f2    dynamic   1251400    F     F  Eth1/1
        #
```

ARP SPOOFING: Address Resolution Protocol (**ARP**) is a protocol or process used for finding an unknown MAC address for a known IP address. All network devices that need to communicate on the network broadcast ARP queries in the system to find out other machines' MAC addresses. In simple terms, for any communication on an IP network, we need to know the MAC address of the next hop in order to place the packet on the wire.

There are two types of ARP messages that can be sent:

- ARP request
- ARP reply

In an ARP request message, the sender broadcasts the ARP request to all computers in a subnet in order to discover the MAC address of the targeted IP address.

In an ARP reply, the target system sends the reply to the sender, giving the MAC address.

For example, the target spoofed may be the internet gateway router. The attacker spoofs the router's MAC address. To divert traffic, you will have to put the same IP on the other device. However, this will cause IP duplication and may alert the network administrator. There are very few ARP requests transmitted by a router because the ARP caching time for such a device may be huge (for example, default CISCO router configuration takes eight hours). All of this magic happens with gratuitous ARP, which automatically causes ARP to broadcast its MAC address to the entire network. In this case, attackers will send **Gratuitous ARP** (**GARP**) to poison the ARP table in a victim's machine:

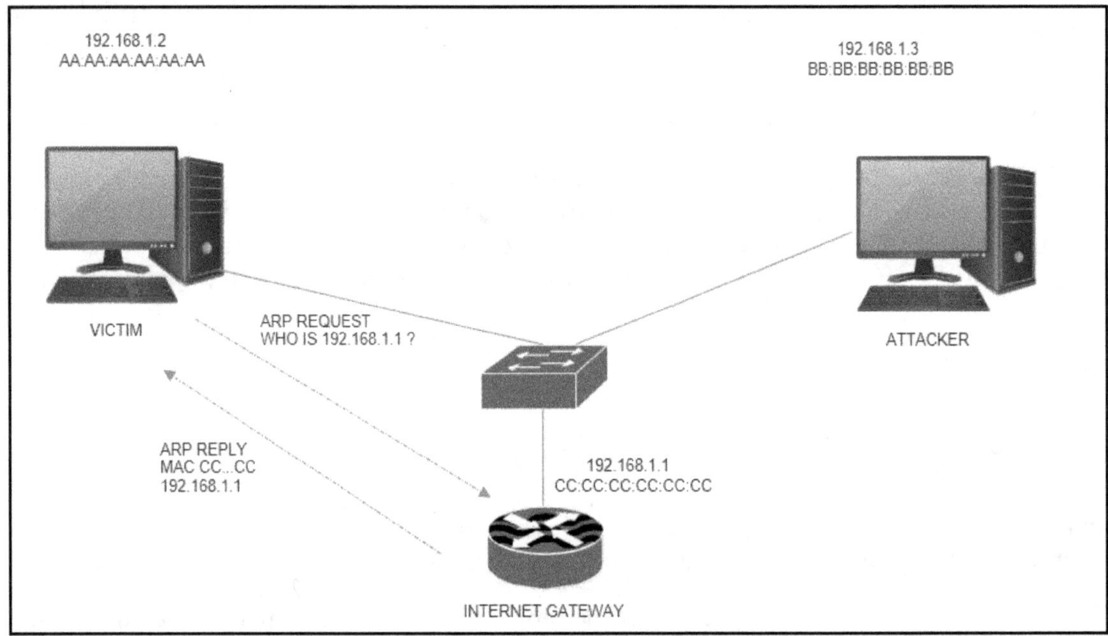

The preceding diagram demonstrates the normal process for learning the MAC address of the gateway. A victim's host machine sends ARP requests to the default gateway `192.168.1.1` and gets a response which contains the MAC address `CC:CC:CC:CC:CC`:

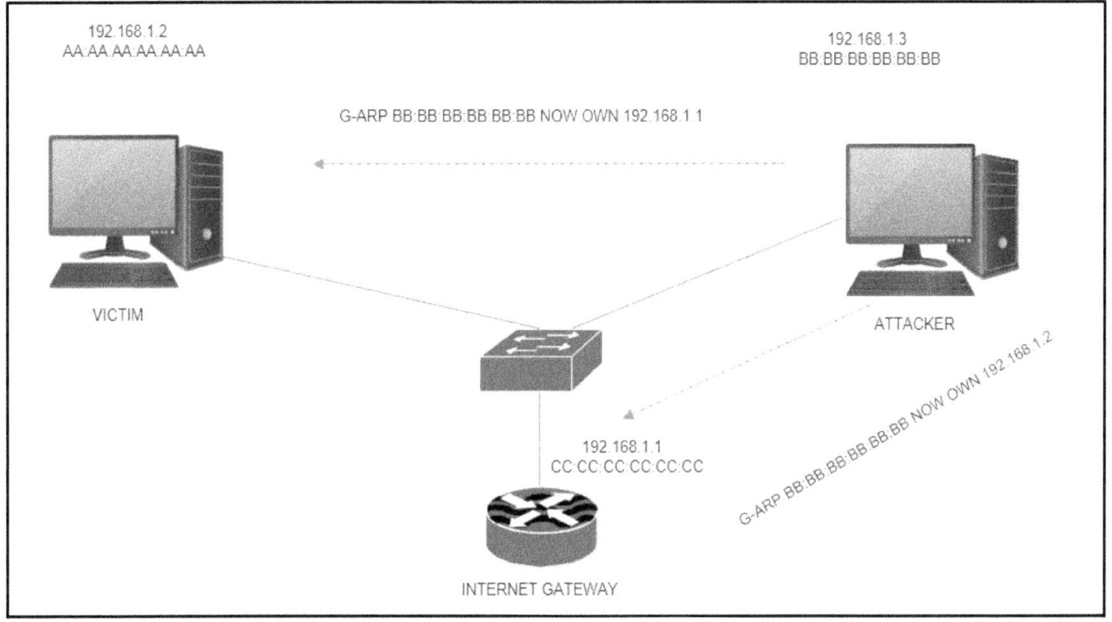

Attackers send G-ARP, which tells the victim that they now own the default gateway `192.168.1.1` and the source IP `192.168.1.2`. This is where the game begins. The communication can now be hijacked with the sniffer. This will enable the victim and the internet gateway to exchange traffic through the attacker's PC without notifying them.

WAN protection: WAN is a geographically distributed connectivity that connects multiple networks. A typical WAN may consist of a connection to an internet service provider's multiple locations, internet connection between ISPs, connectivity to branch offices, collocation facilities, cloud services, public internet connectivity, and other locations. For example, MPLS WAN, INTERNET WAN, PRIVATE LEASE LINES, IPLC CIRCUITS, and DARK FIBER CIRCUITS.

To protect confidentiality and integrity for data travelling over the WAN, we need to ensure data is encrypted. Over internet VPNs, IPsec and SSL encryptions can provide comprehensive protection.

All MPLS service providers use the term **Virtual Private Network** (**VPN**), indicating some level of security. But in reality, MPLS does not provide encryption by default. Instead, technology allows service providers to keep the separate routing tables for each customer. Attackers cannot directly gain access to an MPLS customer network, but they might gain access to the core network. The lack of inbuilt encryption would mean that the attacker could sniff data and analyze it. Just in case the core network is compromised, IPsec offers additional security over an MPLS network.

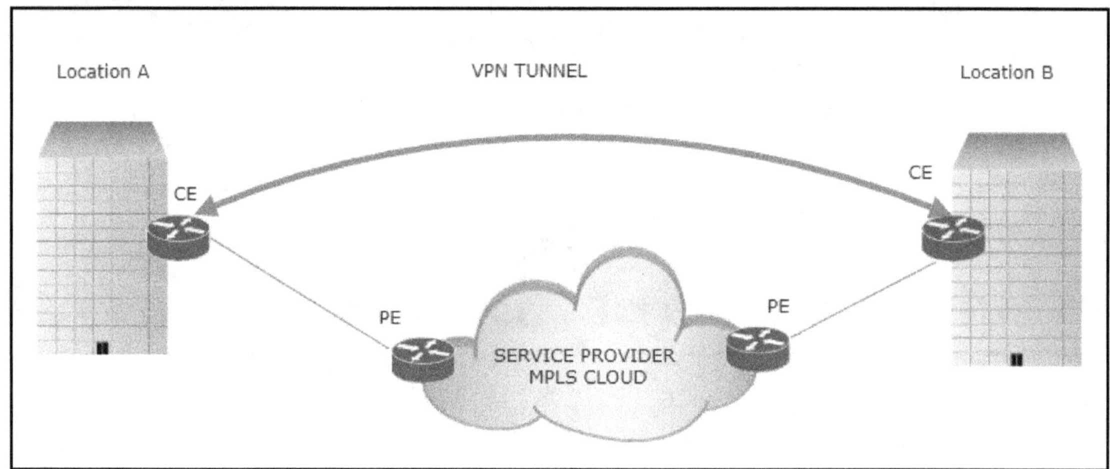

When planning for encryption, we need to decide which layer we want to encrypt.

Why encrypt Layer-1?

Encrypting IP data traffic at higher layers can significantly increase the latency between two network nodes, while Layer-1 encryption gives extremely low latency and high throughput. Keeping in mind the rise of 100 Gigabits (and beyond) network connectivity, the desired results can be achieved by encrypting data on Layer-1. The complexity of the network and encryption management also increases with higher-layer encryption, more devices to manage, and complex encryption key management. Optical encryption includes the encryption and decryption process together with the key distribution between the transmitter and receiver.

The major use case is **data center interconnect** (**DCI**) over dark fiber:

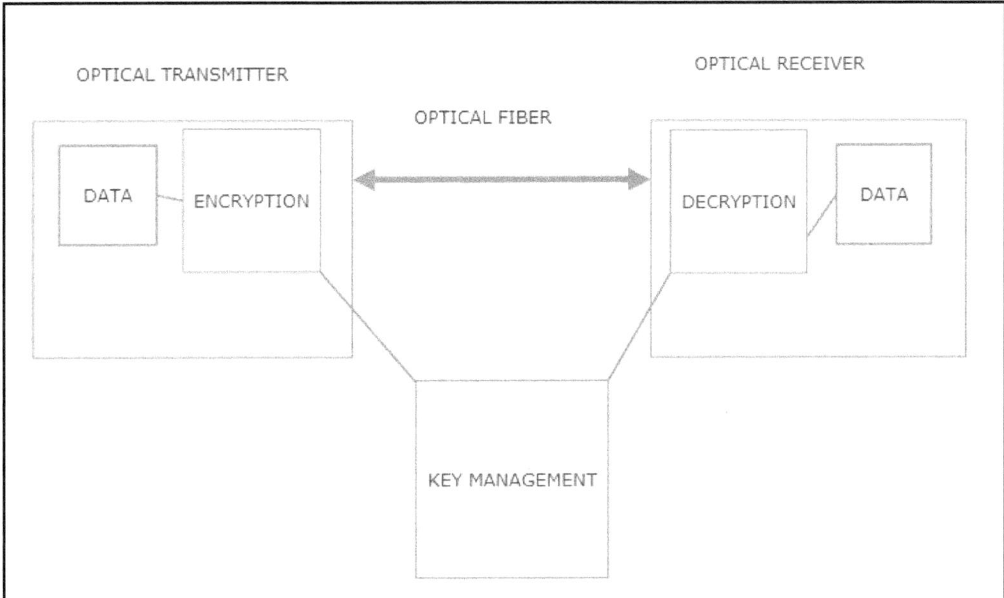

Why encrypt Layer-2?

An Ethernet encryptor that encrypts the network at Layer-2 is the best option when it comes to securing an Ethernet based VPN. The tapping of networks is a common and unpreventable practice. Layer-2 encryption is hardware processed which operates at almost full wire speed and is adaptable to an L2 network (point-to-multipoint and multi-mode links):

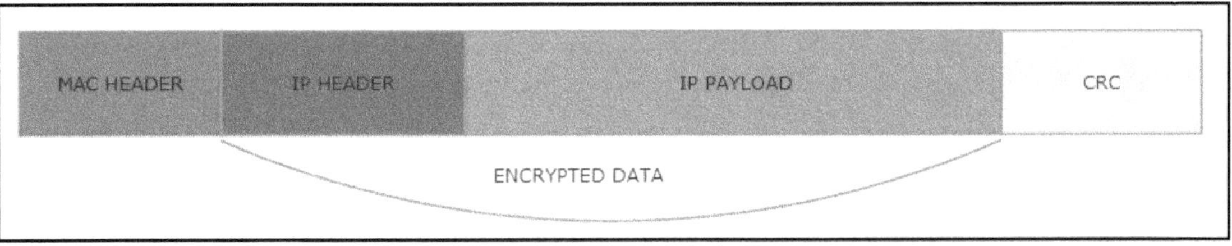

MACsec offers you Layer-2, hop-by-hop encryption. Every hop device will encrypt and decrypt packets, but the IP and IP payload will be encrypted. If you look at a packet in transit, you will only see the Layer-2 header and nothing else. MACsec is the IEEE 802.1AE standard for authenticating and encrypting packets between two MACsec capable devices. Not all switches support MACsec. Check switch capabilities before implementing MACsec.

TrustSec uses AES-128 **GCM and GMAC** (**Galois/Counter Mode Advanced Encryption Standard 128**). MACsec can be configured between hosts - in this mode, the switch is called **Downlink MACsec**. MACsec also works between switches - this mode is called **Uplink MACsec**.

For downlink mode, we need to have NIC, which helps MACsec or Cisco to reply on any connected software:

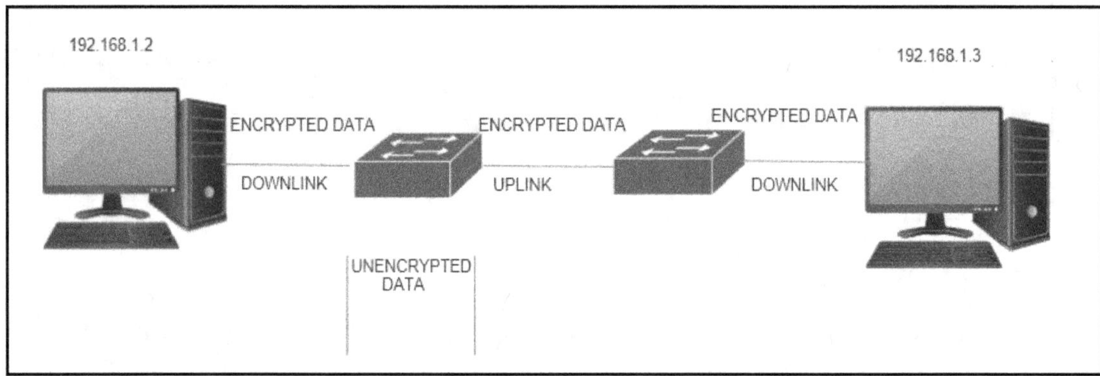

Why encrypt Layer-3?

Public internet is cheap and more flexible. Keeping in mind that public internet is not safe, IPsec provides a lot of flexibility to encrypt data and to provide a framework to maintain confidentiality, integrity, authentication, and anti-replay. IPsec offers a standards based end-to-end encryption solution that is agnostic to the underlying physical network infrastructure. IPsec also has several limitations. This includes the fact that it does not support non-IP traffic flows, including data center storage protocols such as **Fiber-Channel** (**FC**).

IPsec encryption takes place at the network layer (Layer-3) in the OSI model. Layer-2 and Layer-1 encryption technologies provide bump-in-the-wire with 100% throughput at line rate and far lower latency than IPsec VPNs, which operate at Layer-3. Layer-3 encryption is a better choice for low-bandwidth environments:

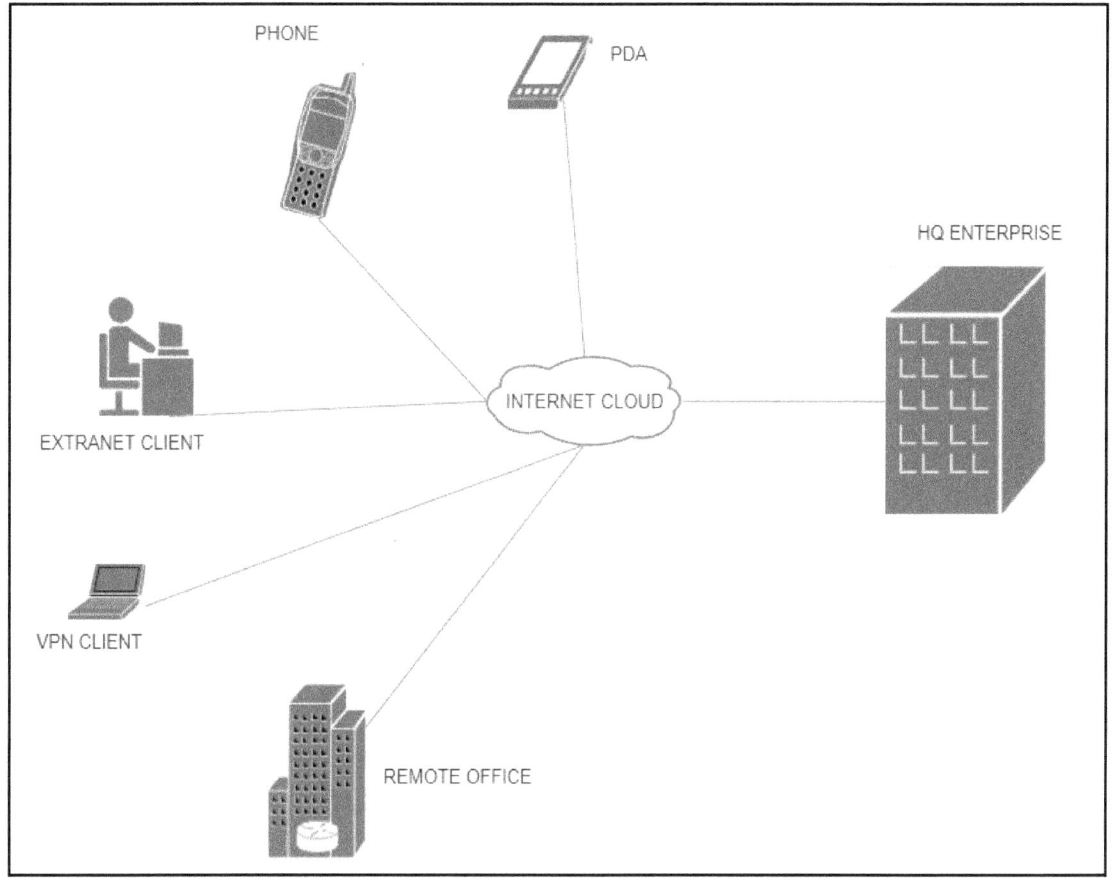

Hardening your TCP/IP stack

For any given operating system, tuning of the TCP/IP stack can be performed by the system administrator. Changing the default values of TCP/IP stack variables provides another layer of protection and helps you to secure your hosts in a better way.

This is all about determining and making decisions about how many connections the server can maintain in a half-open state before TCP/IP triggers SYN flooding attack protection. This simply means that to configure the threshold value of the TCP connection, requests must be exceeded before SYN flood protection is triggered.

The following parameters can be adjusted on an operating system level to tune TCP/IP stacks. These are not only applicable to the operating system, but also to network devices such as firewalls and load balancers, which allow you to fine tune TCP stacks:

- `TcpMaxHalfOpen`
- `TcpMaxHalfOpenRetried`
- `TcpMaxPortsExhausted`
- `TcpMaxConnectResponseRetransmissions`

We will discuss DoS attacks in detail in the next section.

DoS and DDoS attacks

A Denial-of-Service is an attack in which online services do not respond to connections from legitimate hosts due to their resources being overused by malicious requests. This attack becomes a **Distributed Denial-of-Service** (**DDoS**) attack when it comes from multiple sources and it becomes difficult to block the source with IP or Geo-location.

DDoS attacks usually take the form of the following:

- Volume-based attacks
- Application layer attacks
- Low-rate attacks

Volume-based attacks

Volume based attacks are by far the most common type of DDoS attacks.

According to Arbor Networks, 65% of DDoS attacks are volumetric in nature.

Volume-based attacks are characterized by an excessive amount of traffic (sometimes in excess of 100 Gbps). They do not mandate large amounts of traffic to be generated by one location or one source.

The following is an example of such an attack:

- **NTP Amplification**: The NTP amplification attack is a volume based DDoS attack in which an attacker exploits the publicly accessible **Network Time Protocol** (**NTP**) server functionality. This command, called `monlist`, sends the requester a list of the last six hundred hosts that were connected to the queried server. So, for a small query, response data is very high. Let us consider the fact that the ratio of query:response is 1:50. This means that attackers can generate 50 Gpbs of traffic using a NIC of 1 Gbps, and the same thing will be replicated across multiple sources. This can cause multiple terabits of traffic in a network.

  In the following diagram, you can see that attackers generate a query to public NTP servers with the spoofed IP of a victim. In response to an NTP query, the server sends a huge amount of data to the victim's IP, which chokes the network for the victim and make resources unavailable:

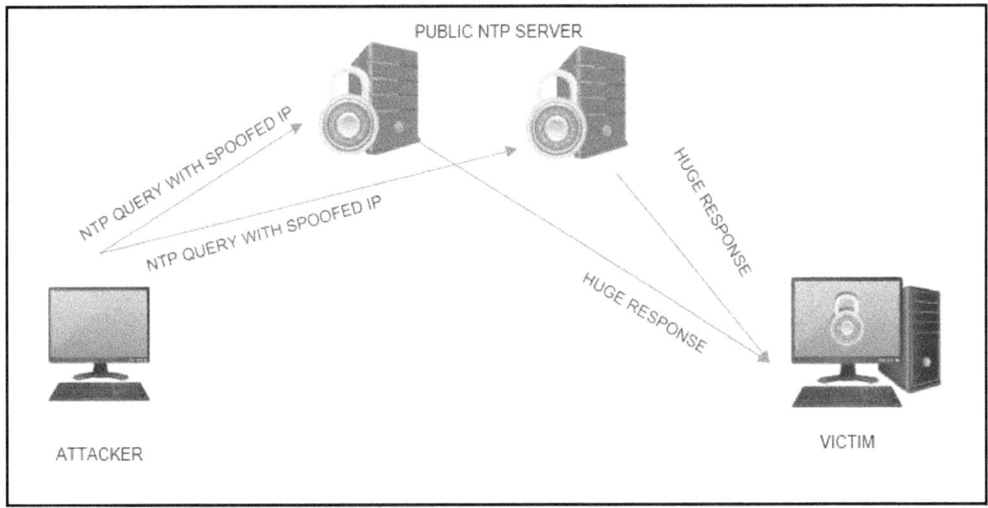

- **Mitigation**: Source IP verification should be activated to prevent spoofed packets from leaving the network.

Other similar examples of volume based attacks are:

- **User Datagram Protocol** (**UDP**) Floods
- ICMP floods
- **Domain Name Servers** (**DNS**) Amplification
- **Character Generator** (**Chargen**)

Application layer attacks

Application attacks are low traffic rate attacks which are very hard to detect. These are targeted at weaknesses in an application or server with the goal of establishing a connection and exhausting processes and transactions. Such attacks do not require a botnet type army; generating a low traffic rate needs few sources and the traffic type seems to be legitimate.

The most famous example of a Layer-7 attack is the HTTP Get/Post DDoS attack.

- **HTTP Flood Attack**: HTTP flood is a very common type of DDoS attack in which the cyber criminal exploits HTTP `GET` or `POST` requests to attack an online web server or application. The attacker forms a botnet army to send the targeted server a very large number of GET (image content) or POST (files) requests. The targeted web server attempts to answer each request coming from the botnet army. In accordance with normal application behavior, the server allocates the maximum number of resources to handle the requests. This prevents genuine requests coming from authentic users to reach to the web server or application. This simply turns into a denial of service:

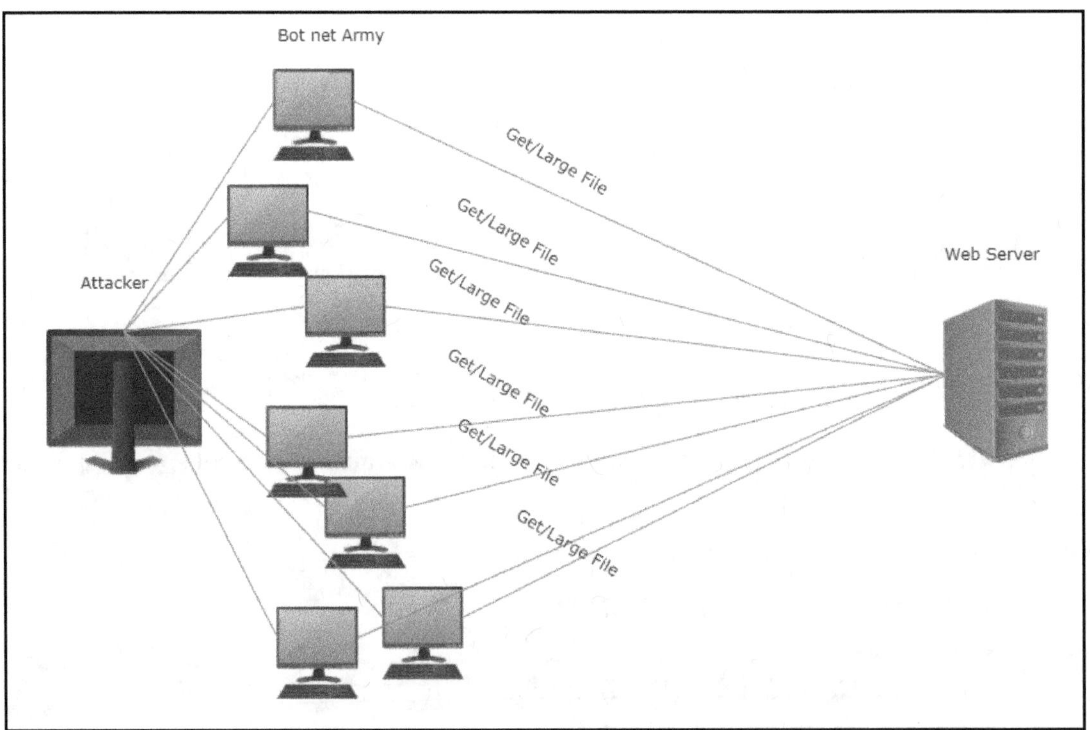

- **Cloud is a new platform for attackers**: To create a zombie botnet army cloud series provides a new platform to hackers. Thousand of VMs/hosts can be created and deleted in a few seconds and the traffic looks legitimate:

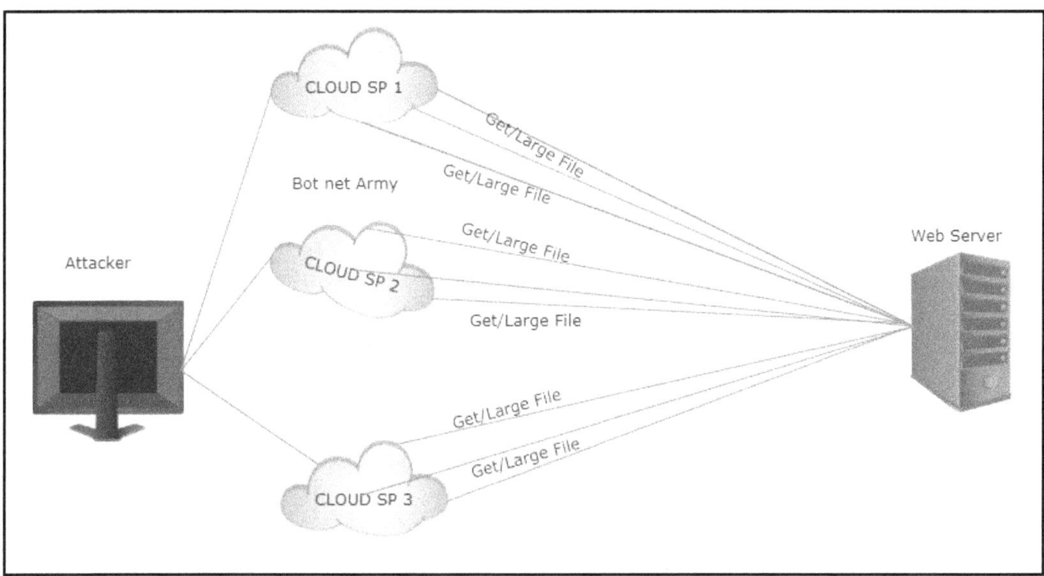

- **Mitigation**: A ring-based Anycast solution offers inbuilt DDoS protection against such flood attacks. The most highly-effective mitigation mechanisms rely on a combination of traffic profiling methods, including identifying the IP reputation.

Low-rate attacks

Low-rate attacks are focused on bringing a target down quietly. This is very different to high rate brute-force attacks. These attacks leave connections open on the target by creating a relatively low number of connections over a period of time and leaving those sessions open for as long as possible. A famous example of these types of attacks is the **Slowloris** tool, which allows an attacker to take down a victim's web server with minimal bandwidth requirements and without launching numerous connections at the same time.

Slowloris is an application layer (Layer-7) DDoS attack which operates by utilizing valid partial HTTP requests. The attacker sends HTTP headers with opening connections to a targeted web server and then keeps those connections open for as long as possible, but never completes a request. To avoid connection timeout, the attacker periodically sends another set of partial request headers to the target in order to keep the request alive. This ultimately overflows the maximum concurrent connection pool, and leads to denial of service for subsequent connections from legitimate users.

Mitigation:

- Increase server availability
- Rate limit incoming requests
- Limit the number of connections coming from one IP address.

IP spoofing

IP spoofing is the creation of IP packets using somebody else's IP address as the source address of an IP packet.

Let's take a look at IP headers in an IP packet:

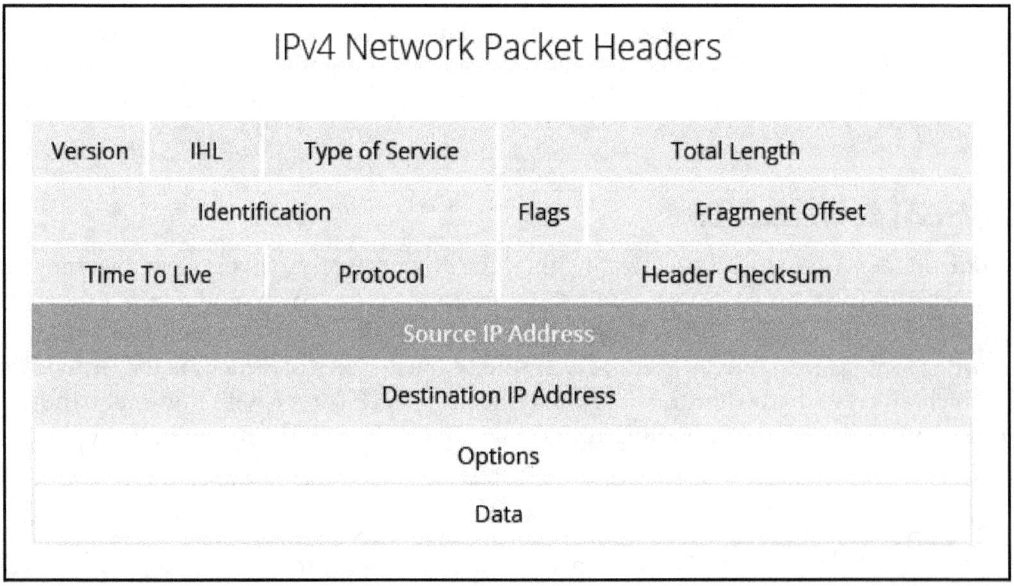

IPv4 Network Packet Headers

Version	IHL	Type of Service		Total Length
Identification			Flags	Fragment Offset
Time To Live		Protocol		Header Checksum
Source IP Address				
Destination IP Address				
Options				
Data				

In the following diagram, the attackers represent someone else's IP address:

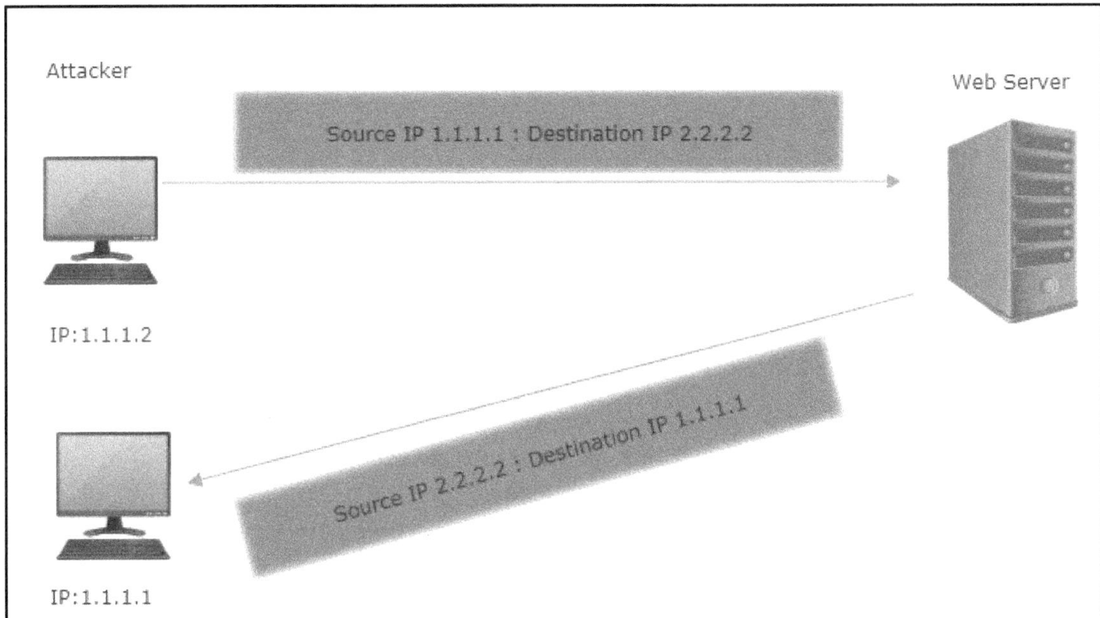

Anti-spoofing using access lists

A network operator can implement an anti-spoofing access-list filter to prevent packets with incorrect source IP addresses from entering and leaving the network. With the following command, the access list will prevent incoming packets that have the internal IP address from coming in. `220.x.x.x` is a network which I own, so I do not expect to encounter any packets coming from outside my own IP address.

Cisco IOS command:

```
access-list 101 deny 220.x.x.0 0.0.0.255 any
```

Encryption

Another possible way to prevent IP spoofing is to encrypt all network traffic to prevent source and destination hosts from being compromised.

Anti-spoofing using RPF checks

RPF is a feature with multi vendor support to prevent IP spoofing. It can be used for both unicast and multicast. RPF checks the source address of a packet as well as the interface it's being learned from. If the source address is present in the routing table, then the packet is accepted by the routing device. If not, it will drop the packet. The only problem with RPF is that it does not work with asymmetric routes and therefore requires strictly symmetric routing patterns.

Ping sweeps and Port scans

Let's try to understand ping before we discuss ping sweep.

- **Ping**: Ping is a tool commonly used to find the status of a host on a network. Ping is based on the ICMP protocol. When a Ping process request is sent out as an ICMP echo to the target host, it replies with an ICMP echo reply.
- **Ping Sweep**: Ping sweep is a technique that can be used to find out which hosts are alive in a network for a defined IP range. Network admins who allow ICMP are vulnerable to ICMP based attacks.

Multiple tools are available for ping sweeps. You can even develop your own tool with a small script. Here is a simple example of how to run a ping sweep from a Windows machine: `FOR /L` loop, which is a counter, the variable is `%i`. It starts at `1` and increases by `1` with each iteration through the loop, going up to `255`. I want to ping through a /24-sized subnet for network `192.168.0.0/24` and ping each IP address once (`-n 1`). Filters can be used `| find "Reply"`, but this will only show the IPs you get a reply from. In my live network, I have four IPs responding to the ICMP ping, as shown in the following screenshot:

```
C:\Users\ajaysinc>
C:\Users\ajaysinc>FOR /L %i in (1,1,255) do @ping -n 1 192.168.0.%i -w 100 | find "Reply"
Reply from 192.168.0.1: bytes=32 time=112ms TTL=64
Reply from 192.168.0.100: bytes=32 time=7ms TTL=64
Reply from 192.168.0.102: bytes=32 time=189ms TTL=128
Reply from 192.168.0.104: bytes=32 time<1ms TTL=128

C:\Users\ajaysinc>_
```

- **Port Scan**: Firstly, let's explore what port is. Any application on a host should have a valid port which acts like a small door to communicate with other hosts on the network. You can have a total of 65,535 TCP ports and another 65,535 UDP ports. Port ranges `0` to `1023` are reserved for privileged services and are designated as well-known ports.

  A port scan is a process that sends client requests to a range of server port addresses on a targeted host, with the aim of looking for active ports and exploiting a known vulnerability of that service.

- **TCP Port Scan**: TCP port scan is the most basic form of TCP scanning. Port scanning tools can scan a target at a very quick speed of approximately one thousand ports per second or more. These tools use operating systems to open a connection to any port on the target machine in order to detect the number of available services for a given target. If the port is listening, an initial connection handshake will succeed, otherwise the port will not be reachable.
- **TCP SYN scanning**: TCP SYN scan is based on the TCP three-way handshake and is also known as **half-open** scanning. The attacker does not open a full TCP connection but sends a SYN packet and waits for a response. A SYN/ACK response from the target indicates that the port is listening and as soon as a SYN/ACK is received, the attacker sends an RST response.

Mitigation

A simple solution to this problem is to stop ICMP totally. ICMP can be stopped on a firewall layer, network layer or even on a host layer. We understand that ICMP is a very common troubleshooting tool for network admin and system admin, but instead of relying upon an ICMP based ping, we should rely upon a TCP ping. Such scans can also be detected and stopped by the IPS/IDS system.

For a host-based example, ICMP Echo can be easily blocked on Windows by configuring an inbound rule. A new rule can be created by using the utility `wf.msc` from the Windows system:

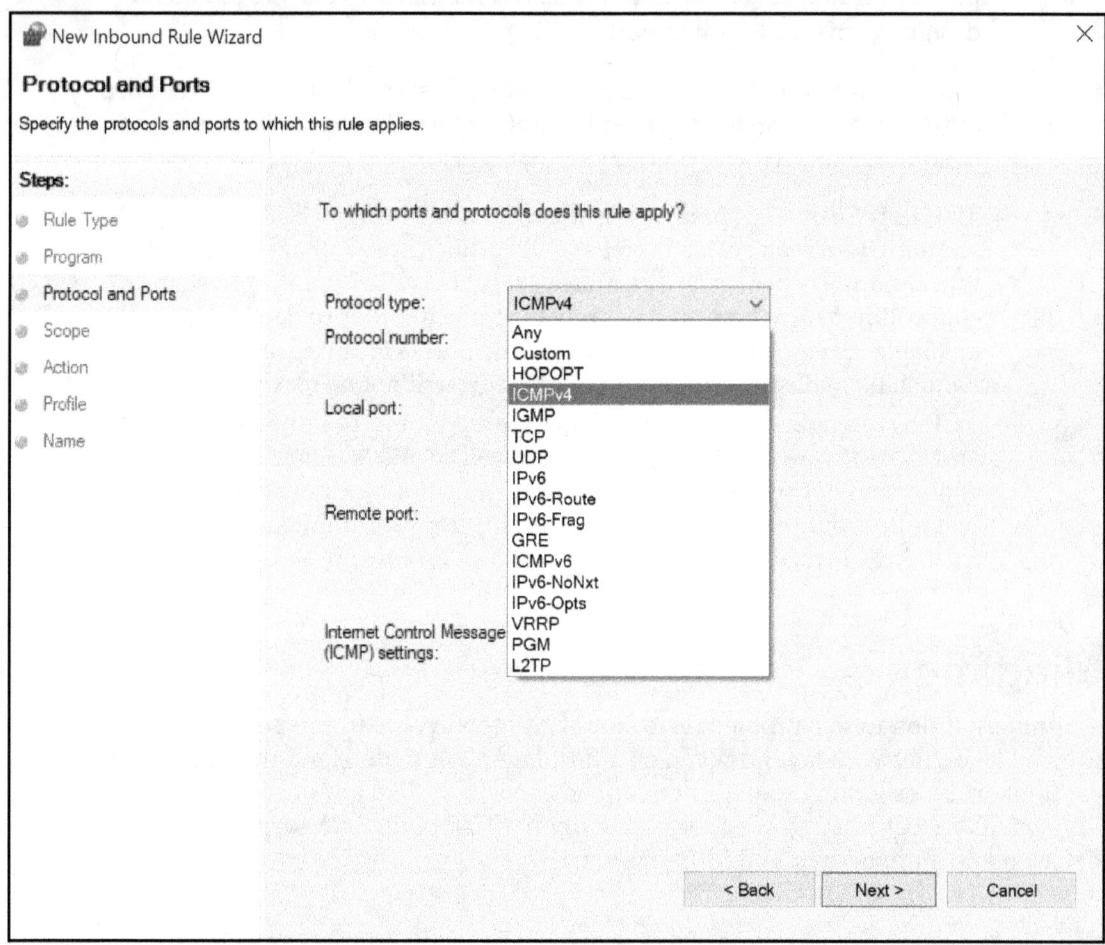

DNS vulnerabilities

DNS continues to be a very attractive target for hackers and a very important piece of network from a user's point of view. We use it seamlessly almost every time we hit a web page or application throughout a day, without even knowing that it exists.

DNS provides a way to resolve the IP address of any host on the internet with directory services.

How does DNS work?

A host sends a DNS query request to a DNS server and, in response, gets the IP address `1.1.1.1` for `www.abc.com`. The host can now make a direct request to `www.abc.com` using the IP address:

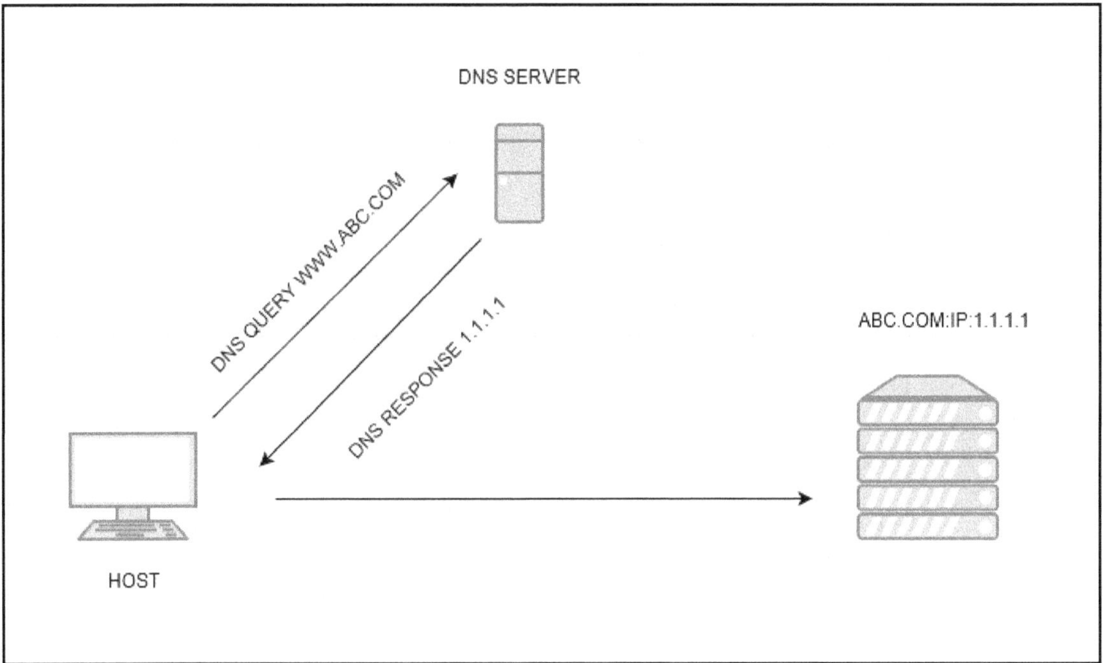

DNS protocol attacks

DNS spoofing or DNS cache poisoning: DNS spoofing occurs when particular DNS server records are altered to redirect traffic to the attacker. This redirection of traffic allows the attacker to steal data because it is hard for users to recognize the difference between an actual web page and a false web page.

In this example, users are trying to get the IP address for a real web server which is `1.1.1.1` but attackers have manipulated the DNS record and, consequently, users are redirected to the IP address for a fake website, which is `2.2.2.2`:

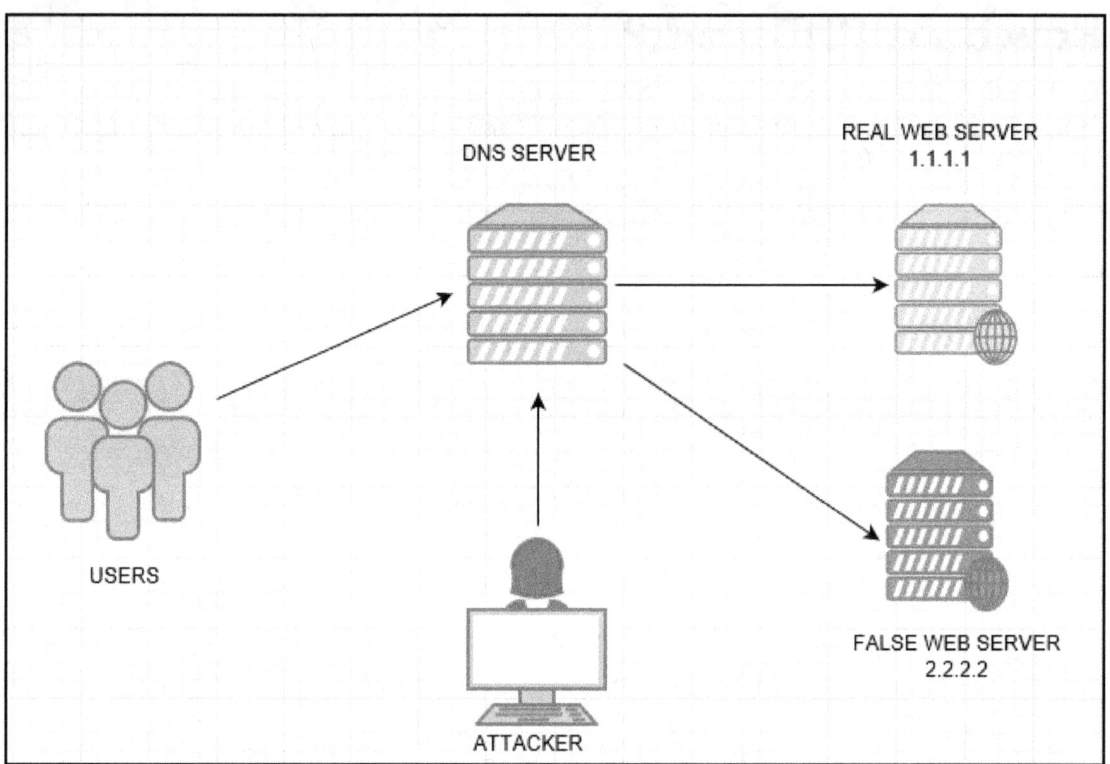

Mitigation

Domain Name System Security Extensions (**DNSSEC**) is a secure technology based on digitally signed DNS records to help determine data authenticity. DNSSEC creates a secure domain name system by adding cryptographic signatures to existing DNS records. The main goal for DNSSEC is to strengthen trust in the internet by helping to protect users from being redirected to fraudulent websites and unintended addresses.

Two factor authentication

Two-Factor Authentication (**2FA**) is an optional layer of security which adds another level of protection to your account. This process combines something you have (a token or code) with something you know (a password). Two-factor authentication is more effective in securing account access than a password alone, making it more difficult for attackers to access your accounts since they become dynamic in nature. The two common methods of 2FA are as follows:

- **Authentication App or Token**: Generate a security code using a trusted app or security RSA token
- **SMS Verification**: Send a security code to the phone number linked to your account via an SMS text message

An example of two-factor authentication:

Most banks now have two-factor authentication available to their customers. A good example of network administration is to combine an RSA feature with Cisco TACACS or Radius to gain access for any network device. VPN users must be authenticated with 2FA to validate an identity.

Hardware tokens (in the form of key fobs or card readers) are difficult to maintain due to logistic support and tokens are also usually small and easily lost. 2FA makes life easier by utilizing mobile phone SMS technology.

Following is an image of an RSA Hardware Token:

Summary

The process of designing a secure network requires identifying an insecure area, understanding the methods of network attacks and the best solutions to meet the needs of a business. The four fundamental technical requirements of network design are scalability, availability, security, and manageability.

We discussed the importance of using the right approach to safeguard against security threats in an increasingly internet oriented world. We also covered the security weaknesses for all networking layers including routers, switches, firewall configuration systems and risks when connected to the internet. We have also learnt the best security methods and how to protect the network from vulnerabilities, threats and attacks by applying security configurations.

In the next chapter, we will discuss more about server security, encryption methods and policy enforcement with regards to data protection.

Questions

1. What does AAA stand for?
    1. Authority
    2. Authorization
    3. Auditing
    4. Authentication
    5. Accounting
2. What are the two most common AAA protocols?
    1. TCP/IP
    2. RADIUS
    3. TACACS+
    4. PPP

3. An attack which attempts to make targeted systems unavailable to its intended users is called:
    1. Denial-of-Service attack
    2. Slow read attack
    3. Spoofed attack
    4. Starvation attack
4. Which of the following is not an attack, but a tool which searches for available services to identify vulnerabilities in order to attack a given target?
    1. Denial-of-Service
    2. Port scanning
    3. Memory access violation
    4. Dumpster diving

Further reading

For references and further information, refer to the following links:

- `https://gcn.com/Articles/2014/08/07/Layer-1-network-encryption.aspx`
- `http://www.uebermeister.com/files/inside it/2016_Introduction_Encryption_Metro_and_Carrier_Ethernet.pdf`
- `http://ieeexplore.ieee.org/document/7781061/`

3
Server-Level Security

In the previous chapter, we discussed how to build a secure network infrastructure. In this chapter, we will discuss how to build and ensure security for servers inside a secure network.

Server/computer security is a critical part of the infrastructure for running business smoothly. Information security has evolved over the years due to an increasing dependency on public networks not to disclose personal, financial, and other restricted information. Consequently, it becomes important to maintain data confidentiality, integrity and availability. This chapter focuses on securing data and implementing various policies to secure a server infrastructure.

We will cover the following topics in this chapter:

- Classification of data
- Physical security
- Disk encryption
- Hardening server security
- Authentication NTLM versus Kerberos
- Password policies
- Server-level permissions
- Server antivirus and malware protection
- Local security policies

Classification of data

The main motive for setting up IT infrastructure is to get your applications up and running. However, after classifying our assets, we need to address the security when it comes to one layer on a server specific infrastructure. In a big network of multi-vendor servers and multi-operating system environments, different sets of applications are expected. A grouping server based on role, permission, and operating system can address multiple security concerns.

Physical security

In most cases, physical access translates to a total loss of security. Even if they can't access your data, an attacker can do a lot of damage. We'll take a look at the most essential security measures everyone should implement, if they haven't already been done:

- **Lock up the server room**: The server room is the power station of your physical network, and someone with physical access to the servers, switches, routers, cables, and other devices in that room can do enormous damage.
- **Set up surveillance**: You need a way to monitor who goes in and out, what they do and when they do it. A better solution is to set up biometric scanners that are required in order to unlock the doors, and the identity of each technician is then recorded. Surveillance cameras can monitor continuously, or they can use motion detection technology to record a person's movement. They can even send an email or cell phone notification if motion is detected when it shouldn't be.
- **Disable the drives**: Of course, for a protected environment, we don't want anybody copying company information to removable media. You should simply disable or remove USB ports and other ways of connecting external drives.
- **Educate your employees**: Apart from technology, this is the most important factor behind security. It is necessary to train staff on security related issues such as password selection, social engineering tactics, and email phishing. This will make it almost impossible for an outsider to intrude.

Disk encryption

It is important to secure any server that manages business critical data and its customers. The fact that servers reside in a secured facility doesn't prevent them from being at risk to data loss or theft. Sometimes storage drives in a server are misplaced during transportation, which can lead to data loss. Another example would be to prevent offline attacks. If data drives are stolen and inserted into another system to boot with another operating system, this basically bypasses the password protection. If that drive isn't encrypted, its information can be retrieved and exposed to unwanted audiences, leaving an organization at risk of regulatory violations, personal lawsuits, and damage to its corporate reputation.

Full-disk encryption

Let's explore the process in detail, looking at how the whole disk encryption works. Full disk encryption encrypts an entire disk drive. When an authenticated user accesses a file from a fully encrypted drive, the encryption technology decrypts the file using the decryption key provided at system startup, and the rest of the drive remains encrypted. This method ensures the protection of the hard drive if a system failure occurs or the system is deliberately shutdown. The primary goal of full disk encryption is that the drive and files remain encrypted during the system shutdown state. On a running system, the encryption is technically not in place for users to access files. This is because the operating system has the decryption key to access files on the disk.

Full disk encryption is a perfect solution for devices like notebooks and desktops, which shutdown at some point. Full disk encryption helps to protect data in the event of the physical loss of a disk and makes more sense for portable devices.

Bitlocker

BitLocker is Microsoft native technology that enables you to encrypt entire hard disks, including the operating system. To get the best results from BitLocker, a hardware system must be equipped with a **Trusted Platform Module** (**TPM**) chip. This is a special microchip that enables your device to support advanced security features. However, you can also use BitLocker without a TPM by using a software-based encryption.

The TPM chip 2.0 can be seen under security devices in the device manager:

Virtual Trusted Platform Module – vTPM

Trusted Computing Group (**TCG**) introduced TPM in 2009. A **Trusted Platform Module** (**TPM**) is a microchip that is often built into the motherboard to provide hardware-based security. This can be also be added later for customized systems if your motherboard supports it. A TPM chip is a secure crypto-processor that is designed to carry out cryptographic operations. If you are using BitLocker encryption on a computer with the TPM, part of the key is stored in the TPM itself, rather than just on the disk. This means that an attacker can't just remove the drive from the computer and attempt to access its files elsewhere.

In Windows server 2016 Hyper-v and Windows 10, you can enable vTPM into a VM. Virtual instance will be mapped to each VM, as shown in the following diagram:

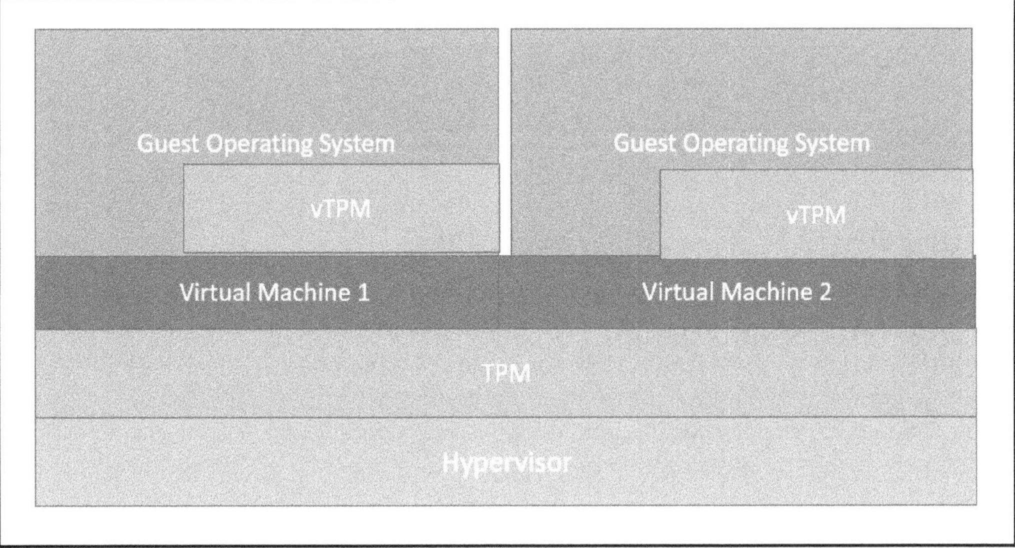

This is what the hardware TPM chip looks like:

Encrypt your Hyper-V Guest VMs

In a virtualized environment, encrypting guest virtual machines is another layer of protection that you can add in Hyper-V. You may wonder what the need is for this if encrypting the Hyper-V host itself can protect against stolen physical disks. Enabling BitLocker inside your virtual machines protects against stolen virtual disks as well. For example, if an attacker manages to gain access to an online Hyper-V, host and VHDX or VHD files can be downloaded or stolen.

Here is the screenshot from Hyper-V 2016 in which the vTPM option is disabled by default. As soon you turn on the feature, it can share virtualized TPM instances with VMs:

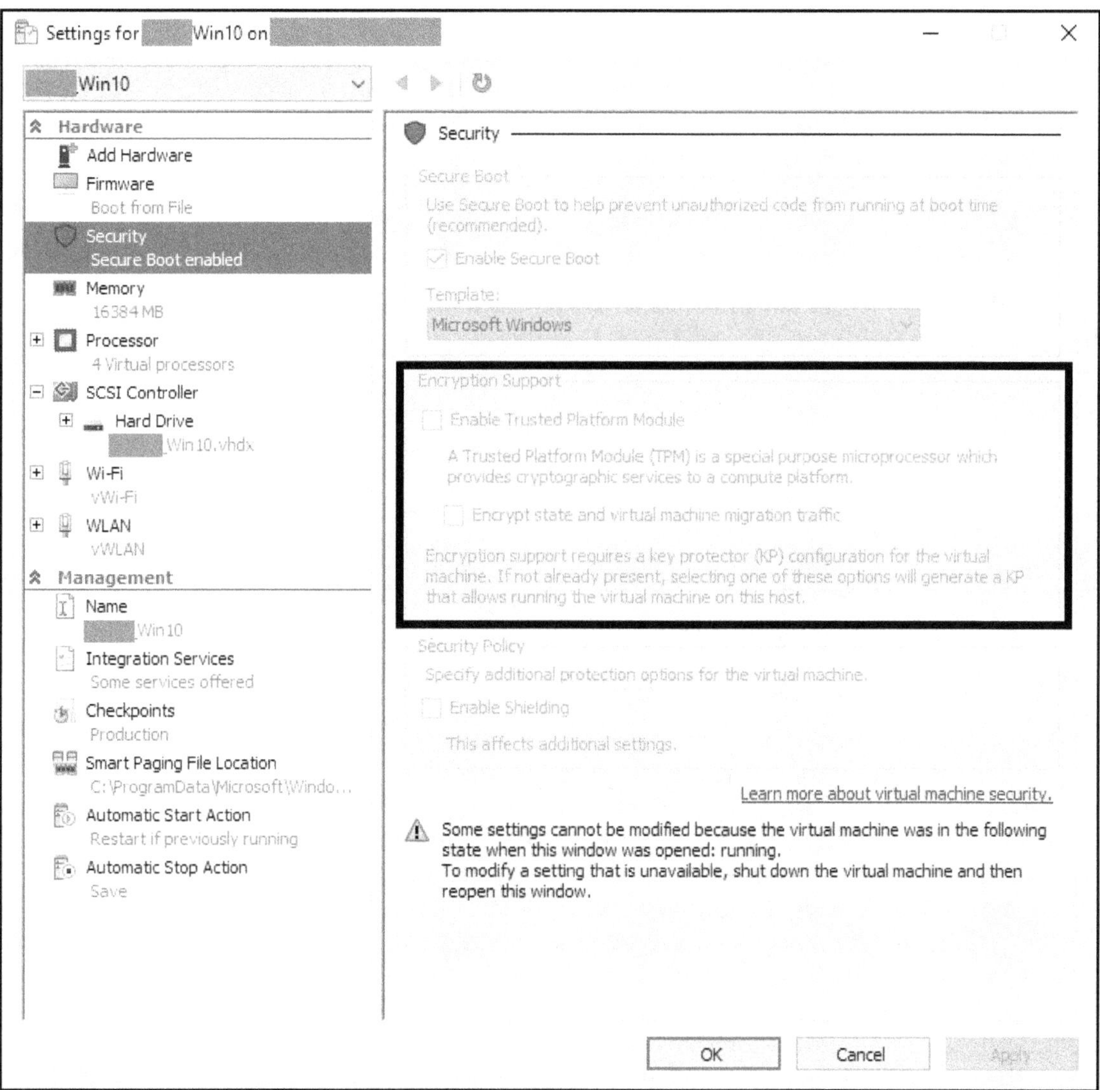

Cloud VM disk encryption

In this diagram, I have taken a screenshot of the running Azure VM which shows a disk associated with a VM that is not encrypted (**ENCRYPTION** not enabled). Having said that, it also states that the disk is encrypted at rest with **Storage Service Encryption** (**SSE**). For more information, you can refer to Azure documentation. Rest is the default data protection technique achieved by encrypting the service provider's full disk in order to protect data in case of physical theft or loss of the disk:

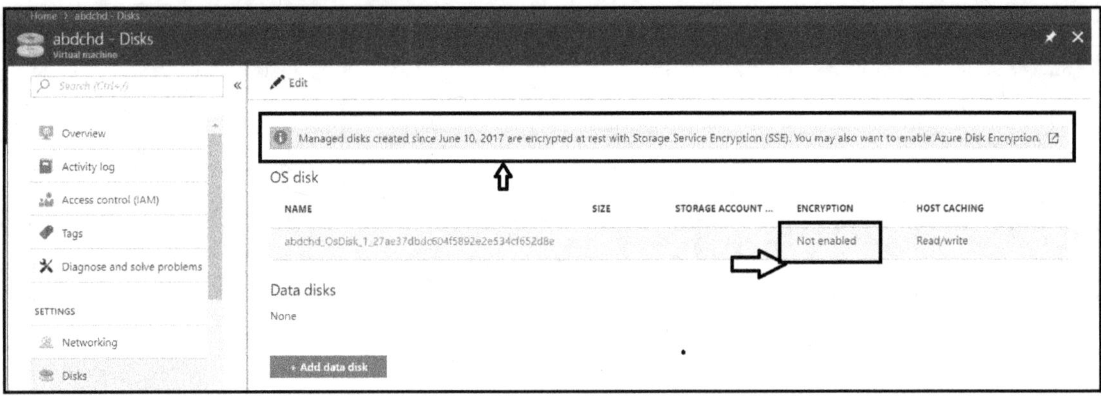

What is encryption at rest?

Encryption at rest refers to the cryptographic encoding of data when it is persevered on physical media. Encryption at rest is supposed to protect data from at rest attacks, including attempts to obtain physical media access where the data is stored. In such an attack, a server's hard drive may have been stolen or misplaced, allowing an attacker to recover data from the hard drive by putting it into a compute device of their own. Encryption at rest is designed to prevent critical data access by unauthorized persons by ensuring that the data remains encrypted when it resides on a disk. An attacker can obtain a hard drive with data in an encrypted format, but without access to the encryption keys, they would not be able to decode the data. Encryption at rest is highly recommended and is a high-priority requirement for many organizations, including cloud service providers, to allow them to comply with state law government regulations and industry standards such as HIPAA and PCI.

Google, Amazon, and Azure Cloud service providers encrypt customer data stored at rest by default, with no additional action required from you.

Hardening server security

Most of us assume that systems or servers are already secure, and this might be a false assumption. Imagine if any system server, firewall or router is stolen without first being hardened. An attacker would probably first try to crack a targeted system with a default username and password. For a Linux based machine, my default username would be `root`, the password would be `root`, and most of us would continue to use it. Server hardening involves identifying and re-mediating security vulnerabilities. We will discuss server hardening and the best practices you can implement immediately in order to reduce the risk of attackers compromising your business's critical systems and data.

Check for open ports or services

Identifying open ports on servers requires the port to be opened and unnecessary services to be disabled or shutdown. The server should have a minimal operating system configuration.

For Windows, run the following command using the Command Prompt:

```
netstat -a | findstr "LISTEN"
```

The ouptu of the preceding command is as shown in the screenshot:

```
C:\Users\ajaysinc>netstat -a | findstr "LISTEN"
  TCP    0.0.0.0:80             abdchd:0               LISTENING
  TCP    0.0.0.0:135            abdchd:0               LISTENING
  TCP    0.0.0.0:445            abdchd:0               LISTENING
  TCP    0.0.0.0:3389           abdchd:0               LISTENING
  TCP    0.0.0.0:5985           abdchd:0               LISTENING
  TCP    0.0.0.0:47001          abdchd:0               LISTENING
  TCP    0.0.0.0:49664          abdchd:0               LISTENING
  TCP    0.0.0.0:49665          abdchd:0               LISTENING
  TCP    0.0.0.0:49666          abdchd:0               LISTENING
  TCP    0.0.0.0:49667          abdchd:0               LISTENING
  TCP    0.0.0.0:49668          abdchd:0               LISTENING
  TCP    0.0.0.0:49670          abdchd:0               LISTENING
  TCP    10.0.1.4:139           abdchd:0               LISTENING
  TCP    [::]:80                abdchd:0               LISTENING
  TCP    [::]:135               abdchd:0               LISTENING
  TCP    [::]:445               abdchd:0               LISTENING
  TCP    [::]:3389              abdchd:0               LISTENING
  TCP    [::]:5985              abdchd:0               LISTENING
  TCP    [::]:47001             abdchd:0               LISTENING
  TCP    [::]:49664             abdchd:0               LISTENING
  TCP    [::]:49665             abdchd:0               LISTENING
  TCP    [::]:49666             abdchd:0               LISTENING
  TCP    [::]:49667             abdchd:0               LISTENING
  TCP    [::]:49668             abdchd:0               LISTENING
  TCP    [::]:49670             abdchd:0               LISTENING

C:\Users\ajaysinc>_
```

For Linux/Unix, run the following command using the shell prompt:

```
netstat -antp | grep "LISTEN"
```

```
ajaysinc@ubuntu-lin:~$ netstat -antp | grep "LISTEN"
(Not all processes could be identified, non-owned process info
 will not be shown, you would have to be root to see it all.)
tcp        0      0 0.0.0.0:22              0.0.0.0:*               LISTEN      -
tcp6       0      0 :::22                   :::*                    LISTEN      -
ajaysinc@ubuntu-lin:~$ 
```

System firewall configuration

To restrict traffic based on firewall rules, traffic should only be allowed into ports that need to be open for services. For example, secure web servers will need to provide access to TCP port `443` to most users, but they do not need **Remote Desktop Protocol** (**RDP**) or **Secure Shell** (**SSH**) management access from all source IPs.

For Windows, you can configure new inbound and outbound rules using advanced security options:

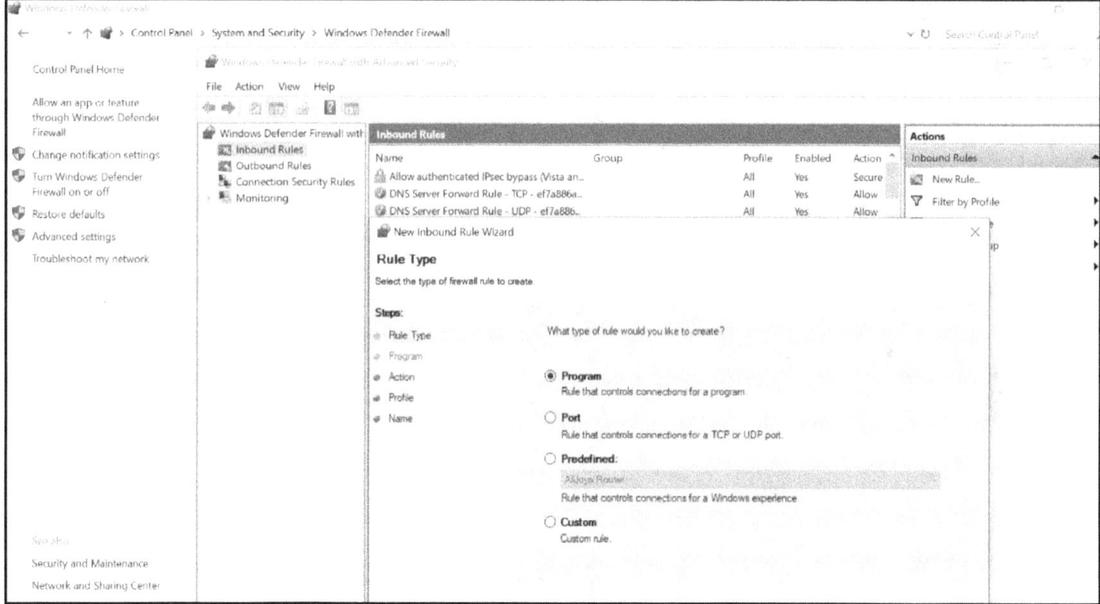

For Linux, `sudo iptables -L` lists your current rules in `iptables`. If you have just set up your server, you will have no rules and the output should be similar to the following screenshot:

```
ajaysinc@ajaysinclinux:~$ sudo iptables -L
Chain INPUT (policy ACCEPT)
target     prot opt source               destination

Chain FORWARD (policy ACCEPT)
target     prot opt source               destination

Chain OUTPUT (policy ACCEPT)
target     prot opt source               destination
ajaysinc@ajaysinclinux:~$
```

System update

The first thing to do after the first boot is to update the system. Critical updates should be applied as soon as possible. Be sure to test these updates in test environments. First, do this to confirm proper function. If there are no compatibility issues, you should then test them in production.

The following screenshot is from 2016 Server, which you can update using the PowerShell prompt:

```
PS C:\Users\ajaysinc> Install-Module PSWindowsUpdate

NuGet provider is required to continue
PowerShellGet requires NuGet provider version '2.8.5.201' or newer to interact with NuGet-based repositories. The NuGet
 provider must be available in 'C:\Program Files\PackageManagement\ProviderAssemblies' or
'C:\Users\ajaysinc\AppData\Local\PackageManagement\ProviderAssemblies'. You can also install the NuGet provider by
running 'Install-PackageProvider -Name NuGet -MinimumVersion 2.8.5.201 -Force'. Do you want PowerShellGet to install
and import the NuGet provider now?
[Y] Yes  [N] No  [S] Suspend  [?] Help (default is "Y"): y

Untrusted repository
You are installing the modules from an untrusted repository. If you trust this repository, change its
InstallationPolicy value by running the Set-PSRepository cmdlet. Are you sure you want to install the modules from
'PSGallery'?
[Y] Yes  [A] Yes to All  [N] No  [L] No to All  [S] Suspend  [?] Help (default is "N"): y
PS C:\Users\ajaysinc> Get-WindowsUpdate

ComputerName Status     KB          Size Title
------------ ------     --          ---- -----
abdchd       -D-----    KB890830    39MB Windows Malicious Software Removal Tool x64 - March 2018 (KB890830)
abdchd       -------    KB4088889    1GB 2018-03 Cumulative Update for Windows Server 2016 for x64-based Systems (KB...
abdchd       -D-----    KB4089510   11MB 2018-03 Update for Windows Server 2016 for x64-based Systems (KB4089510)


PS C:\Users\ajaysinc> Install-WindowsUpdate

Confirm
Are you sure you want to perform this action?
Performing the operation "Windows Malicious Software Removal Tool x64 - March 2018 (KB890830)[39MB]" on target
"abdchd".
[Y] Yes  [A] Yes to All  [N] No  [L] No to All  [S] Suspend  [?] Help (default is "Y"): y

Confirm
Are you sure you want to perform this action?
Performing the operation "2018-03 Cumulative Update for Windows Server 2016 for x64-based Systems (KB4088889)[1GB]" on
target "abdchd".
[Y] Yes  [A] Yes to All  [N] No  [L] No to All  [S] Suspend  [?] Help (default is "Y"): _
```

For Linux, you can run a command to fetch all updates:

```
sudo apt-get update
```

```
ajaysinc@ajaysinclinux:~$ sudo apt-get update
Get:1 http://security.ubuntu.com trusty-security InRelease [65.9 kB]
Ign http://azure.archive.ubuntu.com trusty InRelease
Get:2 http://azure.archive.ubuntu.com trusty-updates InRelease [65.9 kB]
Hit http://azure.archive.ubuntu.com trusty-backports InRelease
Hit http://azure.archive.ubuntu.com trusty Release.gpg
Hit http://azure.archive.ubuntu.com trusty Release
Get:3 http://azure.archive.ubuntu.com trusty-updates/main Sources [415 kB]
Get:4 http://azure.archive.ubuntu.com trusty-updates/restricted Sources [6,322 B]
Get:5 http://azure.archive.ubuntu.com trusty-updates/universe Sources [199 kB]
Get:6 http://azure.archive.ubuntu.com trusty-updates/multiverse Sources [7,368 B]
Get:7 http://azure.archive.ubuntu.com trusty-updates/main amd64 Packages [1,070 kB]
Get:8 http://azure.archive.ubuntu.com trusty-updates/restricted amd64 Packages [17.2 kB]
Get:9 http://azure.archive.ubuntu.com trusty-updates/universe amd64 Packages [450 kB]
Get:10 http://azure.archive.ubuntu.com trusty-updates/multiverse amd64 Packages [14.6 kB]
Get:11 http://azure.archive.ubuntu.com trusty-updates/main Translation-en [528 kB]
Get:12 http://azure.archive.ubuntu.com trusty-updates/multiverse Translation-en [7,616 B]
Get:13 http://azure.archive.ubuntu.com trusty-updates/restricted Translation-en [4,024 B]
Get:14 http://azure.archive.ubuntu.com trusty-updates/universe Translation-en [243 kB]
```

Disable USB

Universal Serial Bus (**USB**) connections are typically plug and play devices. For example, hard disks or pen drives for your computer. Being plug and play in nature, an operating system automatically identifies the device and installs a driver for it. Since USB devices are portable and can be connected easily to computers, these devices can cause real security threats. To prevent employees from saving sensitive information on USB drives, financial organizations do not allow USB devices. The system administrator can disable or block USB devices using group policy. We will now take a look at the steps on how to disable USB devices using group policy.

For Windows, from **Group Policy Management Editor**, you can enable **All Removal Storage classes: Deny all access** as shown in the following screenshot:

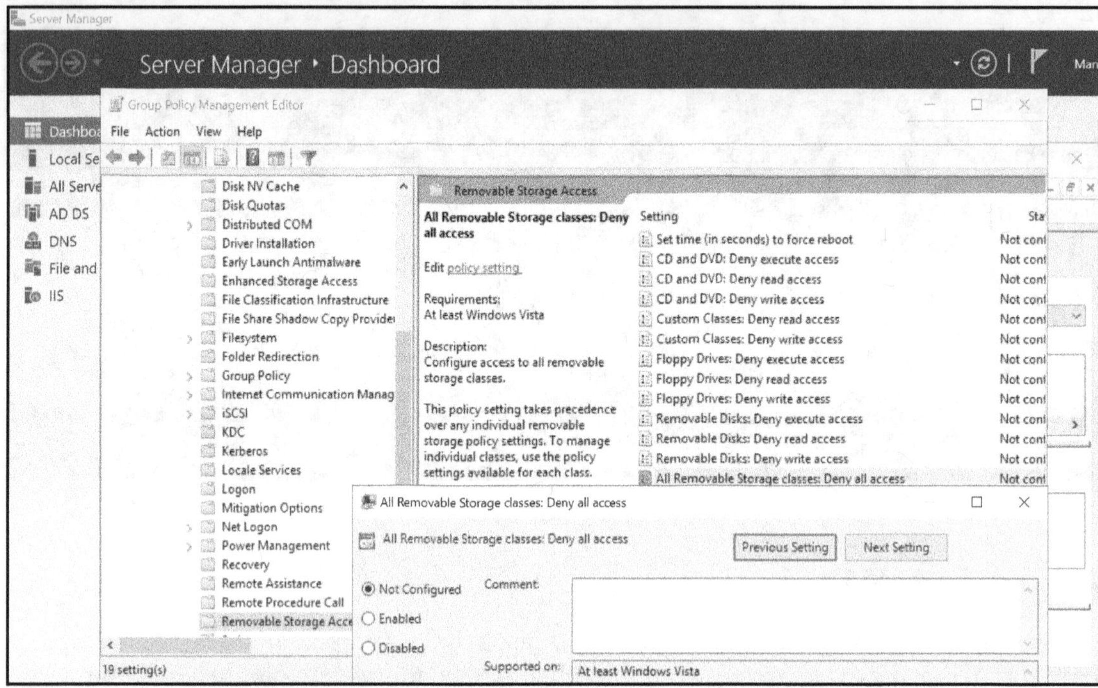

For Linux, you can edit this file by adding `blacklist usb_storage`.

Hard disk encryption

Disk encryption is important in the case of theft. This is because the attackers who stole your computer won't be able to decode your data if they connect the hard disk to their machine and try to retrieve the data. We have already discussed this option in detail in the *Full-disk encryption* section of this chapter.

BIOS protection

It is important to protect the BIOS of the system with a password so that attackers won't be able to use it to change security settings. You also need to disable the booting from external media devices (USB/CD/DVD). BIOS protection is only an authentication mechanism designed to prevent unauthorized physical access to BIOS. BIOS now comes with out-of-band access, meaning that, with the right hardware configuration, you have full remote access to your computer, no matter what state it is in.

Check the installed packages

List all packages installed on your operating system, and remove the unnecessary ones. Disabling unnecessary services will reduce the attack surface. Let's look at how to check installed packages on different OSes.

For Windows, run the following command from PowerShell in admin mode:

```
Get-AppxPackage -AllUsers | Select Name, PackageFullName
```

```
Administrator: Windows PowerShell
Windows PowerShell
Copyright (C) 2016 Microsoft Corporation. All rights reserved.

PS C:\Users\ajaysinc> Get-AppxPackage -AllUsers | Select Name, PackageFullName

Name                                      PackageFullName
----                                      ---------------
Microsoft.AAD.BrokerPlugin                Microsoft.AAD.BrokerPlugin_1000.14393.0.0_neutral_neutral_cw5n1h2txyewy
Microsoft.AccountsControl                 Microsoft.AccountsControl_10.0.14393.1715_neutral__cw5n1h2txyewy
Microsoft.BioEnrollment                   Microsoft.BioEnrollment_10.0.14393.0_neutral__cw5n1h2txyewy
Microsoft.LockApp                         Microsoft.LockApp_10.0.14393.0_neutral__cw5n1h2txyewy
Microsoft.Windows.Apprep.ChxApp           Microsoft.Windows.Apprep.ChxApp_1000.14393.0.0_neutral_neutral_cw5n1h2txyewy
Microsoft.Windows.AssignedAccessLockApp   Microsoft.Windows.AssignedAccessLockApp_1000.14393.0.0_neutral_neutral_cw5...
Microsoft.Windows.CloudExperienceHost     Microsoft.Windows.CloudExperienceHost_10.0.14393.1066_neutral_neutral_cw5n...
Microsoft.Windows.Cortana                 Microsoft.Windows.Cortana_1.7.0.14393_neutral_neutral_cw5n1h2txyewy
Microsoft.Windows.SecondaryTileExperience Microsoft.Windows.SecondaryTileExperience_10.0.0.0_neutral__cw5n1h2txyewy
Microsoft.Windows.ShellExperienceHost     Microsoft.Windows.ShellExperienceHost_10.0.14393.1715_neutral_neutral_cw5n...
Microsoft.XboxGameCallableUI              Microsoft.XboxGameCallableUI_1000.14393.0.0_neutral_neutral_cw5n1h2txyewy
windows.immersivecontrolpanel             windows.immersivecontrolpanel_6.2.0.0_neutral_neutral_cw5n1h2txyewy
Windows.MiracastView                      Windows.MiracastView_6.3.0.0_neutral_neutral_cw5n1h2txyewy
Windows.PrintDialog                       Windows.PrintDialog_6.2.0.0_neutral_neutral_cw5n1h2txyewy
```

For Linux, Telnet comes with a default configuration. Do we need Telnet in a secured environment? Maybe, but personally I don't recommend using it in a secured environment because the data exchange used by a Telnet connection is in plain text.

```
ajaysinc@ubuntu-lin:~$ apt list --installed | grep "telnet"

WARNING: apt does not have a stable CLI interface. Use with caution in scripts.

telnet/xenial,now 0.17-40 amd64 [installed]
ajaysinc@ubuntu-lin:~$
```

Password policies

Don't forget to protect your passwords and do not reuse them. Use a password policy to ensure that accounts on the server can't be compromised or broken by some sort of brute-force attack. If your server is a member of **Active Directory Domain Services** (**ADDS**), the password policy will be set at the domain level. We will discuss password policies in detail in an upcoming section.

Secure and encrypt remote access

SSH uses the cryptography process running at the backend, and therefore is considered very secure. However, you still need to harden this service as well. Make sure you are running the latest version of SSH protocol, and SSH sources can be further restricted with IP subnet. Remote Desktop sessions operate over an encrypted channel, preventing anyone from snooping your session on the network. However, there is a vulnerability in the method used to encrypt sessions in earlier versions of RDP. The best approach would be to update your software, restrict access using firewalls, and set an account lockout policy for additional security. You can also change your RDP port from `3389` to something else, using RDP gateways and then finally using 2FA.

Implement activity logging

You need to make sure that your logs and monitoring are configured and are capturing the data you want so that whenever there is a problem, you can quickly discover who, when, and what you need to fix it. You must set up a centralized log management solution to monitor logs, server health like disk space, CPU, memory, and network activity.

Document the host information

Finally, you should have proper documents which include host information such as the system name, IP address, MAC address, asset tag, and owner information.

Authentication NTLM versus Kerberos

NT LAN Manager (**NTLM**) and Kerberos are both authentication protocols that do not play any role in terms of authorization. NTLM is a proprietary authentication protocol developed by Microsoft, whereas Kerberos is a standard protocol. Starting with Win2K, Microsoft implements Kerberos as the default authentication protocol for the Windows OS. However, if the Kerberos protocol is not negotiated for some reason, then **Active Directory** (**AD**) will use LM, NTLM, or **NTLM version 2** (**NTLMv2**).

Kerberos is a cryptographic network protocol that works for authenticating users to resources, which involves a client, server, and a **Key Distribution Center** (**KDC**). Kerberos was named after Cerberus, the three-headed dog of Greek mythology, because of its three components. KDC has two components: an **Authentication Server** and a **Ticket Granting Service**, as well as the **Client** and the **Print Server** that the Client wants to access, as shown in the following diagram:

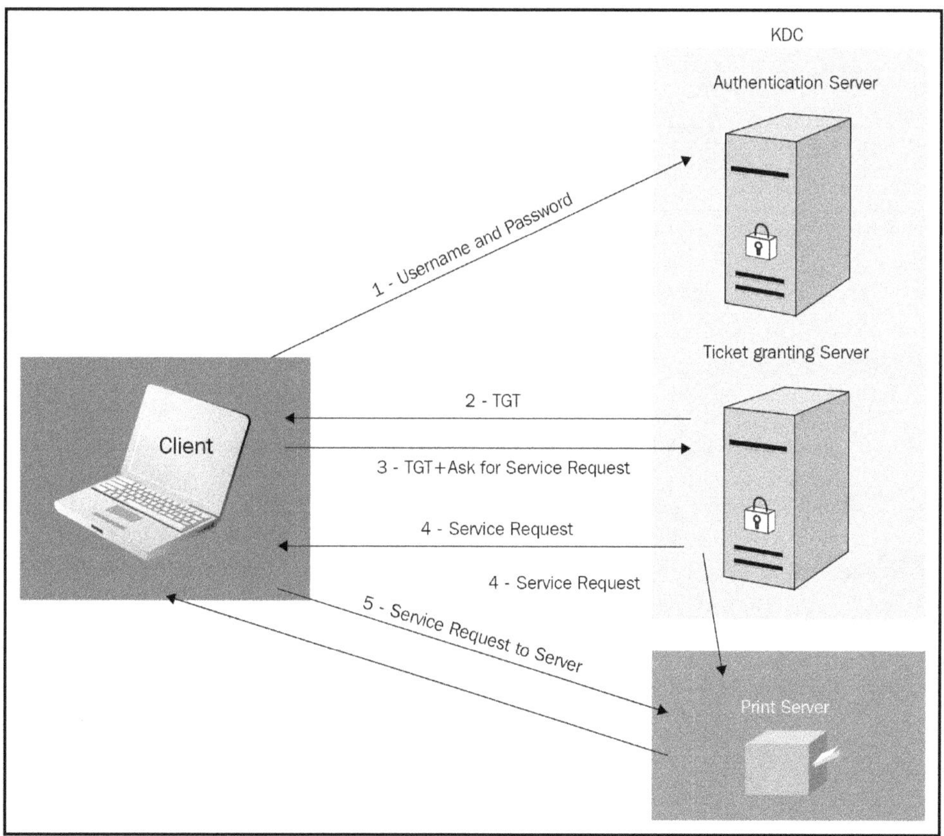

Let's try to understand the process step by step:

1. For network domain authentication, a Client provides a username and a password, which is validated by the Authentication Server, a component of KDC.
2. The KDC grants a **Ticket Getting Ticket** (**TGT**) with a default duration of 10 hours.
3. When the client attempts to access the Print Server in the domain, the TGT is used to make the request instead of entering credentials again and again. The Client obtains a service ticket from the Ticket Granting Server, a component of KDC.
4. A service ticket is created for the Client and the Server that the Client wants to access. The service ticket consists of a ticket and a session key.
5. The Client presents the service ticket to create a session with the service on the Server. The Server uses its key to decrypt the information from the TGS, and the Client is authenticated to the Server.

The major differences can be seen in the following table:

NTLM	**Kerberos**
Challenge-Response based authentication	Ticket based authentication
Microsoft proprietary protocol	Open Standard protocol
The server connects the domain controller [DC] to validate the client's response for the challenge (known as pass-through authentication)	The client contacts the DC to get service ticket.
Due to Pass-through authentication for each session and DC is contacted each Time you access the services, which makes it more chatty.	Faster! The client manages a Tickets cache. No need to contact the DC for additional sessions to the same service if the ticket is still Valid.
Weak cryptographic and easy to crack	Strong cryptography

System admins need to make sure they run Kerberos by default. In any scenarios where you need to turn on NTLM, it should be used with caution, keeping risks in mind.

Password policies

Passwords are an important characteristic of computer security. A poorly constructed, weak password may result in unauthorized access or exploitation of organization IT resources. This password construction guideline applies to all passwords, including (but not limited to) user-level accounts, system-level accounts, web accounts, email accounts, and local router logins. On a Windows system, you can run `secpol.msc` from the Command Prompt:

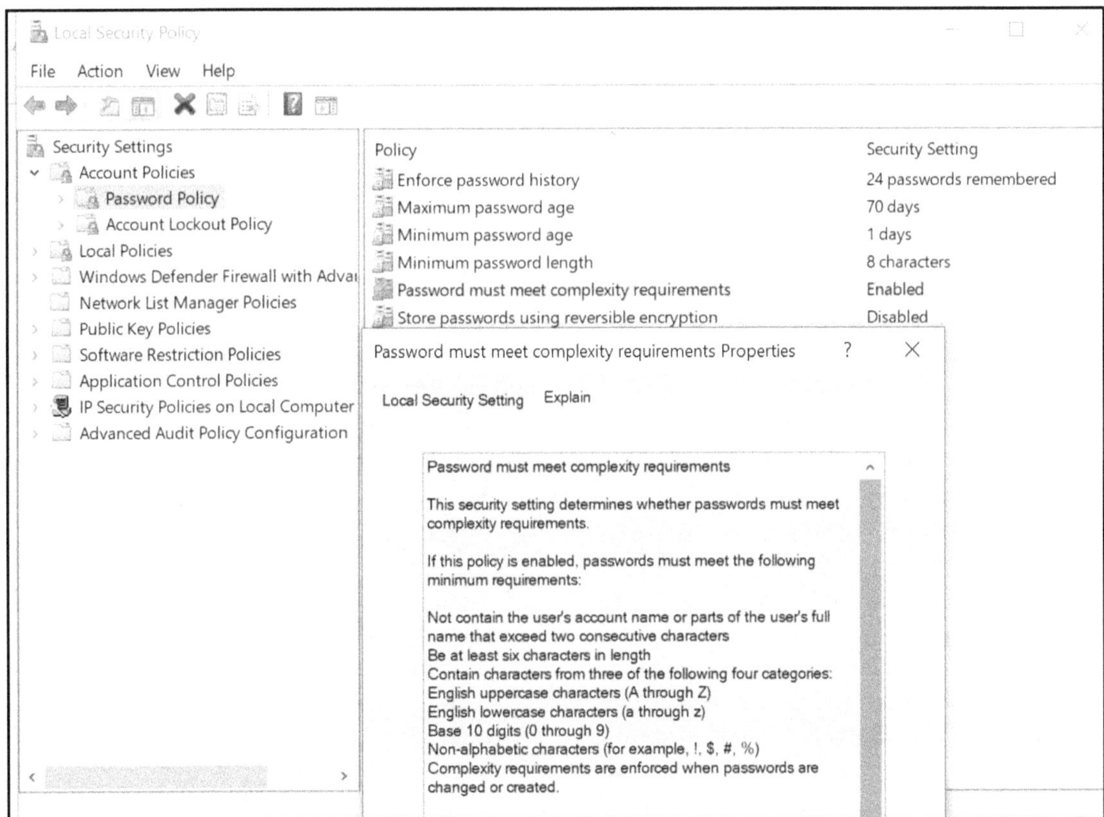

Strong passwords have the following characteristics:

- They contain at least twelve alphanumeric characters
- They contain both upper and lowercase letters
- They contain at least one number (for example, 0-9)
- They contain at least one special character (for example, !$%^*()_+|~-=\`{}[]:";'?,/)

Following are some of the password policies we must remember:

- **Protect your password**: It is very challenging to remember your password without writing it down somewhere, so choose a strong password or passphrase that you will easily remember. If you have a lot of passwords, you can use password management tools or vaults, but make sure you choose a strong master key and remember it. Change your password periodically. Even if it hasn't been compromised, you can set a policy to change the password every 90 days, as a standard guideline. Do not use the same password for multiple websites containing sensitive information.
- **Set a lockout policy**: We've all forgotten a password at some point, and it has taken a few tries to get back into the system. However, you should set an acceptable number of login attempts that when exceeded with unsuccessful attempts, will lock the user out. This will protect your system from any type of Brute-Force attack.
- **Enforce password history**: This security setting determines the number of unique new passwords that have to be associated with a user account before an old password can be reused. The value must be between zero and twenty four passwords on domain controllers.
- **Minimum password age**: This setting determines the minimum number of days a password must be in use before it can be changed. Only when the minimum password age expires are users allowed to change their password. This ensures that users don't change their password too often. The value can be set between zero and nine hundred and ninety-nine days. The default value is one for domain controllers and zero for standalone servers.
- **Minimum password length**: This setting determines the minimum number of characters a password should contain. The value can be set between zero and fourteen. The default value is seven on domain controllers and zero on stand-alone servers.

Server-level permissions

In an organization, firstly you need to identify assets based on the type of server, where each server has a specific role to perform. Server-level roles are server-wide in their permissions scope. You can add server-level principals (server logins, user accounts, and Windows security groups) into server-level roles. Security groups can provide an efficient way to assign access to resources on your network:

- **Security groups in Active Directory**: User rights are assigned to a security group to determine what members of that group can do within the scope of a domain or forest. For example, default domain admins have full permission on all server parts of that specific domain irrespective of server roles. However, we can create user defined groups and add the required user account to that group to limit access.
- **Windows service accounts**: There are applications that run on Windows servers that need an account that is specific to that service. A service account helps in solving this problem and acts as a user identity that is associated with a service executable for the purpose of providing a security context for that service.

Server antivirus and malware protection

Understanding the difference between malware, spyware, trojans, ransomware, scareware, and viruses is very important. For example, a computer virus is the most famous type of malware. *Malware* is short for malicious software or code and is used as a single term to refer to a virus, spyware, worm, and so on, written to disrupt, exploit, steal data, or disable computers over networks. It is important that all users know how to recognize and protect themselves from malware in all of its forms. By nature, computer viruses and worms spread by making copies of themselves. Most of us feel that a firewall does protect us from malware, but, in reality, normal stateful (we will discuss how stateful firewalls work in detail in the `Chapter 10`, *Firewall Placement and Detection Techniques*) firewalls don't protect against malicious content on websites, but anti-malware protects servers and workstations. I would like to clarify here that next-generation firewalls come with antivirus and malware protection, but it has to be configured for the traffic you would like to inspect. You still need endpoint protection.

A robust antivirus software package is the primary layer of technological defenses that every personal and business computer system must have. Well-designed antivirus protection comes with several characteristics:

- Ransomware protection
- Malware protection
- Web security
- Email security
- Scan engine
- Anti-keylogger

The WannaCry ransomware outbreak infected millions of Windows based systems across the globe in May 2017. WannaCry searches for and encrypts 176 different file types. The ransom note indicates that the payment amount will be doubled after three days. If payment is not made after seven days, it claims that the encrypted files will be deleted. WannaCry has affected individuals, as well as government organizations, hospitals, and universities. You can finally remove WannaCry using an antivirus software, but unfortunately this doesn't magically decrypt your files owing to a strong combined encryption of AES-128 with the RSA-2048 being used.
To stay safe from WannaCry ransomware attacks, it's important to keep your software, especially your operating system, up to date. It is recommended to install a second layer of protection through an endpoint antivirus package.

Local security policies

Local security polices are specific to local systems or machines. This makes it possible to enforce many systems, user- and security-related settings, such as password policies, audit policies and user permissions. Most of the default policy settings in Windows are okay, but a few need adjustments for enhanced security. These policies can be modified using the local group policy editor, which normally contains account policies, local policies, firewalls, security, and so on. On a Windows system, you can access the policy editor by running the `gpedit.msc` command, using the Command Prompt. The following screenshot shows the **Local Group Policy Editor**:

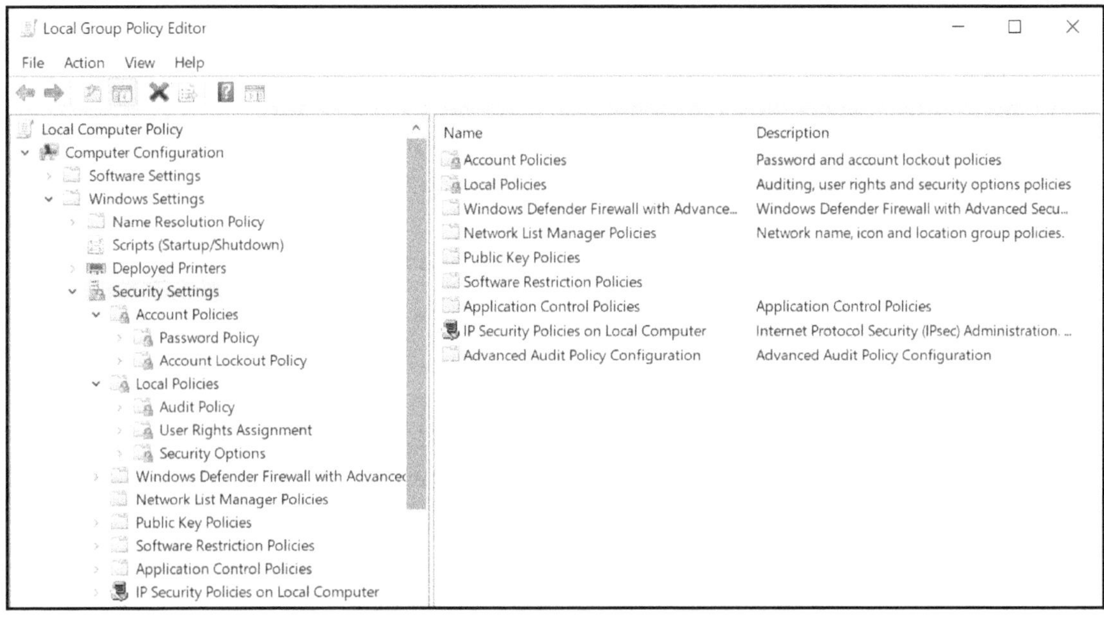

Summary

No matter how secure your network infrastructure is and no matter what services your server runs, there are certain basic hardening techniques you must apply. In this chapter, we focused specifically on hardening steps that apply to any server. In particular, we discussed the physical security of server resources, followed by disk encryption techniques one can use for on-premises and cloud infrastructure. We have established that almost every server has some sort of internet-facing connectivity and has to be protected by antivirus and malware solutions. To complement these security solutions, we can also harden our servers and adjust local security polices and permissions. Finally, we discussed some server management techniques to restrict access to a specific set of IP addresses for SSH and RDP services.

Questions

1. What is not a good practice associated with password policies?
    1. Deciding the maximum age of a password
    2. Restricting password reuse and history
    3. Encrypting passwords
    4. Changing a password every two years
2. What is not a feature of encryption?
    1. Protecting data from unauthorized access during transmission
    2. Ensuring user authentication
    3. Ensuring data integrity
    4. Ensuring data corruption doesn't occur
3. What is not an encryption standard?
    1. AES
    2. TES
    3. Triple DES
    4. DES
4. What is the role of the Key Distribution Center?
    1. It is used to distribute keys to everyone in the world
    2. It is intended to reduce the inherent risks of exchanging keys
    3. All of the above
    4. None of the above
5. Ideally, what characters should you use in a password to make it strong?
    1. Letters and numbers only
    2. Mixed case (upper and lower) characters
    3. Special characters
    4. All of the above

Further reading

For more information, you can refer to the following links:

- https://www.kerberos.org/software/tutorial.html
- https://www.symantec.com/content/en/us/enterprise/white_papers/b-how-drive-encryption-works_WP_21275920.pdf
- https://blogs.msdn.microsoft.com/azuresecurity/2016/01/22/azure-disk-encryption-white-paper-updated/

4
Cloud Security Design

In the previous chapter, we looked at how to secure a server infrastructure inside a secure network. We also looked at the importance of taking server hardening into consideration before moving a system to a production environment. In this chapter, you will learn about the security concerns for cloud infrastructure. As a user, you are not going to manage or secure the physical infrastructure of the service provider for this.

The IT industry is going through a major transformation, and the adoption of cloud computing is clearly a strategic direction for many companies and individuals. This chapter lays out the foundations of cloud computing and provides you with a clear understanding of the topic before moving on to critical applications and migrating data to public cloud networks. Cloud computing offers many benefits, but there are disadvantages as well. It also introduces the difficulty of securing the data outsourced by cloud users. In this book, we will explore cloud security and risk issues in a generic sense.

We are going to cover the following topics in this chapter:

- Cloud offerings
- Public versus private
- Shared technology and shared danger
- Security approach for cloud computing
- DOS attack protection
- Data loss prevention
- Exploited system vulnerabilities

Cloud offerings

This is a small topic with a big debate surrounding it. This debate looks at which cloud model is right for business when an organization plans to migrate to the cloud. Cloud-based virtual infrastructure offers advantages over a traditional data center. Both private and public cloud models have their own sets of pros and cons. Any organization moving to the cloud must first carefully analyze these before deciding which method is right for them.

In this section, we will start by looking briefly at cloud offerings, with a focus on the security benefits for both types of service. The three main models of cloud computing are as follows:

- **Infrastructure as a service** (**IaaS**)
- **Platform as a service** (**PaaS**)
- **Software as a service** (**SaaS**)

The following diagram is self-explanatory. It displays cloud offerings and states which of these should be managed by a customer, and which should be managed by cloud service providers:

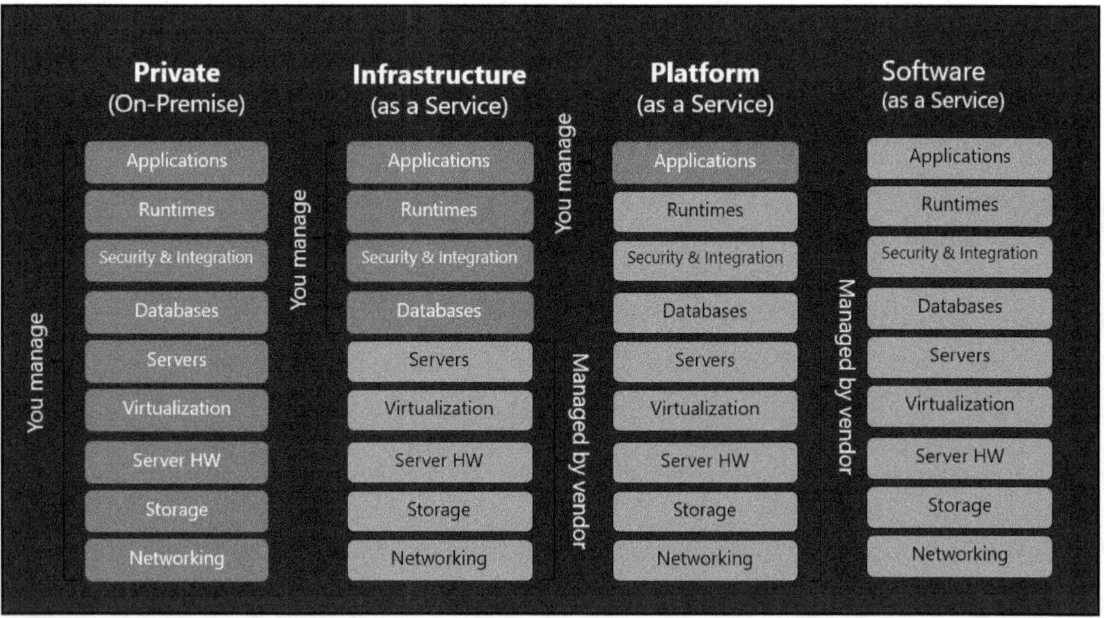

A true cloud service provider does not only offer virtualization in a highly automated environment, but the global presence of resources is what makes it a true cloud service provider. The global presence here is defined by user proximity and how close the user is to the service provider. For example, if I'm at a certain region called *A* and my cloud provider is also at *A*, then my user experience would be much better than other users who are at *B* or *C*. AWS/Azure has global presence to offer the resources needed to bring applications closer to end users around the world. A worldwide presence also enables consumers to specify the location in which their data will be stored.

IaaS

IaaS is a highly automated cloud offering. Here, compute, storage, and networking capabilities are owned by the cloud service provider and services are offered to customers on-demand with self-provisioning IaaS infrastructures. This infrastructure uses a GUI interface or command-line that serves as a customer-managed console for the overall environment provisioning. Cloud users will have full administrator rights on virtual machines. The diagram below shows a typical IaaS model in which compute, networking, load-balancing and storage are provisioned by a cloud consumer:

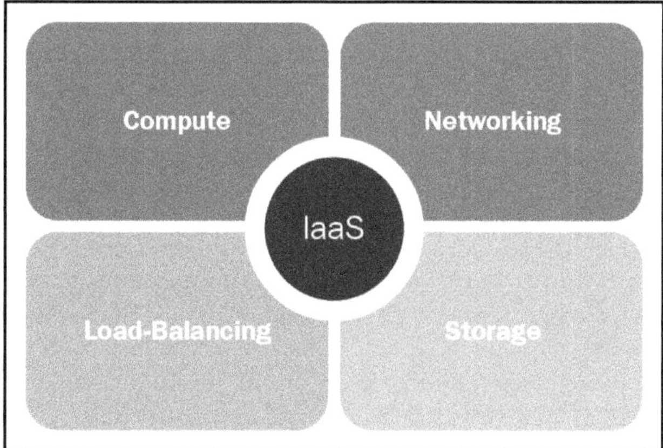

PaaS

PaaS is another offering of cloud computing that works in the middle layer between IaaS and SaaS, and facilitates runtime environment mostly for developers to build and test applications. With PaaS, instead of an end user requesting a VM from AWS or Azure, users can request an actual application and an underlying cloud infrastructure, including networks, servers, operating systems, storage, and security, managed by the cloud service provider. PaaS helps businesses to minimize operational costs and increase productivity by decreasing the time to market. PaaS users have a very common fear of vendor lock-in and the lack of portability when they want to switch between cloud service providers in the future. However, it is a standard offering by all cloud service providers to provide a common platform to avoid vendor lock-in situations.

SaaS

SaaS cloud offering is easy to use and is one of the most popular forms of cloud computing. SaaS also uses a web-based delivery model. Most SaaS applications can be run directly from a web browser, without any downloads or installations required, which eliminates the need to install and run applications on individual compute machines. In simple terms, you are provided access to application services installed on a server. It becomes very easy for enterprises to focus on actual business instead of focusing on IT, because everything is managed by the cloud service provider: applications, runtime, data, middleware, O/S, virtualization, servers, storage, security, and networking. Gmail, Salesforce, and Office 365 are famous examples of SaaS services offered by Google, Salesforce, and Microsoft.

Public versus private

Choosing between public and private cloud models will depend on an organization's business model, budget, security, and compliance factors. Let's discuss some of the major differences between them.

A public cloud is basically the internet-based cloud computing platform. Examples of major public cloud providers include Amazon **Elastic Compute Cloud** (**EC2**) and Windows Azure Services platform. Since a public cloud uses shared infrastructure and a virtualized environment, multiple customers can use services simultaneously without interfering with each other's activities. It is a subscription-based, pay-per-usage model, and the only costs incurred are based on the capacity that is being used.

On the other hand, a private cloud solution pretty much provides the same cloud offerings, but infrastructure is deployed and operated exclusively for an organization or enterprise. The private cloud is also the preferred choice for organizations who depend on legacy applications, might experience poor performance when migrating to the public cloud, or might need to rewrite the entire application.

Public IaaS versus private IaaS

Now let's dig deeper and try to understand the difference between public and private clouds' individual offerings. IaaS components are pretty much defined by the public cloud service provider, and an end consumer has limited options for customizing OS templates, versions and standard configuration options. Service providers roll out standard offerings based on the need for a larger set of consumers and the need to minimize the number of variances for different components. On the other hand, a private cloud offers you the flexibility to customize service components to a much greater degree.

Public PaaS versus private PaaS

It is important for consumers of PaaS services to understand the pros and cons of both public and private PaaS before deciding to use a PaaS deployment model. A public PaaS runs on a shared infrastructure to host multi-tenant environments, whereas a private PaaS runs on an infrastructure that is used exclusively by an organization. A private PaaS is considered more secure, and it avoids business and technical risks that come with public cloud computing. The major concern behind choosing a private cloud is data security. This does not mean that your data is not secure within a public cloud, it simply means that sometimes data is not safe. For example, the banking sector does not host critical data on a public cloud.

Public SaaS versus private SaaS

Private SaaS are SaaS applications delivered on a single tenant architecture. These are hosted either on-premises or off-premises and always on a highly secure network. Application customization is the biggest benefit, as this is very limited with public SaaS.

Shared technology and shared danger

Today, cloud computing is a well-established industry. It is cost-effective, highly agile and flexible, with the ability to provide on-demand, large web-scale cloud computing. Data security is a major concern with a common question: is moving data to the cloud secure or not? In most cases, data is secure. However, when it comes to the fear of losing critical data, organizations tend to opt for a private cloud.

Let's discuss how shared security works in a public cloud. The security implementation of major cloud providers is not the sole responsibility of a cloud service provider, but the shared responsibility of the provider and customer. A service provider is responsible for the underlying infrastructure, but resource access and application security is the responsibility of the customer. This is similar to a situation in which you have a big community with a main entrance secured by many guards. Once you allow a visitor inside the premises, the activity of the visitor becomes your responsibility. In our situation, if a vulnerability is found in Hypervisor, the service provider won't allow you to patch it. If a vulnerability is found in an operating system, the service provider won't patch for VM and the responsibility, therefore, transfers to the customer.

Network security is a major component of a multi-tenancy environment and strict isolation is a must. Cloud providers do provide a networking infrastructure base to build isolated networks, but they do not keep track of what kind of network traffic goes in and out. Infrastructure hardware and software vulnerabilities can cause major failure to maintain isolation between tenants. During the failure, if attackers gain access for one tenant, they can access resources for other tenants as well.

Another major threat exists with cloud consumer data. A consumer has less visibility of where the data was physically stored. A very simple example would be consumer data deletion. Tenant data may be stored on multiple physical hosts; those may be part of the same cluster or may not be. If the consumer opted for geo-redundancy, the data might be located in one region or may be spread across regions. The data deletion process may differ from one service provider to another and consumers have no mechanism to validate data deletion. There must be a chance that this data is available to the next tenant during storage provisioning otherwise attackers might gain access to the data.

So far, we have discussed that threats are generic in nature. In multi-tenancy, a CPU can cause major risks when the CPUs are shared across multiple customers. Interesting, right? Let's discuss this in detail:

Meltdown and Spectre vulnerabilities make data leaking possible for co-hosted tenants, which makes them particularly dangerous when a single device is shared between users. Cloud offers a separate instance to each customer; isolation is tight and has no way to jump from one instance to another. In this case, attackers extract data that is currently being processed directly from the processor for customers sharing the same chip. This might include your passwords stored in a password manager or browser, your personal photos, emails, instant messages, and even critical documents in business. The biggest worry arises when you are not sure if somebody has tried to steal your data. The exploitation does not leave any traces in traditional log files.

Security approach for cloud computing

From on-premises to the cloud application transformation journey, consumers have lost visibility on many things. Network security does *not* offer consumers the visibility required for highly virtualized cloud networks. Cloud technology comes with a certain degree of uncertainty and fear. Relying on cloud to store large amounts of critical data with no network boundaries, less visibility and reduced security control, makes it difficult for administrators to see what's happening with applications and data.

Cloud revolves around data centers and its global presence. Consumers have a lack of visibility into underlying networks and the security infrastructure of a cloud provider. The biggest question for all cloud consumers is whether you are supposed to know about underlying cloud infrastructure builds. The answer to this would be *yes* and *no*. The answer would be *no* with regards to underlying network and security for underlying base infrastructure since you are not suppose to manage and control this. It would also be *yes* as you must have visibility with your pieces on logical infrastructure sitting on top of the physical infrastructure.

Traditional enterprise network model

In traditional enterprise and hosting networks architecture, IT resources such as compute, firewall, storage, load balancer and WAN are fairly static and well-defined under boundaries with a greater degree of control. Network security teams implemented **Security Information & Event Management** (**SIEM**), proper security zones, passive TAPs, net flow based solution and IDS/IPS tools to provide deeper insights into security threats occurring in their network environment:

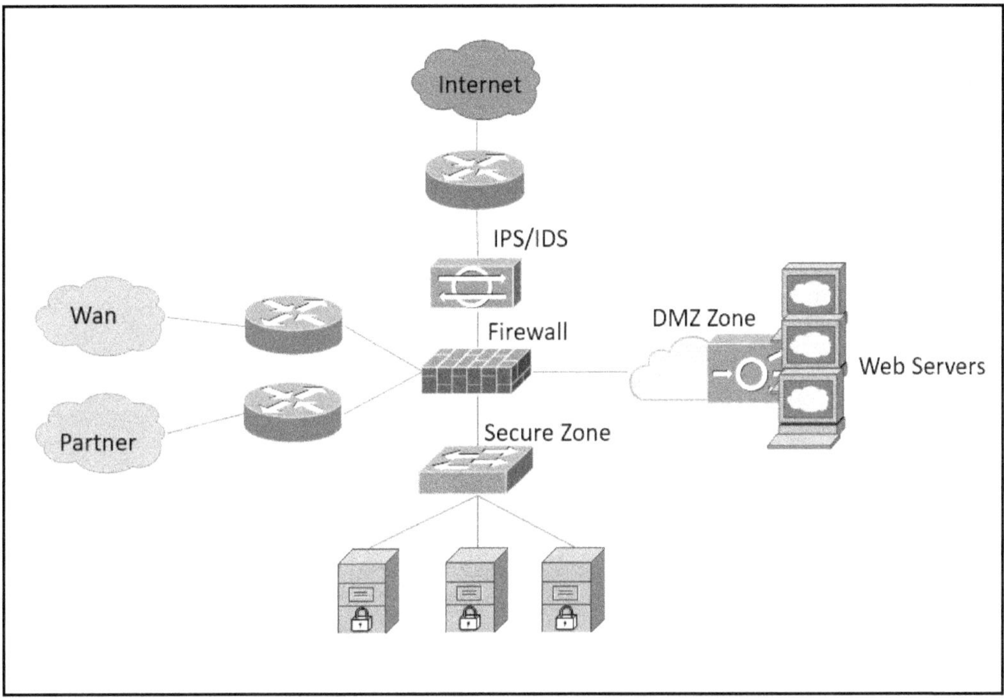

This diagram displays the web servers, network devices, WAN/partner connectivity, and security architecture of a legacy network. Under this model, all systems, network, servers and security were within the organization's control. Achieving full visibility into the network was not a significant challenge.

This is not a perfect model; it has got it own limitations, including:

- Fixed architecture and topology
- Proprietary protocols
- Inefficient use of infrastructure resources
- Hardware-centric
- Manual configuration processes
- Lack of automation and programmability

Hybrid data center and cloud network

The below diagram demonstrates what the hybrid data center looks like from a customer's point of view. In this case, most of your stuff is outside of the network boundaries of the organization, such as a SaaS, IaaS and PaaS, and your currently deployed security solution has lost visibility of an infrastructure deployed on the other side of the world. In terms of network visibility, an IaaS model is more flexible than SaaS. On the other hand, a SaaS model does not allow infrastructure visibility behind the cloud application:

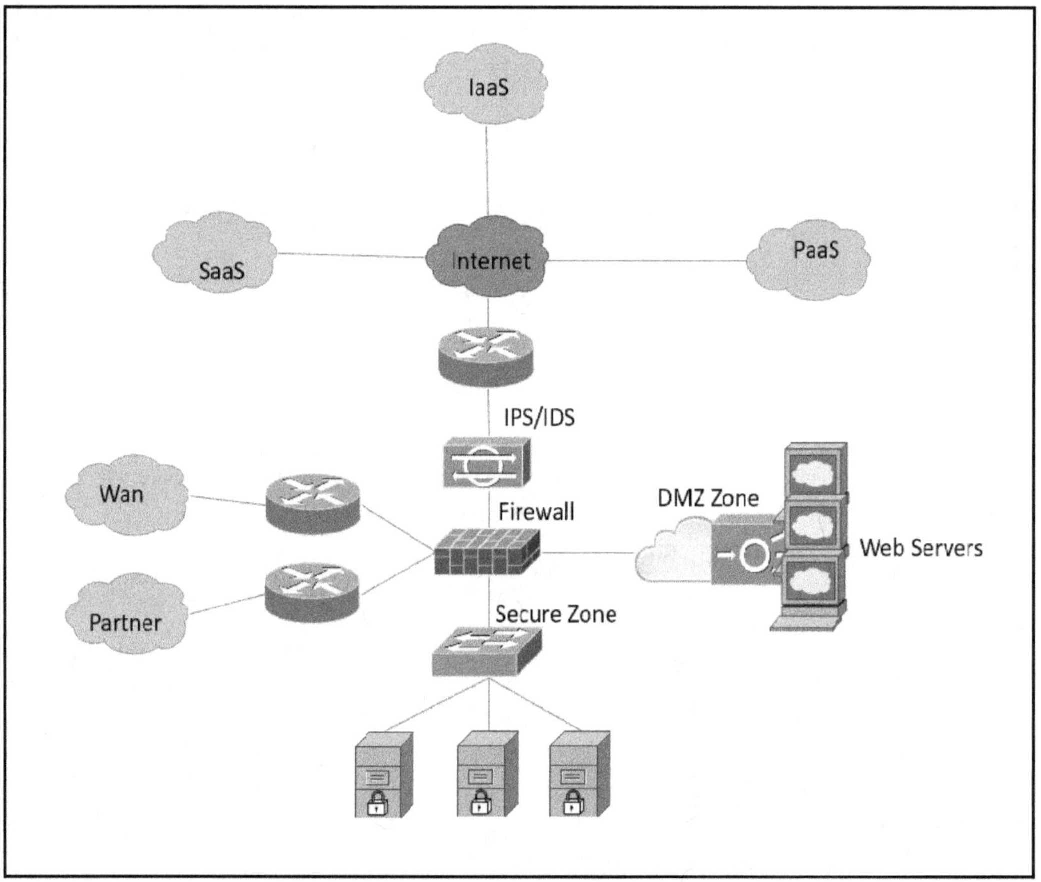

Let's take a look at what the cloud data center network looks like and why we lose total visibility for SaaS from a customer's point of view. Most big cloud service providers have a very agile and resilient fat-free network, which looks similar to the following diagram:

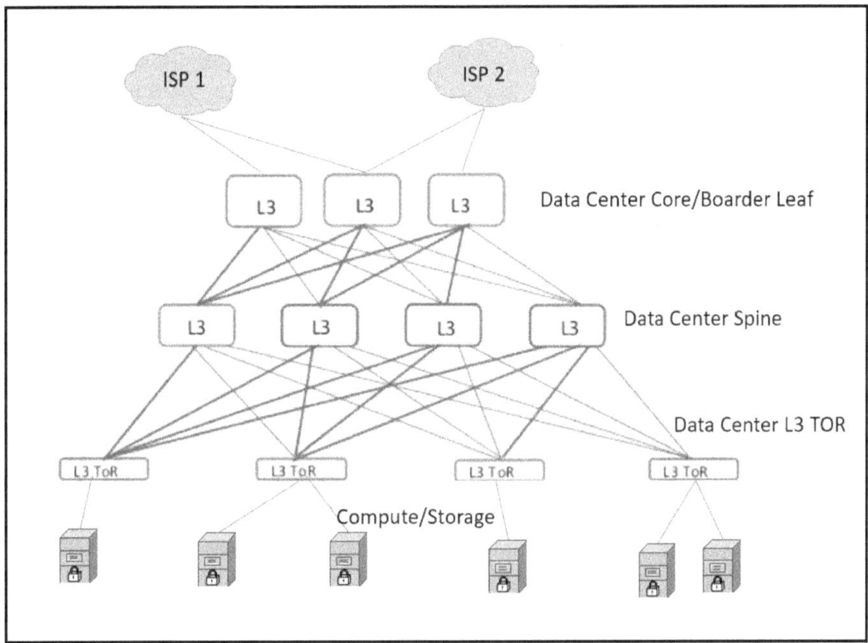

In this cloud design, all networking functions like firewall and load balancer have been moved to a server layer by taking advantage of **network function virtualization** (**NFV**). While this design supports increasing East-West traffic, the legacy model was based on traditional client-sever (North-South) traffic. These servers are also shared resources and virtual machines are allocated to customers. From one VM to another VM, service provider can use either GRE or Vxlan encryption:

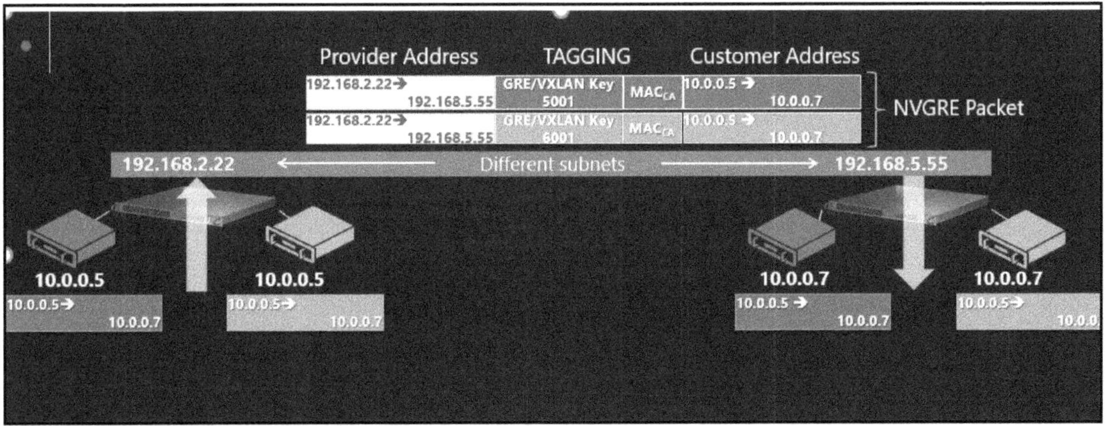

In this model, resources can reside anywhere on server clusters. As a customer, we do not have the control to choose physical resources. From ISP to L3 **Top-of-Rack switch** (**TOR**) and from one physical server to another, communication is encrypted and controlled by service provider, so you have no way of looking at network traffic. IaaS services provide an option to configure virtual appliances such as firewall virtual appliance and virtual TAP. These can provide some visibility, but SaaS is going to be an absolutely zero visibility zone.

Network security devices for IaaS

Virtual appliances can be used to protect or to gain visibility for the customer's environment, specifically to IaaS. This has nothing to do with service provider's baseline environment.

Let's take a look at security layers offered to customers by Microsoft Azure. When it comes to inbound traffic from the internet, Azure DDoS is the first layer of security and helps us to protect against large-scale attacks against Azure customer resources. The next layer is customer-defined public IP addresses (endpoints). Some endpoints are standard and the rest can be defined by the customer, which is used to determine what traffic can pass through the cloud service (public IP) to the virtual network resource. Native Azure virtual network isolation ensures complete isolation from all other customer networks and also provides flexibility to reuse IP space. Network security group is the next layer, and this acts as a firewall access-list by user defined rules. Network virtual appliances is the final layer. This can be used to create security boundaries to protect the application deployments in the protected virtual network:

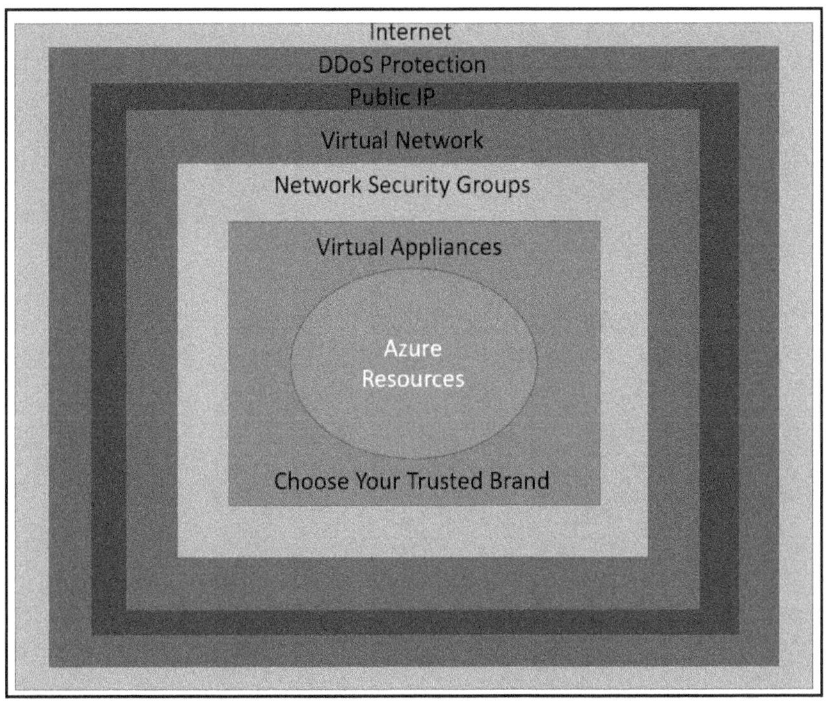

Firewall Virtual Appliance

Multi-tier architecture is common practice for cloud applications. Virtual firewall appliance is a pre-installed software solution which runs on top of virtual machine. All incoming and outgoing traffic passes via firewall. It offers full visibility and better control. Customers can use these firewalls for the purpose of firewall controlled traffic and VPNs.

A typical deployment may look like the following diagram. These products can be chosen from the marketplace under **BYOL**. The major vendors are Cisco vASA, Barracuda, Palo Alto, and Check Point:

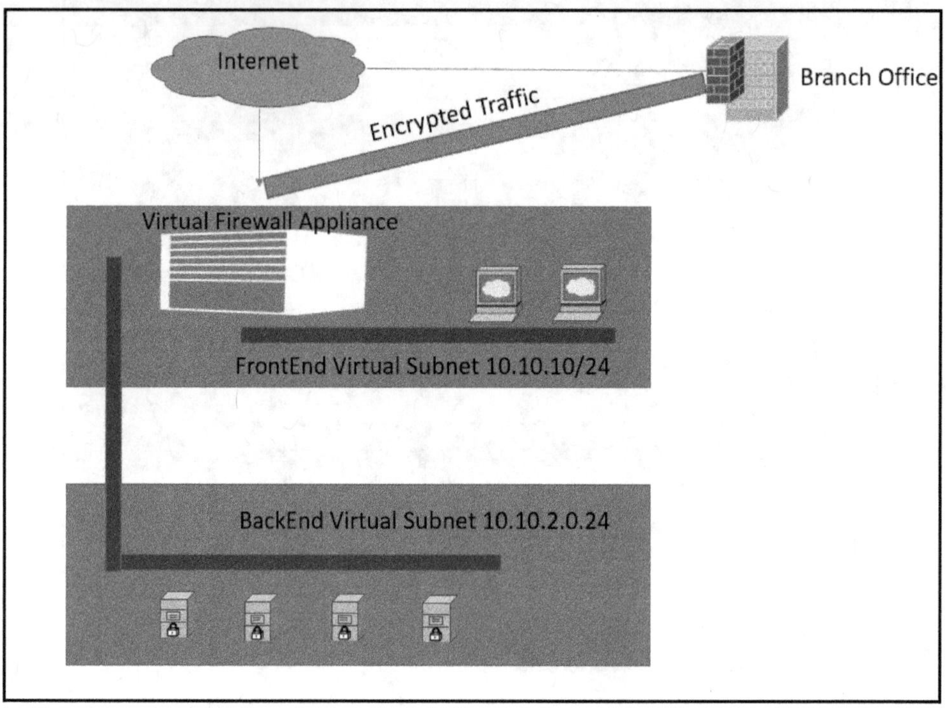

Let's take a look at Network Security Group, which is an Azure inbuilt feature. You can find this option in the *virtual machine networking* section:

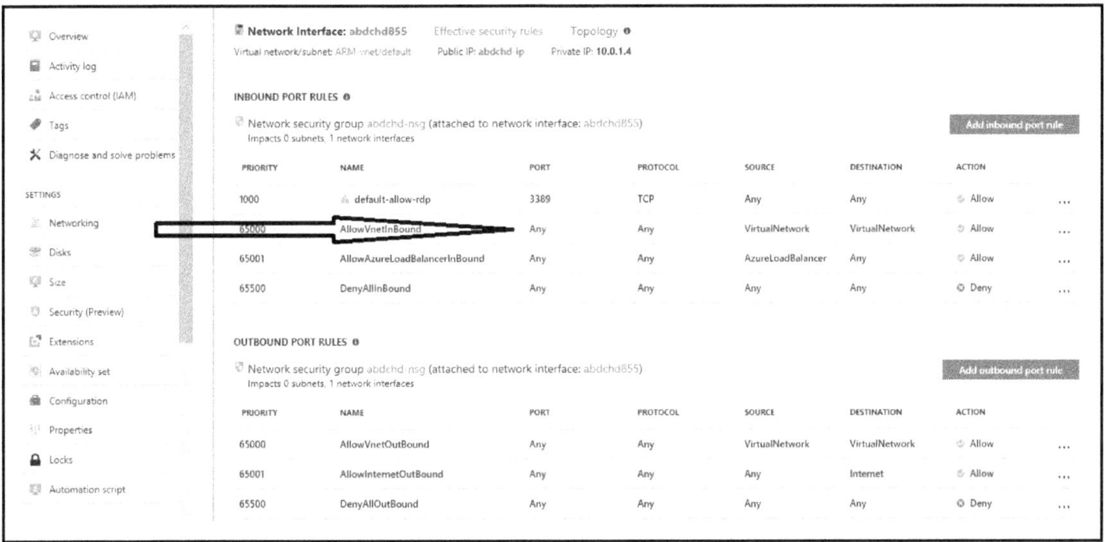

You can also add/delete inbound or outbound traffic rules as per your requirement by mentioning different parameters, like source, destination, port range, protocol, action, and rule priority:

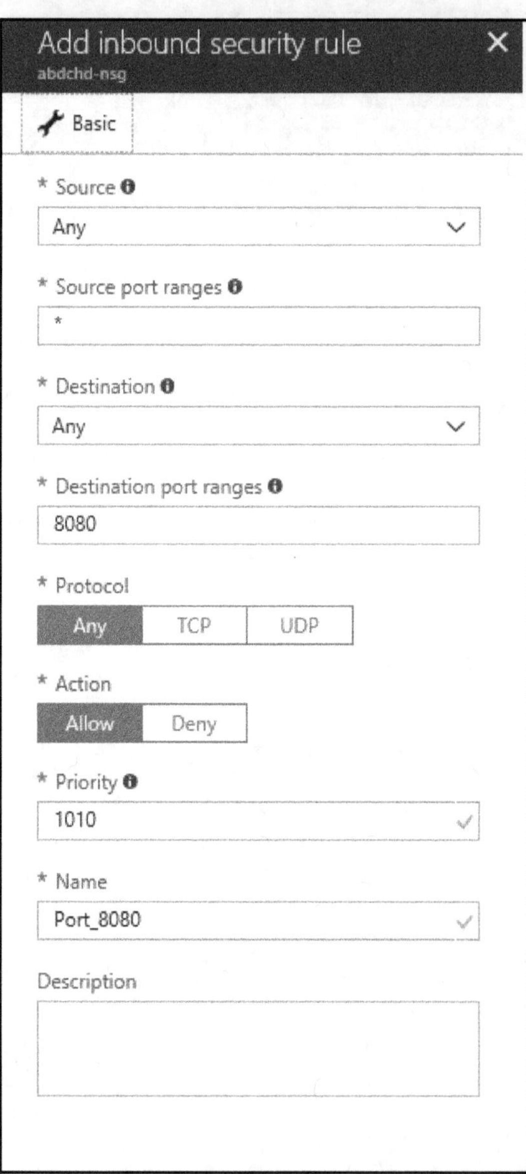

Virtual TAP vTAP

In a traditional network, you have options to TAP data traffic by applying some sort of TAP device or port mirroring (SPAN). Port mirroring creates a copy of packets being transferred between two nodes via a network device. In order to provide this functionality in the cloud, you must use tap-as-a-service. When enabled and configured it will allow the system administrator to run an IDS on his tenant network. Good examples of these solutions are Phantom TAP from Ixia and Gigamon1s GigaVue. Advanced virtual switches like Cisco 1000V also support SPAN port functionality.

Virtual Router

A virtual router is a software function which runs on commodity servers instead of dedicated hardware platforms. You can take advantage of all the offerings provided by traditional hardware routers like firewall, advance routing, access-list and NAT function. A very famous product is CSR 1000v from Cisco.

Virtual web application firewalls

Azure cloud provides web application security by adding **Web Application Firewall (WAF)** to Azure application gateway service. This is a virtual machine appliance from a third party in the Azure marketplace which offers Layer-7 security and can be added to application gateway to perform application layer inspection:

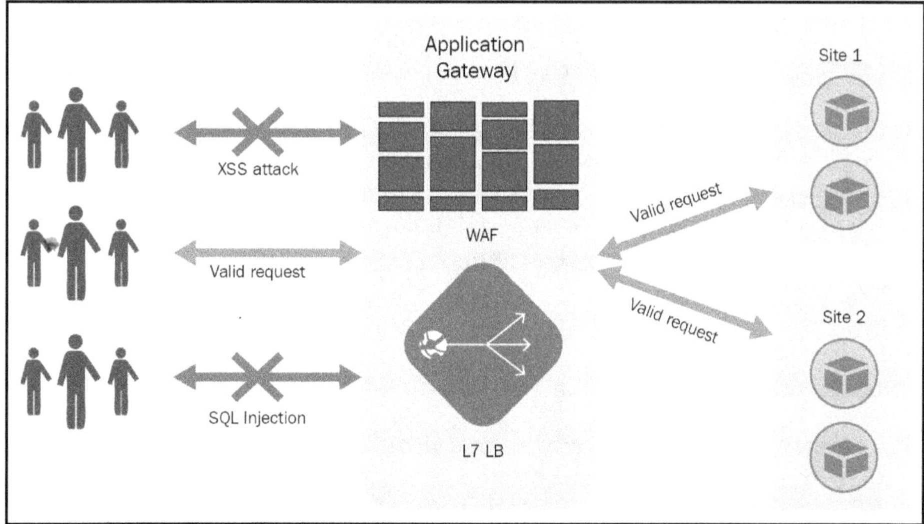

A typical WAF solution protects you against:

- SQL injection
- XSS (Cross-site scripting)
- Common web attacks
- HTTP protocol violations and anomalies
- **Distributed Denial of service** (**DDoS**)
- Botnets and Scanners
- Common IIS and Apache misconfigurations

DDoS attack protection

DDoS attack is one of the top security concerns when you host your application on a public cloud. The gaming industry is mostly abused by DDoS. Since the responsibility of the public cloud is shared, service provider offers basic DDoS protection services free of cost and with customized services by profiling services, altering traffic patterns and providing a telemetry monitoring view.

When writing this chapter, Azure DDoS protection standard is in preview. Azure provides basic and standard DDoS protection, which AWS has named the standard and advanced DDoS protection shield.

Data loss prevention

Data Loss Prevention (**DLP**) is a process for protecting sensitive data at rest, in-transit, and on endpoints to reduce the likelihood of data theft or unauthorized exposure. On-premises backup techniques and processes that protect data in enterprise data centers don't extend to the public cloud well. Intentional or accidental deletion of sensitive data can create serious issues for organizations. Due to lack of visibility, customer data is always vulnerable to data loss. By encrypting data when you transfer it to a cloud or between cloud providers, you provide an extra layer of data protection security and reduce the risk of data loss.

These two tasks would be under major consideration for the Data Loss Prevention Strategy:

- **Automated backups of public cloud data**: Backups of public cloud sensitive data are extremely important and should be highly automated with proper encryption.

- **Deletion control and validation**: If data deletion validation fails, this can have disastrous consequences with subsequent data loss due to lack of visibility. You must have a way to detect and show that data has been deleted either accidental or intentionally. Multi-factor authentication and strict access should be in place to prevent unauthorized access for sensitive data.

Exploited system vulnerabilities

When moving to cloud computing, you have to consider the following security issues in order to enhance your data safety.

Session riding attack works based on session cookies and takes advantage of the user's previously authenticated session. Account hijacking or session riding is not new to cloud service providers and users. Hackers manage to gain access to login credentials and can easily track user activities. A similar attack occurs when attackers access cloud drive files without user credentials. This type of attack works by stealing the password token via a phishing attack or drive-by-exploit, a small file that sits on a user's device for convenience (saving the user from entering their password each time). Once attackers gain access, they can access and steal files, and even add malware or ransomware to the victim's cloud folder, which can be used for further attacks.

`Https://` does not protect from session riding attacks.

Cloud-based DDoS attacks are a big threat now that it's very easy to turn thousands of VMs on and off quickly. Attackers do not launch such attacks from one service provider and one location—the intensity of the attack would be very high if machines are spread over multiple locations with each generating traffic towards the victim. Service providers also have detection mechanisms to detect unusual traffic, so the chance of getting caught is very high if a high volume of attacks are launched from one service provider. Another type of attack is a brute force attack. This can be a very powerful attack if launched from cloud, which can test thousands of password per second and can even break SHA-1 hashes.

A **Cloud Application Programming Interface** (**Cloud API**) is a type of API, generally based on the **Representational State Transfer** (**REST**) that enables the development of applications and services used for the provisioning of cloud hardware, software, and platforms. Cloud networks are typically put at risk by insecure or improper API. We have previously discussed system-specific vulnerabilities like Meltdown and Spectre.

Summary

Cloud computing is the fastest growing computing model and is widely adopted by enterprise. According to Forbes, 83% of enterprise workloads will be in the cloud by 2020. Cloud offers the ability to ease software development, dynamic server provisioning and on-demand IT resources with greater flexibility. This changes the IT operating models for organizations. Data security is a crucial part for organizations that have moved data to public cloud or are planning on deploying applications in the future. In this chapter, we have discussed different offerings by cloud computing and what you should know as part of cloud data security. We have also discussed security considerations for cloud shared infrastructure and shared responsibilities between cloud customer and cloud service provider. In the last section we have covered how to gain lost data on wire visibility and on cloud shared infrastructure.

In the next chapter, we will discuss application security considerations before you launch an application for production and public access.

Questions

1. Which of the following offerings give cloud providers the minimum amount of built-in security?
    1. SaaS
    2. PaaS
    3. IaaS
    4. All of the mentioned

2. Storage drives are a type of cloud computing:
    1. True
    2. False

3. Which of these is not a major type of cloud computing usage?
    1. DDoS as a Service
    2. PaaS
    3. SaaS
    4. IaaS

4. Which can cause cloud resources to become out of service?
    1. Zombies
    2. DOS
    3. DDOS
    4. Backdoor channel attack
    5. Both 2 and 3
    6. All of the above
5. Which of the following is not a cloud service provider?
    1. Amazon
    2. Amazon EC2
    3. Hadoop
    4. SAP
    5. Azure

Further reading

For more information, please refer to the following links:

- `https://meltdownattack.com/`
- `https://docs.microsoft.com/en-us/azure/virtual-network/ddos-protection-overview`
- `https://aws.amazon.com/shield/`
- `https://www.cisco.com/c/en/us/products/routers/cloud-services-router-1000v-series/index.html`
- `https://www.sdxcentral.com/nfv/definitions/whats-a-virtual-router-vrouter/`

5
Application Security Design

In the previous chapter, we discussed data protection and security techniques for cloud hosted applications. In this chapter, we will discuss application security for web-based applications.

While applications can provide efficiency, risks still remain. This is a result of the fact that there are a number of new security threats which could potentially pose significant risks to an organization's IT infrastructure. It is essential to understand the vulnerabilities commonly found in various applications and provide users with a better experience. In this chapter, we will focus on the security aspect of web-based applications with **General Data Protection Regulation** (**GDPR**) around the corner.

We are going to cover the following topics in this chapter:

- GDPR
- SQL Injection
- Web Application Firewall and security
- Blacklisting and whitelisting
- Using HTTPS for everything

GDPR

In a digital transformation era, customers' sensitive personal information held by business organizations pose a significant risk if they are stolen and misused. The data protection laws across the globe have a common goal to protect the privacy of individuals. The general data protection regulation was introduced, which specifies how customer data should be used and protected. Most of us share our personal information on many web portals by clicking **I Agree** or **I Accept the Terms and Conditions**. Personal data contains information about the individual, including who they are, what they do, and where they go. Each of us leaves a digital footprint of our personal data in the cyber world. Data mining is new oil to the industry; it provides insights and a competitive advantage.

The GDPR compliance deadline is May 25, 2018. Every organization that keeps or uses European personal data inside or outside of Europe—regardless of the nature of the business in which it operates—is affected by the new data protection law.

Let's look at an example of how this impacts organizations worldwide.

A US organisation which collects data from EU personnel would be under the same legal obligations as the organisation's head-office which is anywhere within the EU. Even though they do not have an actual physical server or office in the EU, the basic idea was that if the data was not physically located in the EU zone, then the rules didn't even apply. For example, any social networking portal has to keep user information and if the user belongs to the EU, the information is stored on a server which is outside of EU boundaries.

Legislation has to be enforced by 25th May 2018 and this may result in huge penalties for organizations that fail to comply. The maximum penalty is €20 million or 4% of an organization's global turnover. This amount would be enough to close down many businesses. To avoid these steep consequences, preparation is the key to success.

Getting consent

Consent is a key factor of GDPR legislation, which offers individuals a choice and control over how their data is used, with a desire to build their trust and engagement. Your web-portal which collects personal data must make visitors understand exactly how you are planning on using their personal information. They must then agree to each specific purpose. Even if you have someone's email address, phone number, and credit card information after they use a shopping cart feature, you are not allowed to share this information without their agreement.

WhatsApp now lets users see the data that it collects from them.

Access to data

Another key feature of GDPR is to make it possible to view who has access to the personal data that is stored on your website and backend system. The first thing to understand is who these entities are and if they have a valid reason to get access to this data. Also, all data collected from individuals must be linked and a one-click job should be enough to delete all system data which is no longer required.

Encryption

Any data that is submitted to your website must be encrypted in order to comply with GDPR. An SSL/TLS certificate must be installed on your site to encrypt the data in order to avoid man-in-the-middle attacks.

For more information on GDPR you can visit `https://www.eugdpr.org`.

SQL Injection

SQL Injection is one of the oldest and most widely used application layer vulnerabilities used by attackers to steal valuable data from SQL based databases. Attackers leverage an SQL Injection vulnerability to bypass a web application's authentication system and to retrieve information. SQL Injection can also be used to make changes like adding, deleting, and modifying data records. The following diagram shows a 3-Tier application architecture:

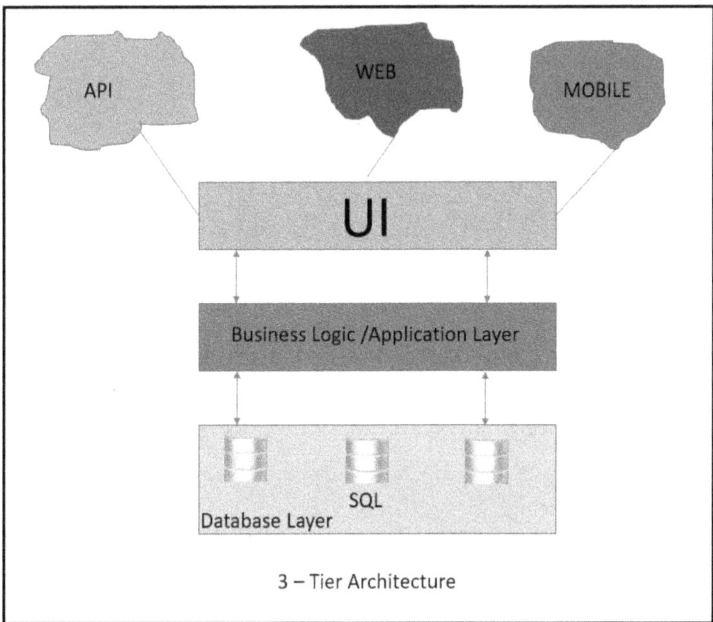

3 – Tier Architecture

The 3-Tier application has the following components:

- **User Interface**: **User Interface** (**UI**) is basically a user friendly way to interact with an actual application. This can be a mobile application, web UI or API method to interact with applications. A UI layer requests data from a business layer.
- **Business Logic**: A business logic can be considered an application layer which is responsible for handling data validation, business rules and task-specific behavior. Business rules fetch or insert data into the database layer.
- **Database Layer**: This is the third and most critical layer of the 3-Tiers, which hosts the actual data and is responsible for feeding data to the other above-mentioned two layers.

It's worth mentioning here that running a SQLi attack against a website without the owner's permission could well land you in legal trouble with the state law enforcement.

Let's discuss how SQLi works in detail:

- On a web portal login page, when you submit a username and password, the SQL query will look like the following. If the correct credentials have been provided, everything will work fine:

```
SELECT id FROM customer_data WHERE username = 'xyz' AND password
='abcd';
```

- The same method becomes vulnerable due to a small trick which bypasses the login forms on web portals:

```
SELECT id FROM customer_data WHERE username = '' AND password = ''
OR '1'='1'';
```

You can see that the username field is empty and the password field has a closed apostrophe. The magic starts here with the `OR` statement `'1'= '1'` which will always return true and the whole query returns all `username` and `password` from the entire database.

We have discussed the basic idea of what an SQL Injection is and how it works. The preceding example is a very basic attack that can run very complicated queries to crack databases. It is highly recommended to test the system or a website with databases against this type of attack every time it is launched for public access. Just think, if you can play tricks with a banking system which is vulnerable to SQLi, you can probably rob the bank by manipulating the amount reflected on your account or by transferring an amount to someone else.

Do remember that this SQL Injection test should only be tested in the test environment.

Prevention of SQL Injection attack on web applications

The good news is that there is actually a lot that website owners can do to prevent SQL Injection. The bad news is that there is not one complete, foolproof solution to database security:

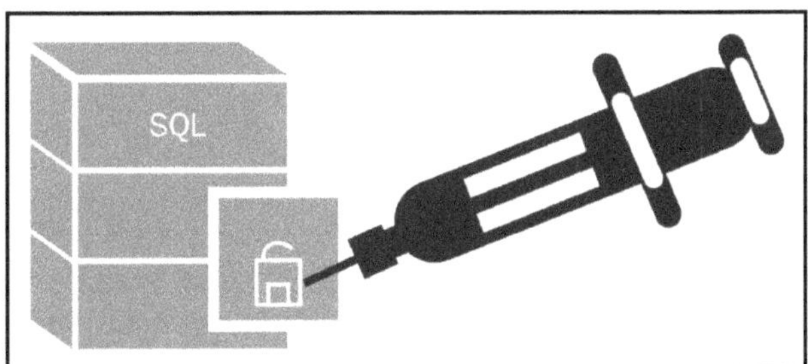

Employing comprehensive data sanitization

It is very important for all websites to filter all user inputs and to exploit works because of weak input filtering or no filtering at all. You can also call this *validation*. For example, if the input field is supposed to be a cell phone number, you can certainly validate that field to make sure that it contains only numbers and, of course, is the length of a cell phone number. This will not just protect your application from SQLi but it will also protect you from undesired behavior.

Deploying a Web Application Firewall

Web Application Firewalls (**WAFs**) are essential security mechanisms used on almost all commercial websites today. Using a WAF is a very effective way of preventing known attacks. The WAF combats commonly known attacks against web servers using a number of security checks to filter inbound HTTP/HTTPS requests. In addition to managing requests, you can apply WAF security checks to modify the responses sent back to users. Despite the excellent protection they offer against many types of attacks, WAF is inadequate for protecting against today's sophisticated **SQL Injection** (**SQLi**) attacks. You can consider WAF a rule-based second layer of defense for protecting web servers against known threats XSS, SQLi, and DDoS attacks.

Limit database privileges

The key element of database security is access control privileges for everyone, from DBA to application schema. To limit database privileges, create multiple database user accounts with a minimum level of privilege for their usage environments. You should also grant an application with the minimum possible access to the database. Unless absolutely necessary, do not allow DROP, DELETE, and so on.

Finding vulnerabilities

Once you have written your application, we do not know if it is vulnerable to SQL Injection. Obviously, you could examine the source code and find any instances of concatenating user input with SQL, but that could be very tedious and time consuming. You must use a good, updated vulnerability scanner to find the most frequently found vulnerabilities. Performing SQL Injection generates high network bandwidth and sends a lot of data, so make sure you are the owner of the website you are testing. If not, make sure you have taken prior permission from the owner. A few famous tools such as sqlmap, Acunetix, Vega, and Netsparker can be used for scanning.

WAFs

WAFs provide additional security between users and web applications to protect web servers from unauthorized access and malicious attacks. WAF vendors offer hardware, software, virtual, and cloud-based firewall solutions. Web applications are extremely vulnerable and are also the backbone of business, so they must be protected. The biggest challenge in application security is detecting a vulnerability in your application, at which point the trouble begins when you are patching and fixing the code, as these are time-consuming tasks. This is where WAFs come in; as soon as a vulnerability is detected, you can apply patches to WAF. Any request which comes after the WAF patches are updated will stop attacks associated with the vulnerability that has been found.

Let's take a look at the following diagram. Non-HTTP/HTTPS attacks are blocked by a perimeter firewall, but the perimeter firewall does allow HTTP/HTTPS connections. These HTTP/HTTPS connections can also become attacks and are therefore blocked by WAF, which acts as a second layer of security. Consequently, only a clean connection is passed by both layers and reaches the application server:

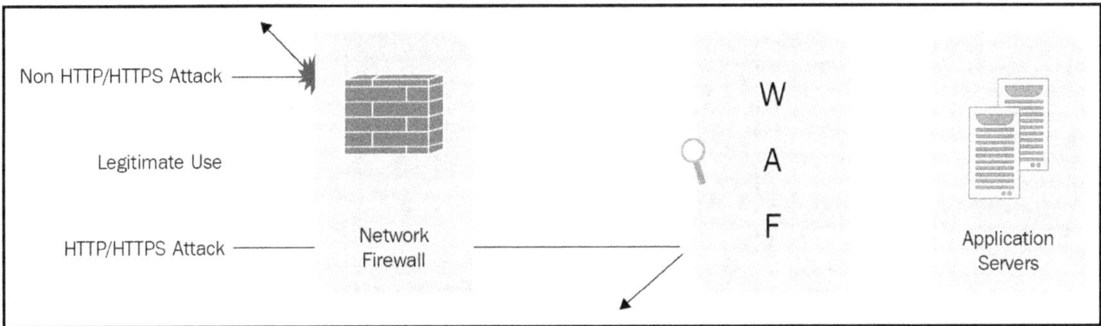

WAF protection against common web attacks

A WAF protects your web servers from common threats which can compromise the security of websites. We will list the common threats and WAF security checks you can use to counter these attacks:

- Buffer overflow attacks
- Cookie tampering
- Forceful browsing

- Web form security attacks
- Request protection
- Bot check
- Brute force and credential stuffing
- Layer-7 DoS
- Cross-site scripting (XSS)

Blacklisting and whitelisting

A simple approach and fundamental principle in IT security is to allow what is really needed. Security is all about access control and keeping track of activity with identity. In cyber security, access is granted based on identity and intent. Whitelists are identities with good intent and blacklists are identities with bad intent. This is a debatable topic and we will discuss it further with regards to requirements and implementation:

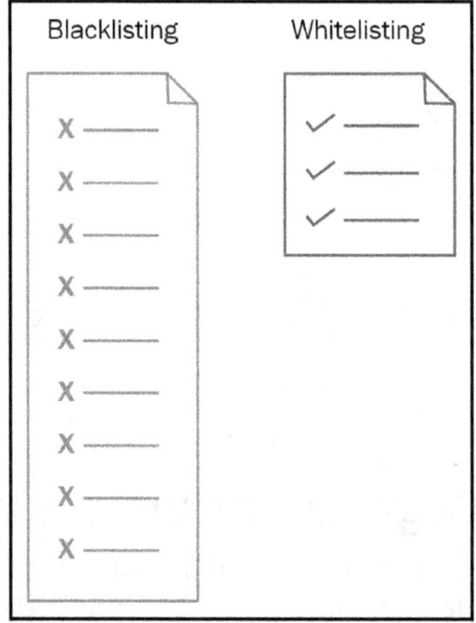

What is blacklisting?

Most of the antivirus suites on the market work with a blacklist approach to detecting and preventing viruses and malware. In the 1980s, antivirus was first introduced with blacklist. Today, the antivirus industry still follows the same principle. This works similar to creating a list of all cyber criminals in the world. However, what happens if you miss a few criminals, or if they are new and are not on the list? Depending on the IT environment, blacklisted entities might extend to users, applications, processes, IP addresses, and organizations known to carry threats to an individual or other organization.

Blacklisting delivers almost no value against zero-day threats.

Benefit and disadvantage of blacklisting

The primary advantage of blacklisting is its simplicity. You can exclude known threats from the system and the intelligence lies with the software vendor. Its effectiveness totally depends on how often the vendor releases or updates the known threat database. From a user's point of view, all of the updates are fetched automatically. Users do not have an option to differentiate between good and bad data traffic until the software says it's bad. The major drawback of blacklisting architecture is knowing how to deal with unknown threats. For example, ransomware continues to evolve with new patterns and variants that have not been seen before.

What is whitelisting?

Application whitelisting uses the reverse logic. Here, you can create a list of trusted entities such as applications, emails, users, trusted partners, services and IPs. These are allowed to access IT resources and block everything which seems to be unwanted for your business. With whitelisting architecture, you must have a tight access control policy and grant appropriate permission to users. Since you block all unwanted entities, this reduces the attack surface which gives automatic protection from zero-day attacks.

Benefit and disadvantage of whitelisting

The primary goal of whitelisting is to protect high-risk security environments. This approach only allows trusted software, applications, users and IPs, which drastically reduces intrusion. The main advantage is that nothing comes inside the network which is outside of the list, and nothing that is not on the list can come inside the network. A good example would be the way the salesforce application portal operates. With this, you gain access to an application only for the allowed IP range and users. We all know that salesforce is a critical application. This does not scale well for a large network or every time you need to add new entries, making it tough to manage.

Which is better?

Each approach to security has its advantages and disadvantages. It may sound strange, but you need both. A typical business organization which uses a limited number of applications and knows about the users and network connections required for this application should follow a whitelisting approach. The next step is to combine this approach with blacklisting to ensure that if authorized users enter the network with a known threat, your network will still be protected. Of course, there is less of an administrative effort involved in blacklisting compared to whitelisting, and the difference increases with the size of the whitelist. You can take a whitelist approach for applications which can be opened from all over the world, such as banking web portals and online shopping carts.

Using HTTPS for everything

Around two billion people are connected to the internet all across the globe, and the internet world has become the backbone of the species. HTTP is one of the most famous protocols which has become critical in today's digital era and it is the primary protocol for applications used on computers, tablets, smartphones, and many other devices. You should always protect all of your websites with HTTPS, even if they don't handle sensitive communications. This is because in today's world, there is no such thing as non-sensitive web traffic.

Beginning in July 2018 with the release of Chrome 68, Chrome will mark all HTTP sites as *not secure*.

HTTPS is a very serious and sensitive subject, and in this section we will discuss website security.

HTTP versus HTTPS

Hypertext Transfer Protocol (**HTTP**) is a protocol that allows communications between client and server. Most commonly, it is used for transferring data from a web server to a browser to view web contents. The main problem is that HTTP does not encrypt the data being transmitted and can be snooped by someone else. As the first part of the diagram shows, a web server running on service port `80` and all the content being transferred between client and server are in plain text. In the next section of the diagram, the web service is running on the service port `443` and data is being transferred in encrypted mode:

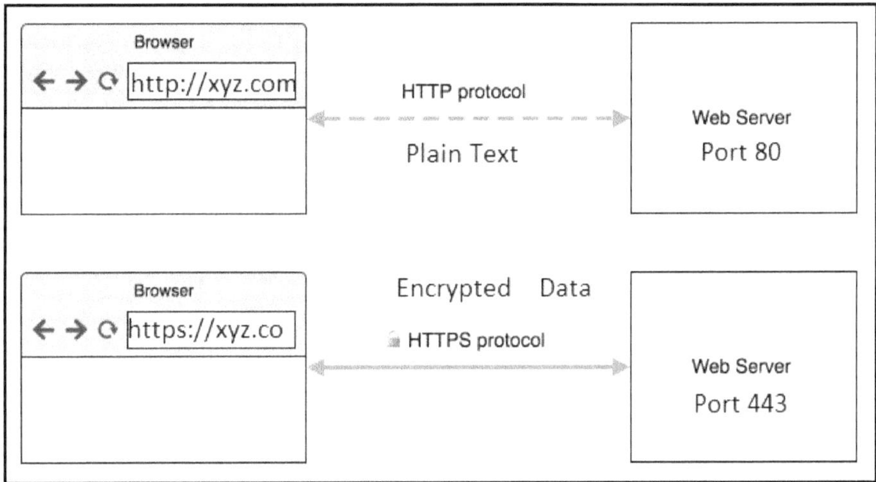

HTTPS is the secure form of HTTP, which simply means that the information being exchanged between the browser and web server you are visiting is encrypted. Any web servers currently using HTTP can be migrated to HTTPS. However, there is a small cost if a **Secure Sockets Layer** (**SSL**) certificate must be purchased. HTTPS helps to prevent attackers from hijacking communication sessions between your web-server and user browsers when using public infrastructures such as public Wi-Fi, ISPs, or hotels.

Web application security

Every developer wishes their application could be more secure. This section highlights some of the top security considerations and best practices when designing or migrating to HTTPS.

SSL/TLS deployment

Choose a **Certification Authority** (**CA**) that is reliable and serious about its certificate business, security and reputation. A reliable CA will also provide a wide variety of certificate types and flexible licensing models.

SSL/TLS key size

It is always preferable to have longer key lengths, but for public-key cryptography (asymmetric ciphers), 2048-bit keys have the same sort of property, so longer keys are meaningless. **National Institute of Standards and Technology** (**NIST**) suggests that a 2048-bit RSA key has a strength of 112 bits, therefore there are theoretically two thousand, one hundred and twelve possibilities to crack the private key. RSA claims that 1024-bit (asymmetric) keys are likely to be cracked sometime between 2006 and 2010, and 2048-bit keys are sufficient until 2030. At the same time, longer key sizes like 4096 significantly decrease server performance, which directly impacts browser response time.

The NIST recommends 2048-bit keys for RSA.

Signing algorithm

Secure Hash Algorithm (**SHA**) is a hashing algorithm used in secured connections to provide the integrity and authenticity of a message to the receiver. SHA algorithm is the default hash algorithm set in SSL/TLS certificates. SHA-2 is a set of hash functions including SHA-224, SHA-256, SHA-384, SHA-512, SHA-512/224 and SHA-512/256. The most common hash function used is SHA-256. Generally speaking, SHA-2 = SHA-256 and that is the minimum requirement.

Secure Hash Algorithm 3 (**SHA-3**) is the latest member of the Secure Hash Algorithm family of standards, released by NIST on August 5, 2015. A wider implementation for SHA-3 is probably many years away.

Secure protocol

Do not use SSL 3.0. For secure implementation, configure a server and software that supports the latest versions of the TLS standards TLS 1.1 and TLS 1.2.

Preventing an authentication hacking attack

Authentication plays a very critical role in the security of web applications. Attackers will try to find passwords or session IDs and get access to the desired information. Here are a few ways to prevent an authentication hacking attack:

- Prevent an automated brute force attack by adding CAPTCHA. However, this is not perfect. Along with CAPTCHA, use account lock-down. This is a very effective deterrent against brute force attacks.
- Transfer session keys in cookies (do not show session IDs in the URL) and session keys should be unpredictable. Showing session IDs with the URL is a method that is normally used when cookies are blocked by client side or a fallback method.
- Keep the duration shorter for session IDs and ensure that they are rejected by the server after logout.
- Use two-factor authentication.
- During a session fixation, the attacker wants you to access your account with a Session ID of his choosing. An easy fix for this problem is to not let a client choose session IDs.
- Do not leave your session active once you are done with your activity; ensure that you log out at the end of every session. Session logout also forces attackers to log out automatically.

Use cookies securely

Cookies are a set of information stored on the client browser, which are then sent to the server with every subsequent request made by the client during the session. Cookies are primarily used for authentication and maintaining sessions. It becomes very important to secure cookies effectively in order to avoid session hijacking. Cookies can be secured by properly setting cookie attributes. These attributes are:

- Secure
- Domain
- Path
- HTTPOnly
- Expires

A developer only encrypts the main login page. Other sensitive and non-sensitive information is sent to the server in an unencrypted format. Keep in mind that cookies are also sent along with these requests. If they are unencrypted then this gives an attacker the opportunity to sniff data to steal session information from these cookies. To avoid leaking session information to attackers, make sure that the cookies are also only transmitted over HTTPS connections, not HTTP connections. This can be done with the help of the secure attribute of a cookie. You can also play with all other attributes such as HTTPOnly. This protects you from XSS cross site scripting, which can steal data from cookies.

Vulnerabilities scan

With the adoption of digital transformation by businesses and organizations, web applications have become a lucrative target for attackers. Web applications are often plagued by vulnerabilities and misconfigurations due to poor coding and broken hardening policies. Network and security admins must use web application security scanners to perform testing on a web application and identify security vulnerabilities. Scanners do not access the actual source code, they only perform functional testing and try to find security vulnerabilities.

Server security

Prepare your server for safe and secure operations. Here are a few steps you need to perform:

1. Update the server to the latest operating system
2. Turn on inbuilt firewall

3. Enable automatic critical updates for OS security
4. Enable logging or integrate with SIEM system

Introduce a bug bounty program

Bug bounty programs are incentive-based and result-oriented programs designed to encourage security researchers to find the vulnerabilities and security risks associated with a product. They are then encouraged to report them to the sponsoring organization. These programs are considered highly beneficial as they represent a global community of professionals and researchers that are available all the time.

Summary

By now, you are familiar with the basics of application security. We have covered enough background information in this chapter to understand a multi-layer security approach. Although web applications can efficiently exchange information, the fact still remains that these applications can be attacked. A number of new security threats have also arisen. If not handled properly, these issues could potentially pose significant risks to an organization's information technology infrastructure. Since it is all about data security, individual data is very important. Consequently, it becomes very important for organizations to design a robust web system aligned with GDPR to protect users' information.

In the next chapter, we will discuss an overall approach for infrastructure security and future technology.

Questions

1. Which of the following is not a factor in securing the environment against a security attack?
    1. The education of the attacker
    2. The system configuration
    3. The network architecture
    4. The business strategy of the company
    5. The level of access provided to DBA

2. What does the `http` you type at the beginning of any site's address stand for?
    1. Hyper Text Transfer Protocol
    2. HTML Transfer Technology Process
    3. Hyperspace Terms and Technology Protocol
    4. Hyperspace Techniques and Technology Progress
3. SQL Injection is an attack in which what kind of code is processed to the database server?
    1. Malicious
    2. Redundant
    3. Clean
    4. Non-malicious
4. Which of the following is not a security exploit?
    1. Eavesdropping
    2. Cross-site scripting
    3. Authentication
    4. SQL Injection
    5. None of the above
5. Which of the following is the most vulnerable to injection attacks?
    1. Session IDs
    2. Registry keys
    3. Network communications
    4. SQL queries based on user input
    5. None of the above are vulnerable to injection attacks

Further reading

For more information, please refer to the following links:

- https://www.sans.org/reading-room/whitepapers/analyst/started-web-application-security-36735
- https://www.eugdpr.org/
- https://www.sans.org/reading-room/whitepapers/application/web-application-firewalls-35817
- https://www.cisecurity.org/wp-content/uploads/2017/05/SQL-Injection-White-Paper2.pdf

6
Threat Detection and Response

In the previous chapter, you learned how to identify the common risks involved when designing and launching an application. You also learned the common safeguarding methods to help users to surf applications securely.

In a hyperconnected world, responding to cyber threats is the new reality for organizations and security professionals. In this chapter, we will explore the basics of threat detection and ways to mitigate ongoing threats. Finally, you will learn to choose and deploy an advanced threat protection system for your business goals. The typical network contains information about users and also includes security information. A critical step towards protecting your organization includes having end-to-end visibility into usual and unusual traffic patterns, URL scanning, blocked traffic, ranking-based websites during visits to malicious websites, detecting botnets, DDoS protection, and defense against unknown threats.

We will cover the following topics in this chapter:

- Network threat detection
- Endpoint threat detection
- Security information and event management

Network threat detection

In order to protect information, organizations need to change the way they think. Administrators need to stop thinking that the firewall, IPS, IDS, and antivirus suites will be able to protect their system from all types of cyber threats. Most traditional security detection models are old and outdated and even they cannot differentiate between malware and regular network traffic. An organization's data security programs can ideally stop a majority of known threats. However, there are many *unknown, evil* threats that an organization aims to detect and has not encountered before. This can be a result of brand new methods and technologies.

Detection methods

Network intrusion detection systems themselves are not perfect, and are always bombarded with both false positive and false negative notifications and warnings. Consequently, any threat detection system needs both a human element and a technical element. The human element may come in with security analysts who analyze trends, data traffic patterns, behaviors, and reports, as well as those who can determine if anomalous data indicates a potential threat or a false warning.

Let's take a look at different methods.

Intrusion detection system

An **intrusion detection system** (**IDS**) is a type of signature-based software designed to monitor or scan network traffic to find suspicious activity and trigger alerts when something is trying to compromise an information system through malicious activities or security policy violations. Alerting information contains information about the source address of the intrusion, the target/victim address, and the type of attack that is suspected. An IDS is referred to as attack detection technology, but it cannot prevent or stop attacks. In contrast, an IPS device can be used to prevent attacks by detecting them and stopping them proactively before they reach a target.

Types of IDSs

Intrusion detection systems can be further divided into two broad categories based on their placement: host-based IDSes and network-based IDSs.

- **Host-based intrusion detection system (HIDS)**: This is a small, agent or sensor-based piece of software installed on single or multiple hosts on a network. It protects the individual host by monitoring and reporting the system configuration and by keeping track of application activity. A host IDS is passive in nature, provides functionality to gather information by identifying, logging, alerting, and reporting. You can always install a HIDS on different DMZ servers such as web servers, mail servers, database servers, or any server that you want to monitor or protect on the network. Any masking techniques such as insertion, padding, fragmentation, or out-of-sequence delivery bypass a network-based IDS but can be easily caught by a host-based IDS. The primary goal of any HIDS is to monitor and analyze data traffic passing through the **network interface card** (**NIC**) of a host, but can also be expanded to monitor application behavior and activities.

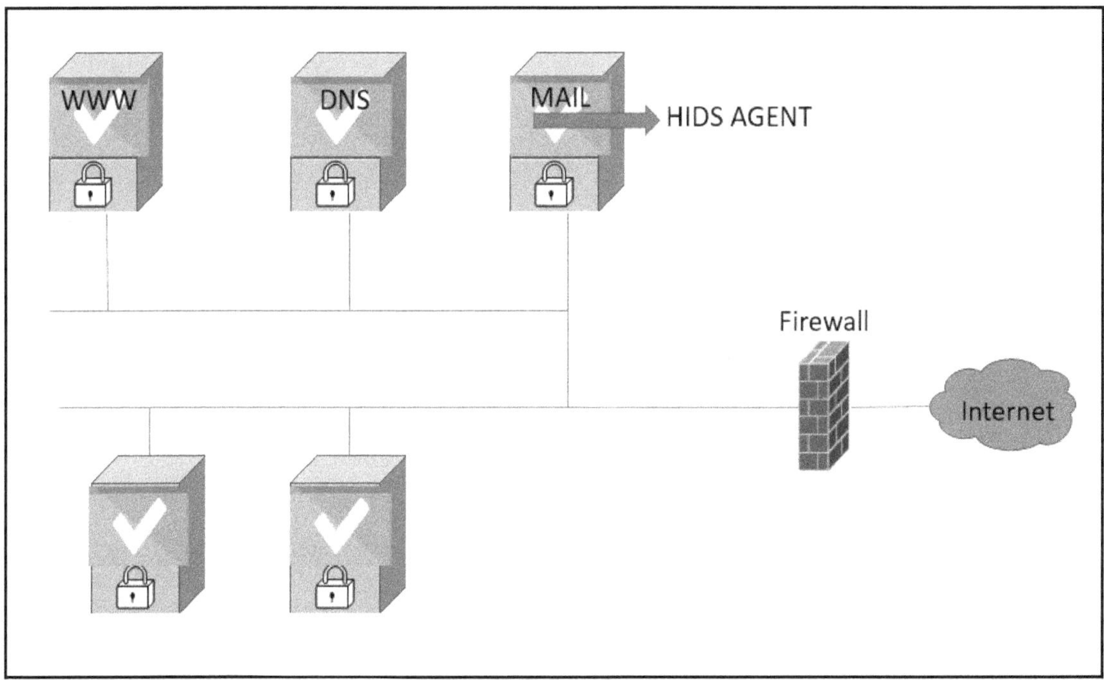

- **Network-based intrusion detection system (NIDS)**: This offers a different approach and monitors activity on the overall network traffic, rather than on each separate individual host. NIDS operations are based on the concept of wiretapping and the system comes with known attack signatures, which can also be customized. Signature updates are released by vendors from time to time. The major issue with NIDS is performance. For small organizations, this might be a suitable solution that deals with gigabytes of traffic. However, for larger organizations with high speed networks, it simply cannot handle it:

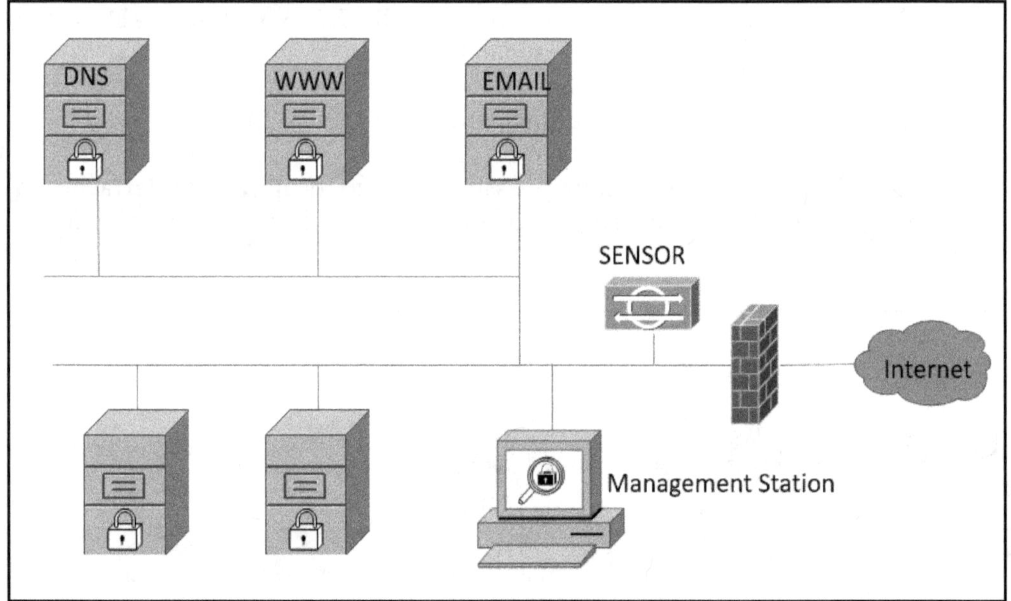

NIDS does not decrypt encrypted traffic.

Network capture solution

The IP traffic within a network can be sniffed by deploying network TAPs on a network and redirecting traffic via a network TAP or SPAN port to a security analyzer. The following diagram demonstrates the process of traffic travelling from a router and a switch into the network TAP. From there, it is directed to a port which hosts a network sniffer analyzer. This method provides full visibility into all network flows that reside in the network. One of the biggest advantages of network TAPs is their ability to monitor traffic without any interference.

However, there are also disadvantages. This includes the fact that the deployment of TAP is disruptive and expensive in nature, and can be difficult to manage for large scale networks. Significant expenses can be incurred as a result of the security analyzer used to correlate all packet captures, to identify and mitigate security attacks, the network TAP's deployment, and data storage. These significant expenses derive from a number of physical links in any given network topology.

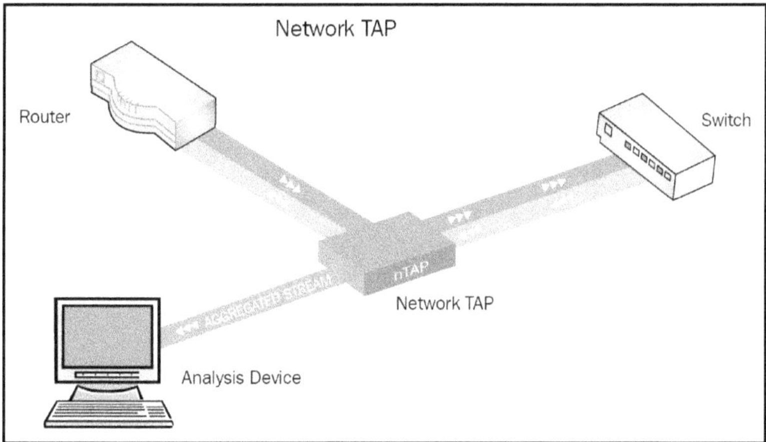

Network TAPs can be divided into two categories :

- **Passive TAP**: Passive TAPs are passive devices that make a copy of the network data and distribute it to a third-party appliance that is passing between network nodes.
- **Active TAP**: It is what occurs on the inside of the TAP, which makes the difference. Active TAPs are used in networks where copper cabling or optical budgets do not allow for passive TAPs.

Installing a TAP generally involves some network downtime, and this downtime could be increased if there are problems with a TAP.

Threat detection with Netflow/IPFIX

When looking at cloud scale and high speed data networks, the trend is to monitor and trigger events for suspicious flows based on NetFlow and **IP Flow Information Export** (**IPFIX**). Most network devices, routers/switches, and firewalls support NetFlow and IPFIX. These flow methods make the data traffic passing through devices visible. You can relate these methods to Wireshark capture, which holds information such as source IP, destination IP, and TCP/UDP ports. Wireshark capture works in a similar way to a phone call recording, while flows are the call logs containing metadata information. A flow reporting system continuously monitors flows and has the ability to connect host reputation databases in order to check any odd traffic patterns:

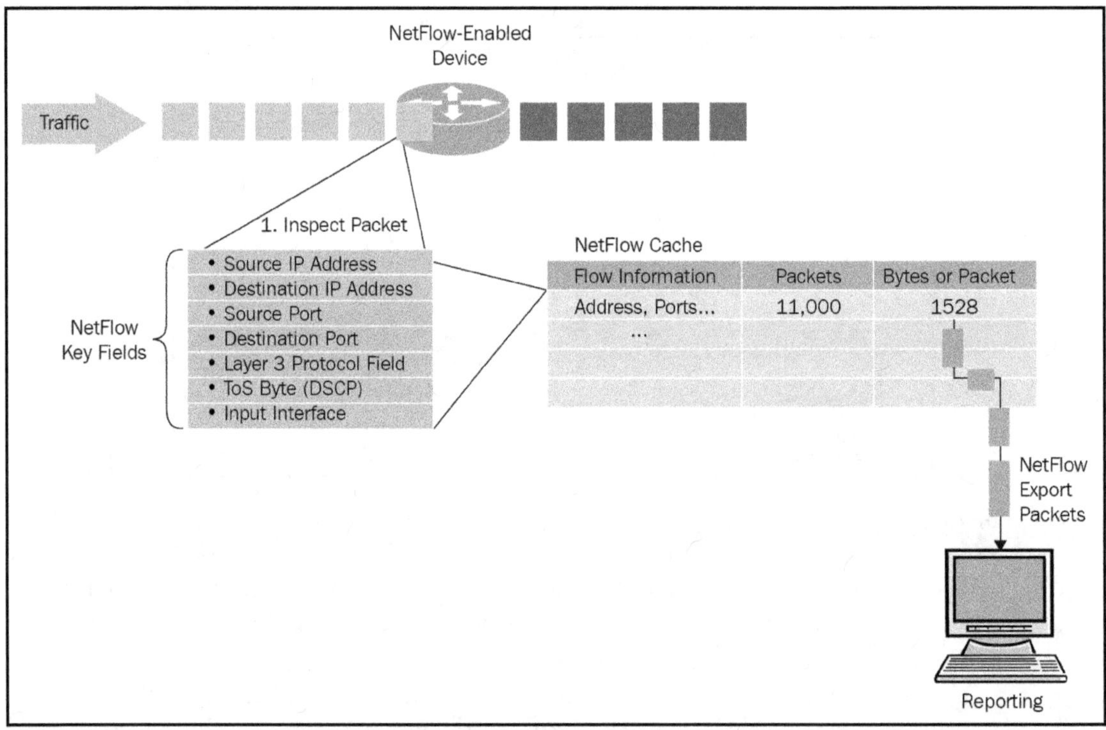

On a Cisco router, this configuration can be done for NetFlow v9. Before the release of NetFlow v9, flows were limited to roughly 20 common fields and the rest of the packet contents were discarded. The introduction to NetFlow v9 made it possible for data export logic to be used for any details found within a packet:

```
match ipv4 protocol
match ipv4 source address
match ipv4 destination address
match transport source-port
match transport destination-port
match interface input
collect routing source as
collect routing destination as
collect transport tcp flags
collect interface output
collect counter bytes
collect counter packets
```

Let's assume that you are exporting TCP flag information along with traffic flow, and you also know the source and destination for network flows. Having this information makes it easy to detect SYN (a TCP flag) attacks. With flow technologies, cyber threat detection focuses primarily on monitoring traffic behavior rather than performing DPIs (such as a firewall) and triggering events based on a threat signature match. DPI methods do not scale very well for large infrastructures, such as cloud service providers, in which traffic comes in Tera/Peta bits per second. Due to a lack of traffic handling capabilities, this makes it almost impossible to scan all traffic with expensive equipment, such as firewall and IPS systems.

NetFlow vs. IPFIX

First of all, IPFIX is an enhanced version of NetFlow v9, widely considered as NetFlow v10. IPFIX is an IETF standard specifically designed to make it easier to open up flow to a broad range of vendors.

As you may already know, IPFIX RFC 5101 and RFC 5102 are derived from the NetFlow v9 RFC. IPFIX is also backward compatible with v9, which was fuelled by vendors' desire to move away from Cisco-driven standards. This essentially allows hardware vendors to specify a vendor ID, to put any proprietary information into a flow, and to export it out of the collector/analyser for further dissecting and monitoring. NetFlow v9 now supports Flexible NetFlow, which is almost equal to IPFIX. By default, IPFIX listens on UDP port `4739`, while NetFlow v9 listens on 2055, 2056, 4432, 4739, 9995, 9996, and others. NetFlow v9 defines 79 field types and IPFIX defines the same 79, but continues on to reach 238.

Endpoint threat detection

Regardless of how powerful your defenses are, there's always a chance that attackers will evade your security system and gain access to your environment. Endpoint security generally refers to a well-described method for protecting an organization's data and networks that are accessed by endusers and connected devices. Laptops and desktops are not the only devices that are considered to be endpoints; smartphones and other wireless devices also have network access that becomes a target and entry point for security threats.

What's an endpoint

An endpoint is any connected device used to access an organization's data and network resources. Looking at how to handle endpoint devices in order to safeguard the data assets that can be accessed through these systems is a challenging job for security administrators.

This becomes more complicated for security administrators when you allow employees to **Bring Your Own Device** (**BYOD**). Futuristic technology such as IoTs are also considered as endpoints.

The following diagram shows a hierarchy for different types of assets found in any organization network. The bottom-to-top approach reflects device counts and business values in terms of risk. As far as the counts are concerned, there are more end-user devices than anything else among the endpoints, with relatively fewer network devices and business-critical endpoints:

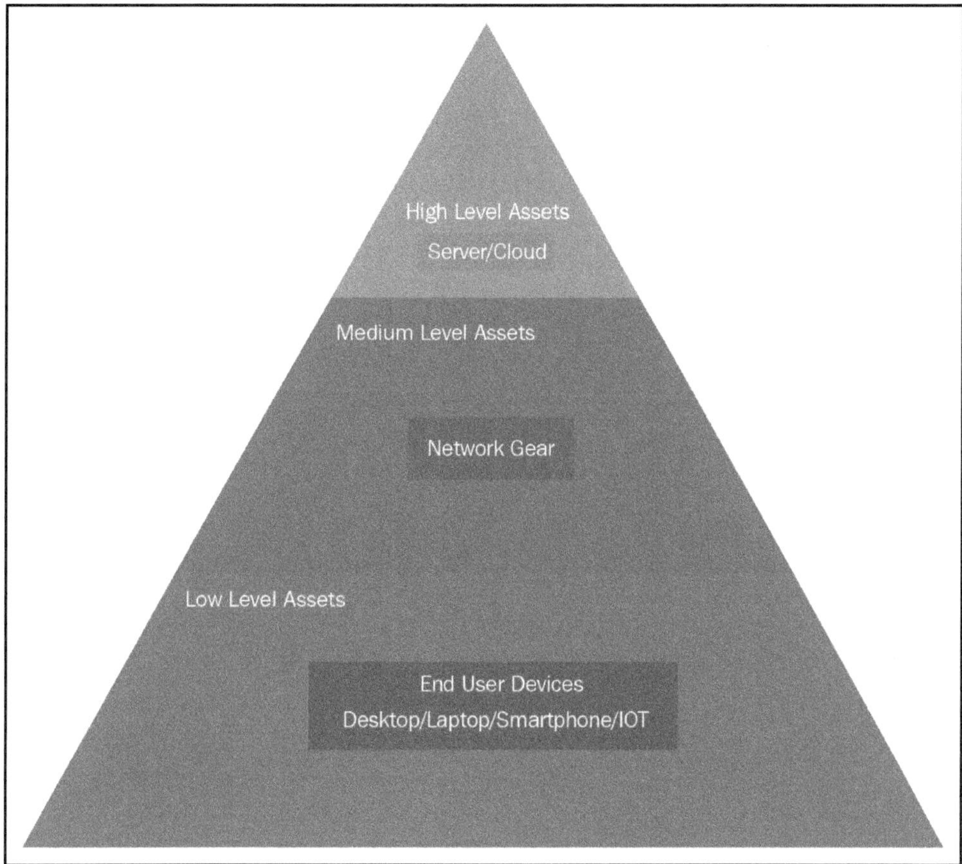

From a business point of view, the pyramid shows a risk of being compromised. Devices at the bottom of the pyramid are more vulnerable to serious threats, and this opens the door for an attacker to move toward high level assets. The higher an attacker climbs on the pyramid, the bigger the impact is.

Endpoint Detection and Response (EDR) system

Every point of network interaction is a potential part of the network attack surface. Endpoint security simply involves hardening devices to reduce the attack surface and limiting network attack vectors. **Endpoint Detection and Response** (**EDR**) is a critical part of the overall security strategy, which addresses the need for continuous monitoring and responds to advanced threats. Securing endpoints starts with endpoint discovery as it is important to know what's on a network. The discovery of assets helps in building an inventory that includes firmware, OS, and many attributes. Security administrators can now assign the appropriate security policies to endpoints, and they can continue monitoring to help with any policy violations, unwanted changes, and unauthorized access:

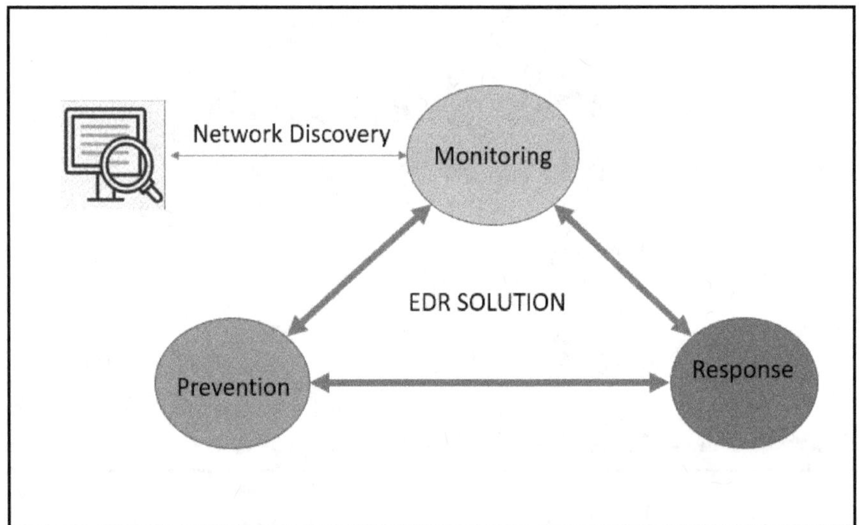

EDR systems can also be lightweight programs called agents that run on each endpoint in the form of an application. They may even run in the form of a kernel-level plugin on devices that may not support hosting applications directly. For some scenarios, an agentless approach can also be used. An agent provides real-time monitoring for data traffic passing through NIC, analyze, and alert. Your endpoints can be hosted on an on-premise network such as an enterprise data center. They may also be hosted on a cloud network using a variety of devices such as virtual desktop or a wide range of operating systems such as Amazon Web Services and Azure deployments.

Case Study – Why EDR system is required?

Endpoint Detection and Response (**EDR**) solutions are essentially a Next-Generation set of security tools which focus on monitoring, detecting, investigating, and mitigating malicious activities as well as possible attacks on endpoints, beyond the legacy signature-based approach used in traditional security tools.

Let's take a look at one example of where the EDR system can help:

An online shopping company's **Network Operating Center (NOC)** started receiving alerts for 500 internal server error logs, with 10% of transactions resulting in failure. During initial investigation, the NOC thought it was some sort of DDoS attack, but their firewalls and network intrusion detection system events didn't report anything at all. They then thought it was an exploited system vulnerability, but their vulnerability scanner also reported nothing relevant to the event. Finally, using EDR with configuration management determined that an operating system update patch had been deployed incorrectly on four systems in a server farm of 20 servers by looking at the system state history. The patch was redeployed and the error disappeared!

Security policy

A security policy is a document which defines the plans to protect all type of assets, both physical and virtual. The following areas must be addressed:

- Risk assessment policy
- Password policy
- Email policy
- Internet policy
- Disaster recovery
- Intrusion detection

Any violation of these policies should be monitored and prioritized for analysis and response. These can be used for the early detection of any security breach. Any organizations that seek to attain a high level of security maturity should review and adjust their endpoint security policies from time to time.

How to choose an EDR solution ?

Increasingly, cyberattacks have been targeting organizations, resulting in multiple data breaches in recent years. Not only have these attacks increased in volume, but they have also become highly sophisticated in nature as well. These sophisticated new methods are much more complex and harder to find and stop. EDR differs from other **endpoint protection platforms** (**EPP**) such as antivirus (AV) and anti-malware, and its primary focus isn't just to automatically stop threats in the pre-execution phase of an endpoint. The need for an EDR solution is the highest priority for any organization serious about business and that wants to ensure it is as protected from the threat of an attack.

There are many EDR solutions available on the market. However, capabilities may differ from platform to platform. When evaluating EDR platforms, you must consider capabilities including the level of visibility, reporting, automation, response effectiveness, ease of deployment, impact on the environment, and finally a solution that fits your budget. Here are what organizations need to consider when choosing the right EDR solution:

- An EDR solution should run as a managed service based on complex analysis, and organizations need to have visibility into EDR operations and management. This might differ on the basis of whether the organization just needs prevention or if it also requires visibility.
- Any viable EDR candidate must support all type of endpoints on their network.
- Deploy tens or hundreds of thousands of endpoints quickly, in a scalable and cost effective way.
- The solution should be intelligent enough to correlate activities across multiple endpoints.
- The solution should not consume a significant portion of endpoint resources like bandwidth and CPU.
- Finally, the cost of purchase and deployment, plus all recurring costs must fit within your security budget.

This link gives you a comparison between different EDR solutions available on the market: `https://www.gartner.com/reviews/market/endpoint-detection-and-response-solutions`

Security information and event management

Understanding what's going on inside your network is the key element to securing it and ensuring continued surveillance. Managing the data feed coming from servers as well as security devices on activity and the use of these available services is key to providing this security. SIEM is a tool which aggregates incoming information from network sensors such as IPS, IDS, Honeypot, firewalls, or anything which can detect security events and feed information to the SIEM tool. SIEM provides you with the current state of your network and offers a 360-degree view of the IT environment. The correlation with log events makes it possible to view what is going on in your network, and including this feature means that an incident response team can react.

SIEM—Event versus incident and data breach

If you have been a network or security professional, you may be familiar with terms such as logs, alerts, notifications, incidents, and events. All of these terms depend on how you label an occurrence, which will dictate your response.

What is an event?

According to the **National Institute of Standards and Technology** (**NIST**), "*Any observable occurrence in a system or network, such as sending an e-mail message, SSH to any device, or a firewall blocking an attempt to connect, are defined as an event.*"

What is a security incident?

A security incident is an event that violates an organization's security policies and procedures and compromises the integrity, confidentiality, and availability of information assets. For example, a simple login to an SSH server is considered an **event** but a brute force attack using multiple logins to an SSH server is considered a security incident. All types of security incidents should be actionable either in an automated way or by a security analyst.

What is a data breach?

Data breaches are the most the critical and confirmed security or privacy incident. These incidents may involve personal or business sensitive information. Storing sensitive data is always governed by the legal definition given by state laws. Data breaches also require notifying the affected individuals or users, regulatory agencies, sometimes credit reporting agencies, and the media.

So far, the Facebook–Cambridge Analytics data scandal was the worst data breach that has occurred in 2018 so far.

How do SIEM systems work?

SIEM can provide a real-time analysis of security alerts generated by any system that we can produce in a collectable log feed.

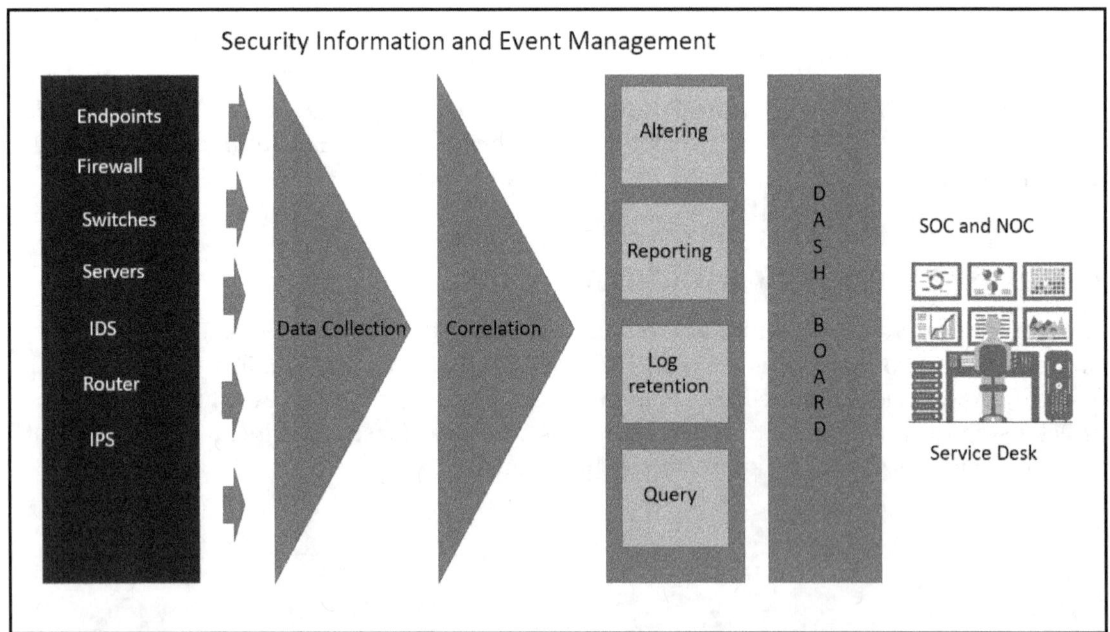

Event generator sensors

Logs are the key and primary requirements for visualizing what's going on in your network and who's attacking. Every organization wants the logs coming from the all-critical resources of your network and business. As security administrator, you always want the logs from your firewall, IPS, and IDS. You will also want logs from your key servers sitting in DMZ, and of course you would also include Active Directory server and your key application, endpoint, and database servers.

Event and log collection or data aggregation

Log collection or aggregation is the heart and soul of a SIEM solution. A SIEM should not be confused with SYSLOG data, which is a simple log generated by devices. Someone has to look at this log to find out the root cause of the alert. The idea is not only to collect log data, but to create a meaningful context from log data. SIEM platforms collect event logs from thousands of different sensors installed on various devices, and these events provide activity data, which is required to analyze the security of our IT environment. In order to get a 360-degree view, we need to consolidate what we collect onto a single platform to find out the pattern. Aggregation is the process of transformation for data transferring from different types of sources into a common repository and meaningful standard format.

For example, Event ID 10509 has resulted in login failure, and the logs are coming to the SIEM solution. It is very easy to read or correlate this event with an attack or an incident:

Event ID	Source IP	Destination IP	Username	Time Stamp	Count
10509	1.1.1.1	2.2.2.2	ajays	2:00:01	1
10509	1.1.1.1	2.2.2.2	ajays	2:00:02	1
10509	1.1.1.2	2.2.2.2	ajays	2:00:04	1
10509	1.1.1.3	2.2.2.2	ajays	2:00:05	1
10509	1.1.1.5	2.2.2.2	ajays	2:00:06	1

⇩

Event ID	Source IP	Destination IP	Username	Time Stamp Start	Time Stamp Stop	Count
10509	1.1.1.1	2.2.2.2	ajays	2:00:01	2:00:06	5

Correlation

Event correlation is the process in which a SIEM relates a series of events to generate an incident or a more meaningful event. In our previous example, there were five failed login attempts to the same user account from multiple source machines. For a security analyst, it might be worth investigating this. Logging the correlation is the best way to raise alerts:

INC 100001 - Multiple Login Failure

Event ID	Source IP	Destination IP	Username	Time Stamp Start	Time Stamp Stop	Count
10509	1.1.1.1	2.2.2.2	ajays	2:00:01	2:00:06	5

Reporting and Alerting

Alerting is a feature that enables SIEM systems to trigger alerts based on the rule configured. All solutions will at least alert the SIEM console, but some may offer extended alerting capabilities.

Dashboards

For massive SIEM deployment, a SIEM solution must have effective dashboards for compliance, infrastructure, and security analysis. Dashboards make it easier for security administrators to visualize a report on trends and activities, as well as to spot anomalies, to track security indicators, and to assess the overall security posture of an IT environment. Most SIEM products come with pre-built dashboards, but these can also be customized according to requirements.

Automation

Security professionals invest a lot of their time in running customized queries to get the required data. They also give a lot of time to navigating through multiple dashboards and data feeds just to find the details required to investigate a single alert. With an ever-growing number of cyberattacks, there comes the requirement to develop improved identification and response times to potential attacks and security threats.

To illustrate this, let's take a look at the following scenario:

It's a Saturday night, and you receive alerts for a malware infection like WannaCry in your IT environment. The first thing you do is try to remotely access your network, but for some reason this does not work. Do you have an alternative option? You could get changed, travel to the office and start checking IPS/IDS reports as well as analyzing security reports, but this might take a lot of time. Investing time in reports can cause more damage because such attacks spread quickly. Here, the easiest method is to isolate networks by shutting down devices or by unplugging the cables. But is that possible? Yes, but only if you have a small network with just a few racks of servers and a few networking gears. However, this approach is almost impossible for a large scale Geo-spread network.

Now imagine an automated incident response machine, which will raise an alarm as soon as malware is detected and will send you an SMS to your cell phone. Your SIEM solution will respond to such threats by isolating the infected machine from the network, and then peace will be restored when you recieve an SMS to notify you that the problem has been temporarily fixed in this way. When you return to the office on Monday, you can then analyze security reports and recover your critical systems.

Let's take a look at a few more examples:

- **Blocking a Malicious IP address**: The first layer of security in any organization is a perimeter firewall. We know firewalls work according to rules, and this situation can be addressed by creating a new rule to block the malicious IP as soon as suspicious activity is detected.
- **Node isolation**: SIEM can automate vulnerability scans to identify systems at risk. The response tool can take action by disabling networking on an infected system and isolating it from the network.
- **DDoS attack**: By using only log monitoring, a SIEM tool can be used to detect Denial of Service (DoS) attacks, one of the most dangerous and common types of network attack. Based on log analysis, an alert can be generated for a DoS attack, which can be further automated to redirect traffic to DDoS scrubbers.

Log management

The basic premise of log management is very simple. Network devices and operating systems all generate events and notifications. The SIEM solution organizes and archives these log event data based on the time period. Any logs older than the duration defined by the security administrator are usually moved to some sort of backup.

SIEM commercial products

Here is a list of the most famous products on the market according to a survey that took place in 2017 :

- LogRhythm
- LogPoint
- Splunk
- QRadar
- AlienVault OSSIM
- RSA Security Analytics platform
- ArcSight

Summary

Security is defined in multiple ways, but for IT security professionals it's a simple competition against cyber criminals. In this game, the winner owns the network. We cannot protect what we do not understand—it is as simple as that. In this chapter, we discussed how to detect potential security threats before they compromise our network, host infrastructure, and applications. We have also discussed the fact that it is very tough for a human to read all of the logs coming from various devices. Keeping that in mind, we have discussed SIEM tools and its future with automation and automated threat response techniques.

In the next chapter, we will discuss vulnerability assessments and why these are required in every organization for protecting information.

Questions

1. What elements would you typically expect to make up a SIEM environment?
    1. Client, server, agent
    2. Archive, cloud processor, contribution network
    3. Central processing node, sensors, database/logging
    4. Agents, sensors, logging, reporting, Central processing node

2. How can SIEM directly support enhanced security services?
    1. By increasing the integrity of event messages
    2. By overlaying additional contextual information using authentication messages. This will achieve a correlated view of authentication
    3. By improving the overall availability of a processing environment
    4. By increasing the confidentiality of event messages

3. When considering the budget of a SIEM service, what are the components that should be considered?
    1. Monitoring agents and console
    2. Software licensing, implementation fees
    3. Implementation project, hardware (platform/storage), software, operational costs
    4. Archivel storage system and processing nodes

4. Which phase of hacking performs an actual attack on a network or system?
    1. Reconnaissance
    2. Maintaining Access
    3. Scanning
    4. Gaining Access

5. What is the best statement for taking advantage of a weakness in the security of an IT system?
    1. Threat
    2. Attack
    3. Exploit
    4. Vulnerability

Further reading

For more information, visit the following links:

- `https://www.sans.org/course/siem-with-tactical-analytics`
- `https://www.cisco.com/en/US/technologies/tk648/tk362/technologies_white_paper09186a00800a3db9.html`
- `https://www.sans.org/reading-room/whitepapers/detection/understanding-intrusion-detection-systems-337`

7
Vulnerability Assessment

In the previous chapter, we learned about various aspects of security IT infrastructure, including monitoring and responding to incidents, threat detection, and diverting attackers.

In today's digital world, information is accessed, stored, and transferred electronically. The security of this information and the systems storing it are critical to companies' reputations, as well as for providing a better user experience. Consequently, the need to analyze and remediate vulnerabilities from IT infrastructure have become the most important tasks for any security expert, system admin, or network administrator. Even if an organization has a well-managed security infrastructure in place such as a firewall, antivirus, and intrusion detection system, an attacker can still gain unauthorized access by exploiting the vulnerabilities. In the context of software security, vulnerabilities are specific flaws or oversights in a piece of software that can be exploited by attackers. Using assessment methodology, we will focus on security functions and security evaluations in this chapter.

We are going to cover the following topics in this chapter:

- Infrastructure concerns
- Nessus installation and vulnerability assessment methodology
- Sample report

Infrastructure concerns

With the increasing threat of cyber attacks (including those originating in one's own network) it is now becoming more important for organizations to secure their IT resources. The world is moving faster than ever before—every year cyber criminals launch more attacks than there are patches released by software developers. No single system is managed by one vendor—instead, it is a multi-vendor environment: motherboard manufacturers are different; operating systems are provided by someone else; and storage comes from different vendors. On top of this never-ending list, you have multiple applications installed on operating systems, and then to protect your IT resources you have firewall and cryptography systems. None of these systems are foolproof and they are always vulnerable to attacks.

Changing the whole ecosystem would be a huge, tedious task. Every day new technology arrives, daily patches and releases are released and vendors offer free upgrades. Consequently, it becomes very tough for an IT organization to keep all resources up-to-date.

Apart from the previously mentioned factors, a few common assumptions are listed below:

- We're highly protected and guarded by firewalls and an **intrusion detection system** (**IDS**)
- Many organizations do not audit until disaster strikes and they are forced to react
- My organization isn't a target for attack due to the nature of our business
- Vulnerability assessments are too expensive and I do not see any ROI
- Attackers are smarter that us; we cannot beat them
- My infrastructure is running fine, we never saw a need to audit
- We do not know our own network infrastructure

What is vulnerability assessment?

In an IT space, vulnerability assessment is the process of identifying and classifying security holes in an organization's system, network, and communication infrastructure, which can be affected by an internal or external threat. Vulnerability assessments typically involve the use of highly automated testing tools such as cloud-hosted instances and network security scanner appliances for internal scans. The results of this are typically provided along with weakness and appropriate solutions. When it comes to identifying such security loopholes, we now need to decide whether we opt for an FAQ, vulnerability assessment, penetration test or compliance test. In fact, vulnerability assessment and penetration tests are both different exercises. From a regulatory compliance point of view, the selection of a vulnerability assessment or a penetration test will depend on the specific control objective you are trying to meet. In a constantly evolving digital era, organizations' methods of data management and security have to be compliant with the standards dictated by regulated bodies or institutions such as PCI, HIPPA, GDPR, ISO or SOX. This is an important factor in ensuring the minimum security requirements are met for running a business.

The following diagram summarizes the vulnerability assessment:

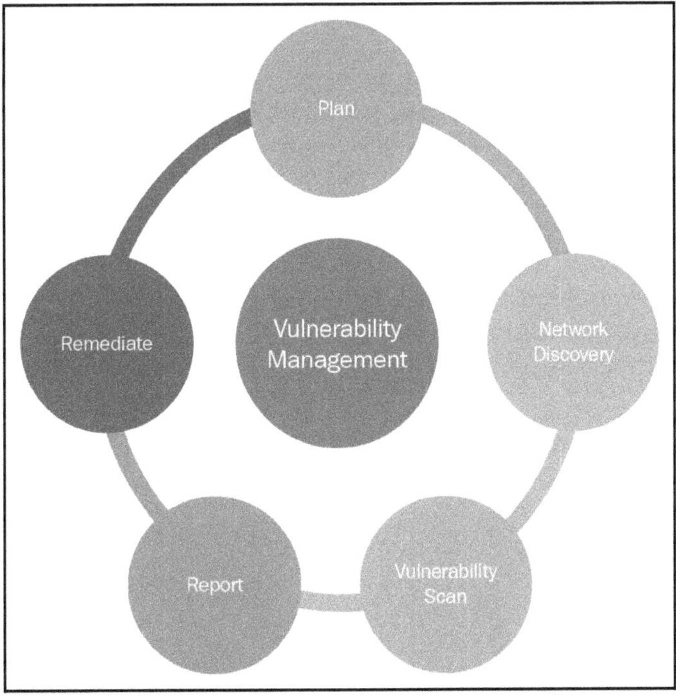

Plan

Everything begins with planning. The planning component will include gathering all relevant information defining the scope of activities, secure permission, roles and responsibilities, and making others aware through the change management process.

Network discovery

Network discovery is basically used to discover a number of live hosts on a given network. There are many methods that can be configured for this.

Vulnerability scan

The most effective method for keeping your system safe and up-to-date is to regularly run a vulnerability test to uncover vulnerabilities and highlight actions that help you to make informed decisions to reduce risk across your business.

Report

A vulnerability report is important when it comes to including every bit of important information within your scan report. A report should contain details of the type of issue, severity, product and services, the type of vulnerability, potential threats, and proof of concept.

Remediation

A remediation plan should have detailed bottom-up technical measures such as application patches, configuration changes of firewalls or other network-based devices, changes to governing policy, processes and procedures, or configuration standards.

Why do we need vulnerability assessment?

The overall objective of a vulnerability assessment is to scan, investigate, analyze, and report on the severity of risks associated with any vulnerabilities discovered on the external facing resource. It should also provide your organization with an appropriate mitigation plan to address the weaknesses or vulnerabilities previously discovered. Network vulnerability scanning can help an organization to identify weaknesses in their network security. Whether results are good or bad will depend on who runs the scanning first - a system admin or attackers.

Types of vulnerability assessment

Vulnerability assessment can be divided broadly into two major groups:

- Network-based assessment
- Host-based assessment

For maximum effectiveness and security, both of the vulnerability assessments mentioned above are required. This is because vulnerabilities can be exploited by an insider, a legitimate user, bad guys outside of the perimeter or an unauthorized user.

Network-based assessment

The network-based vulnerability assessments are completed by scanner tools which are internally or externally installed. These allow a network administrator to discover and eliminate their organization's network-based security vulnerabilities.

A network vulnerability assessment generally includes tasks such as the following:

- Password analysis for network devices such as Router/Switches/Wi-Fi
- Reviewing network strength against **distributed denial of service** (**DDoS**)
- Network intrusion
- Device-level security analysis (router, switch, computer)
- Scanning for known and potential threats and vulnerabilities

Some common tools are:

- Nessus
- OpenVAS
- Qualys

Nessus is a free, open source tool. It is as powerful as some of the best commercial vulnerability assessment scanners.

Most famous network scanners come in the form of both virtual and physical appliances. These are hardware boxes designed to be placed on customer premises such as data centers or office locations. These scanners provide continuous security and compliance monitoring of IT assets and send that data to the Cloud Instance backend scanning engine. Scanning engines are updated in the background with the latest vulnerability signatures. Customers don't have to touch these boxes once they've been deployed. The diagram below demonstrates a typical network-based scanner architecture:

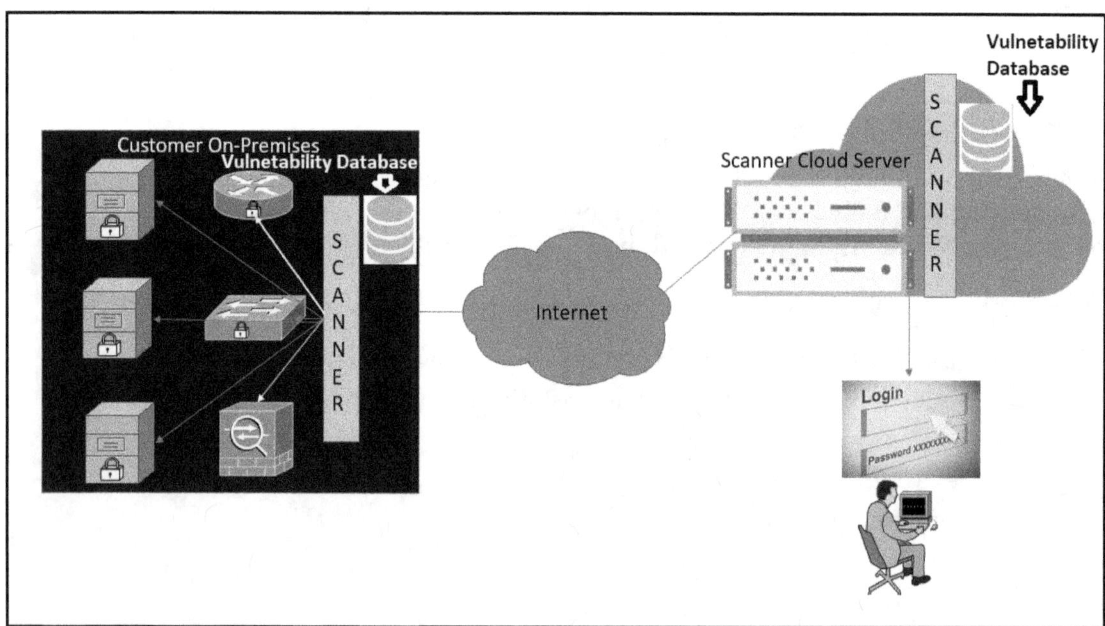

Host-based assessment

The host-based vulnerability assessment works on a client-server model where the client performs the scan and sends the report back to the server/manager. A host-based scanner is installed on every host on the system that you want to monitor. Host-based vulnerability assessment tools can provide an insight into the potential damage that can be done by insiders and outsiders once some level of access is granted or taken on a system. They are generally useful for discovering weaknesses behind an initial access control setting. Network-based scanners cannot perform a deep low-level security check because they do not have direct access to the file system on the target host. A few famous open source tools include OSSEC, Prelude and SNORT.

Nessus installation, configuration, and vulnerability assessment methodology

Nessus is a pretty strong remote security scanning tool which scans devices and raises an alert if it discovers any vulnerabilities that hackers could use to gain access to a computer you have connected to a network. Within days of the vulnerabilities being released to the public, there will be plugins for new vulnerabilities. Nessus utilizes Nmap for port scanning.

Let's take a step-by-step look at how to scan a specified network and hosts.

Installation

To download Nessus' latest release, please visit `https://www.tenable.com/downloads/nessus`. I have chosen to download the package for Windows 2016:

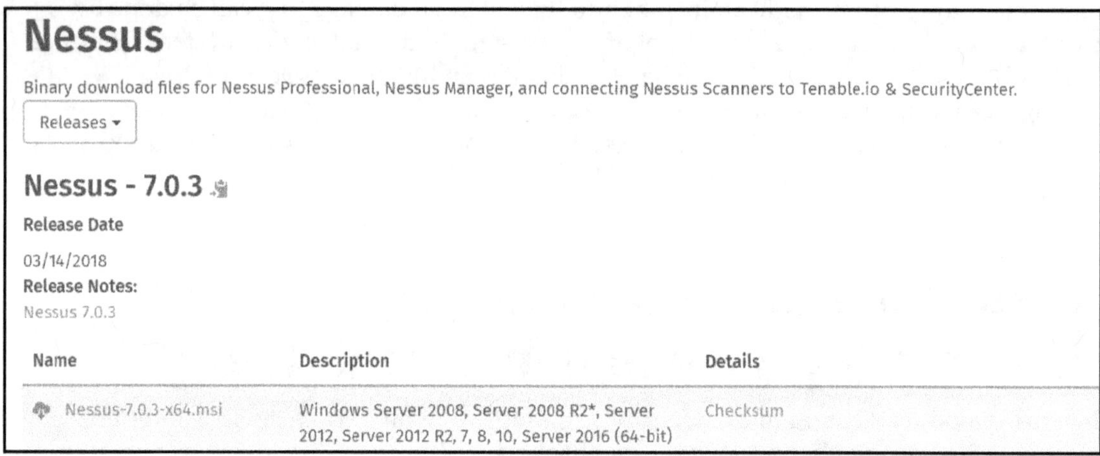

After a successful installation, the console can be accessed on the port `8834` `https://localhost:8834`. Firstly, you will be prompted to provide an activation key and asked to create a username and password. Nessus will then install all the required files and plugins to scan your assets. Once plugins and files are downloaded, you will be redirected to the login page.

Policies

After login, you will see the home page. Follow these steps:

1. Click on **Polices**:

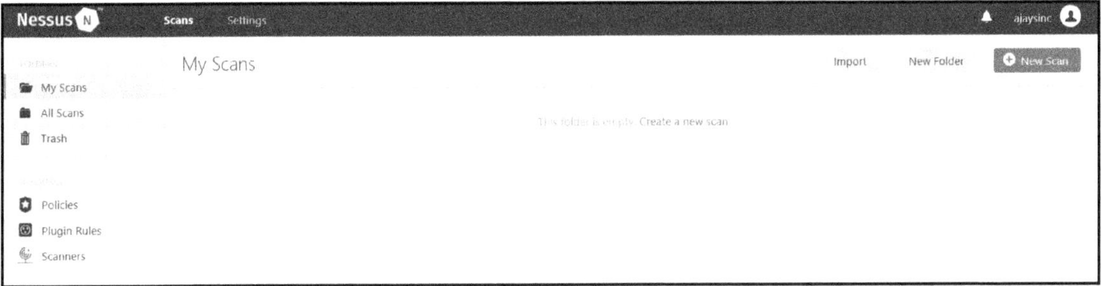

2. Click on new policy. Here, you will see many policies which are default and inbuilt. You have the option to use these default policies or to create your own customized policy to scan by choosing a policy:

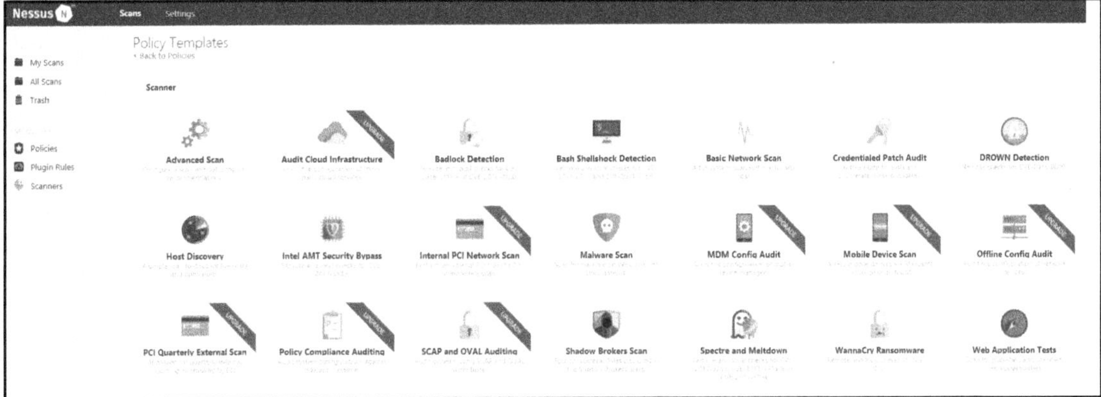

3. Let's do a basic network scan. Click on the **New Scan** and select the **Basic Network Scan** policy.
4. Assign a unique name that reflects the objective or purpose of this scan.

5. In targets, put the target IP address scope. You can also put the range here. For example, `10.0.0.1-255` or the entire subnet, `10.0.0.0/24`:

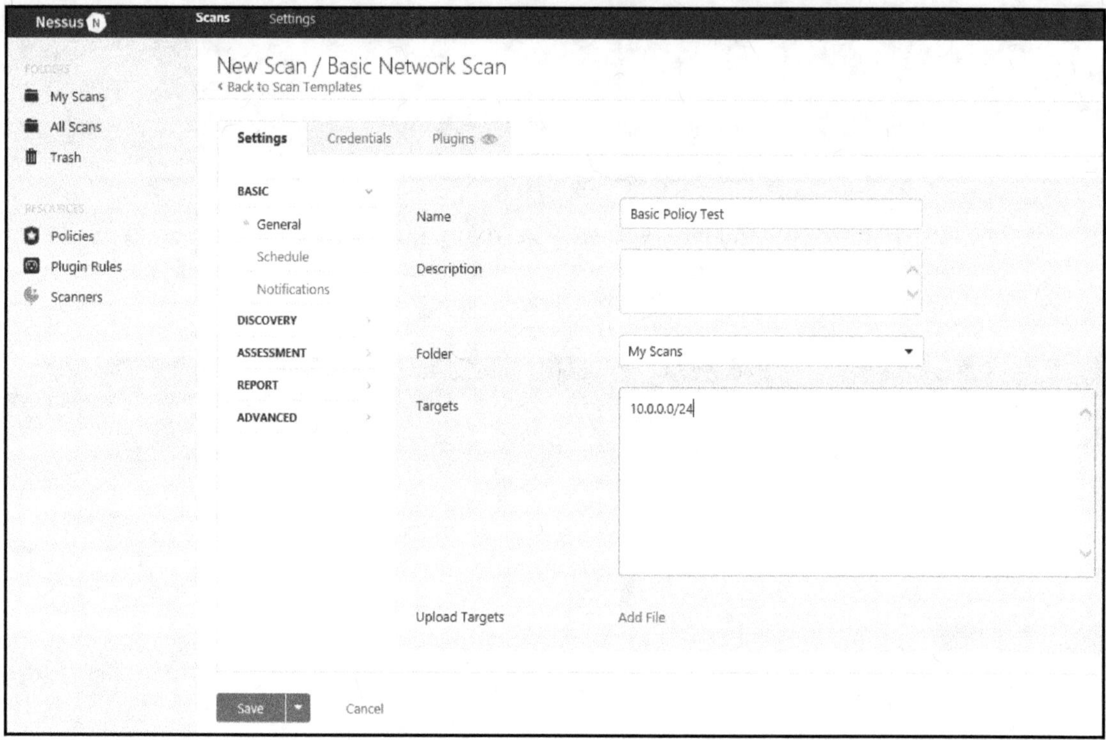

The second most important factor is the credentials. You should provide the necessary credentials before scanning the network, depending upon which type of host you have inside the network. You can add credentials for the Windows, SSH, Databases (MySQL, Oracle, and so on), virtual machines, and the ports (FTP, POP3, and so on):

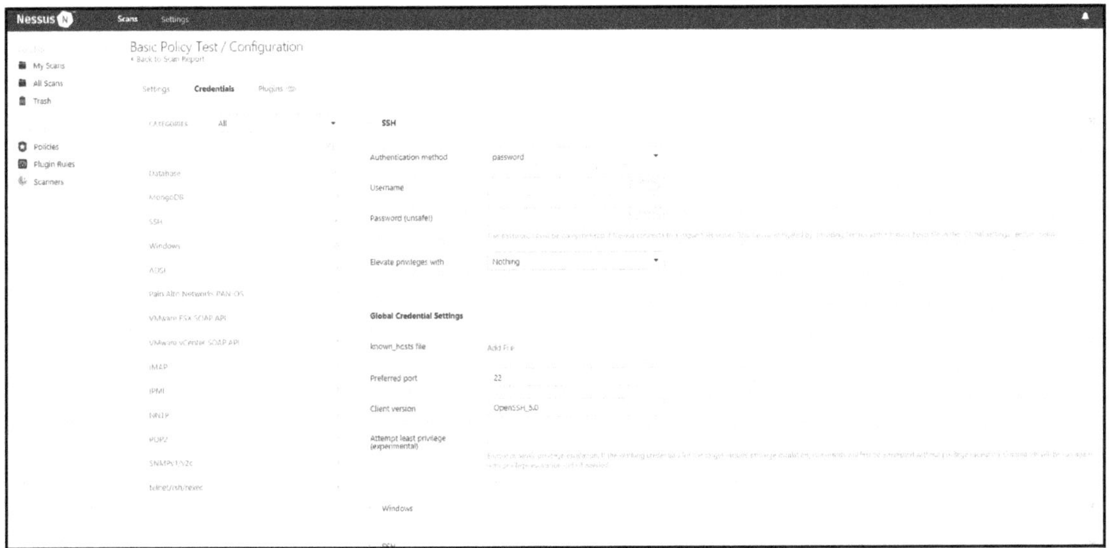

I have passed credentials for SSH and Windows. In the same way, you can add more credentials from the list as shown in the following diagram:

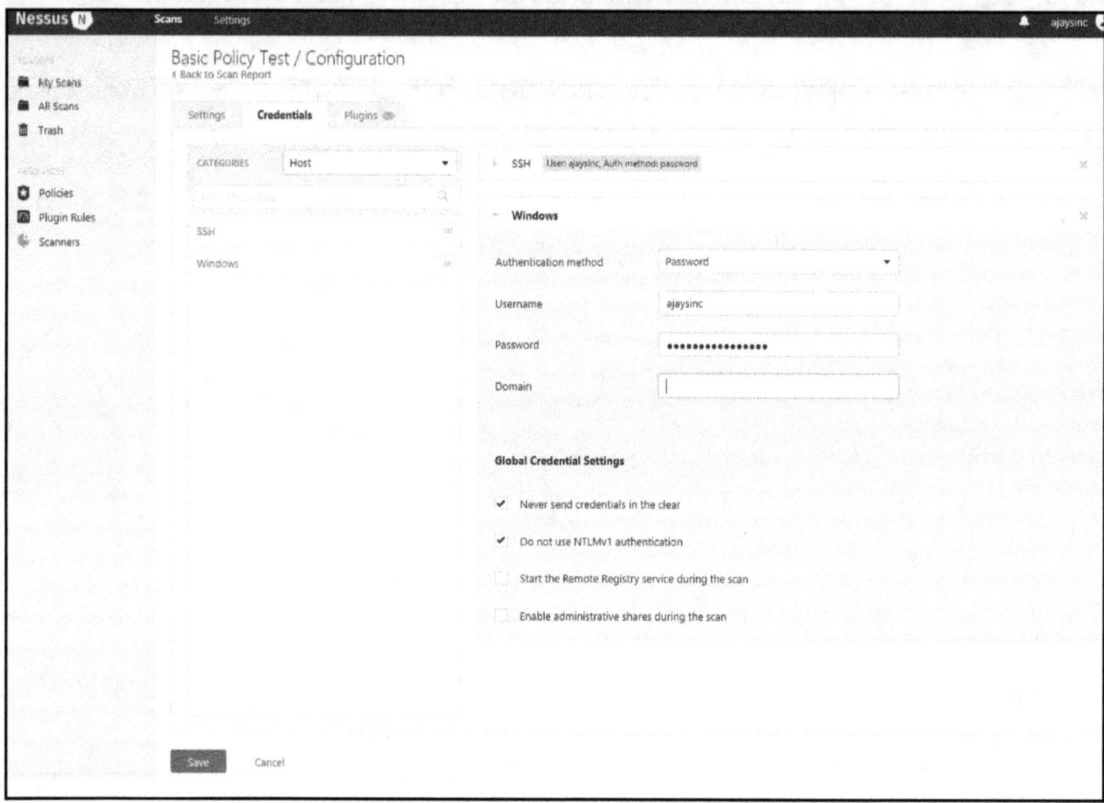

By default, a network scan runs on common ports and protocol, as shown in the following screenshot:

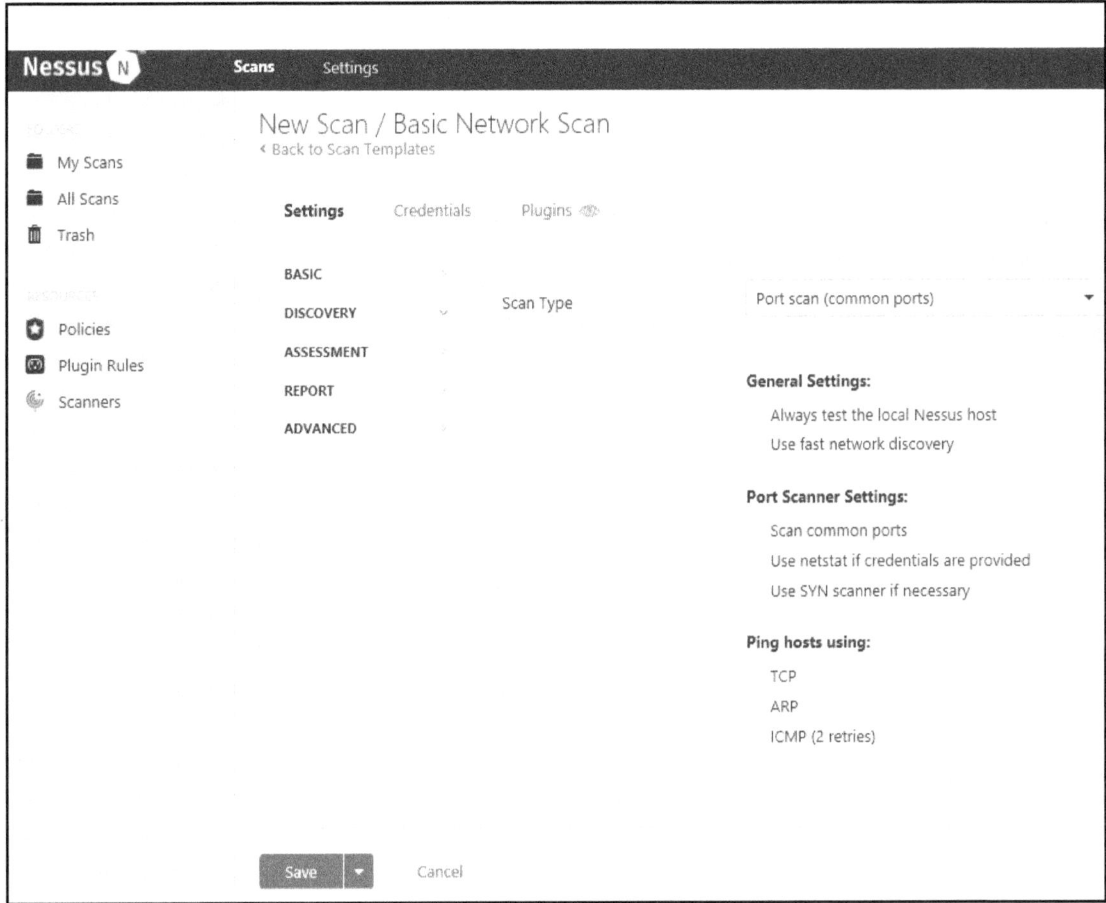

You can customize discovery by changing the scan type to custom, which gives you the option to customize host discovery, port scanning, and service discovery:

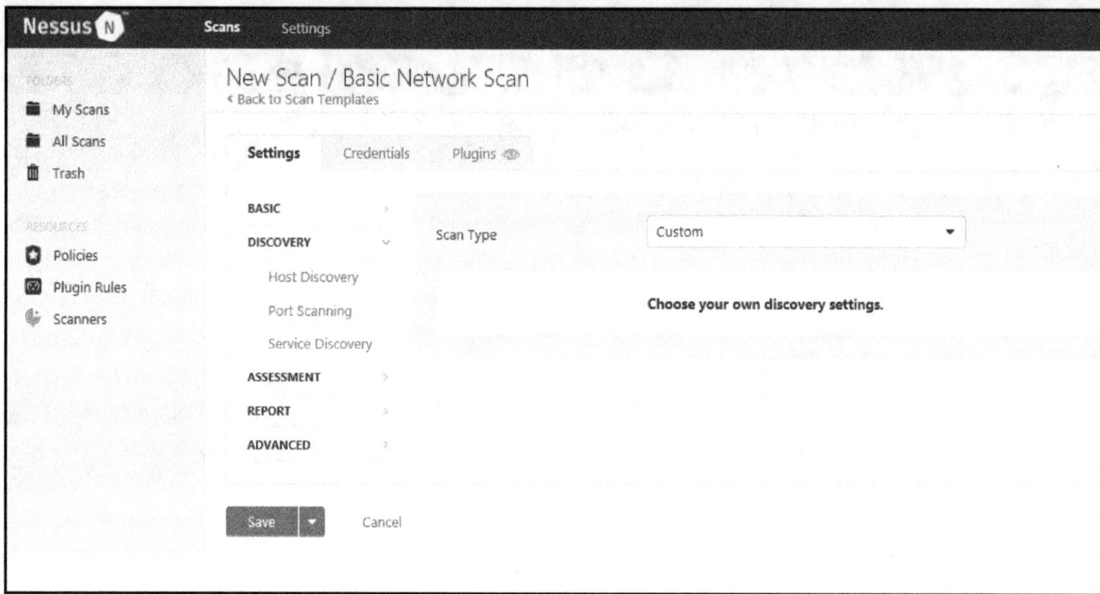

The discovery module has been divided into three parts:

- Host discovery
- Port scanning
- Service discovery

Let's discuss these modules in detail:

- **Host Discovery**: Host discovery is a method which is used to check the number of live hosts in a given network or network range. The fast network discovery option can be used when you want Nessus to finish scanning as soon as possible. Personally, I would not choose this option as Nessus will not probe the network deeply using it. Nessus can also use TCP Ping, and the specific port numbers can also be defined. For security purposes, most system admins block ICMP. The last method is ICMP-based, which works well if there is no firewall blocking ICMP. You can also upload the list of MAC addresses to scan. UDP might not be a good choice because it is a connection-less protocol and is sometimes undetectable.

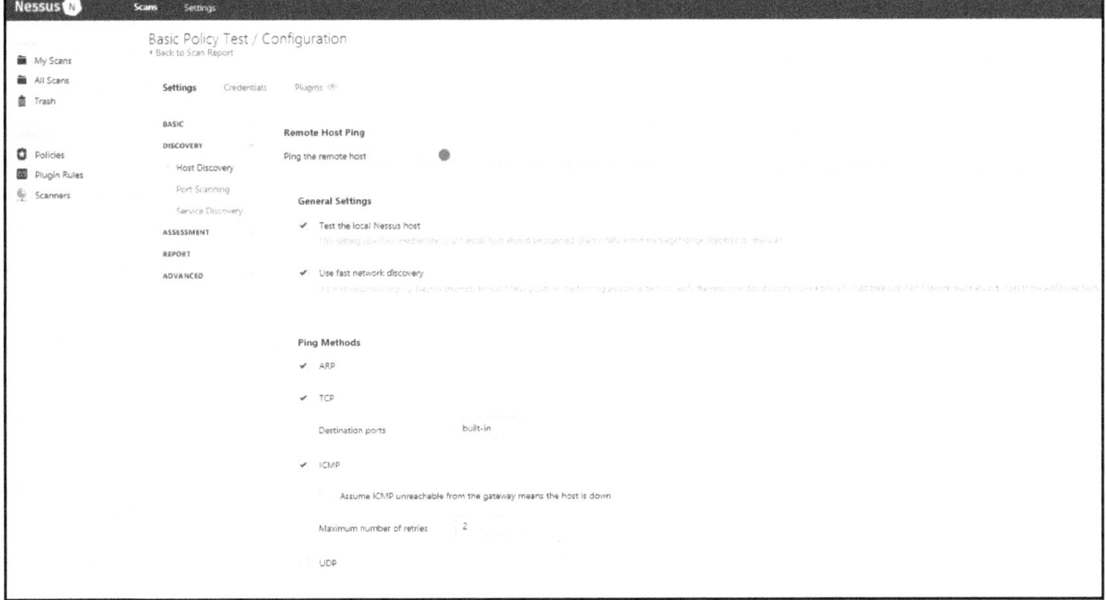

- **Port Scanning**: By default, Nessus will consider all unscanned ports as closed. You can define a range of ports to be scanned, but by default only `4790` common ports will be scanned and listed in Nessus. While **All** represents all of the `65365` ports to scan, a typical system can have a maximum total of `65365` ports. The range of port numbers can also be selected, for example, from 1-99. The local port enumerators is a credential-based scan. The `netstat` utility is made specifically for a Unix-based system and uses the `netstat` command to find the open ports with the status on any running system. In contrast, WMI (netstat) is for Windows-based systems and also requires the credentials to utilize the `netstat` commands which can also be launched using the Windows Command Prompt. TCP uses the three-way handshaking process, starting by sending a SYN packet to a remote host. The scanner sends the SYN packet to the target and, after getting the ACK message from the target machine, predicts the operating system based on signatures. The backend process of Nessus utilizes an NMAP signature to detect the operating system:

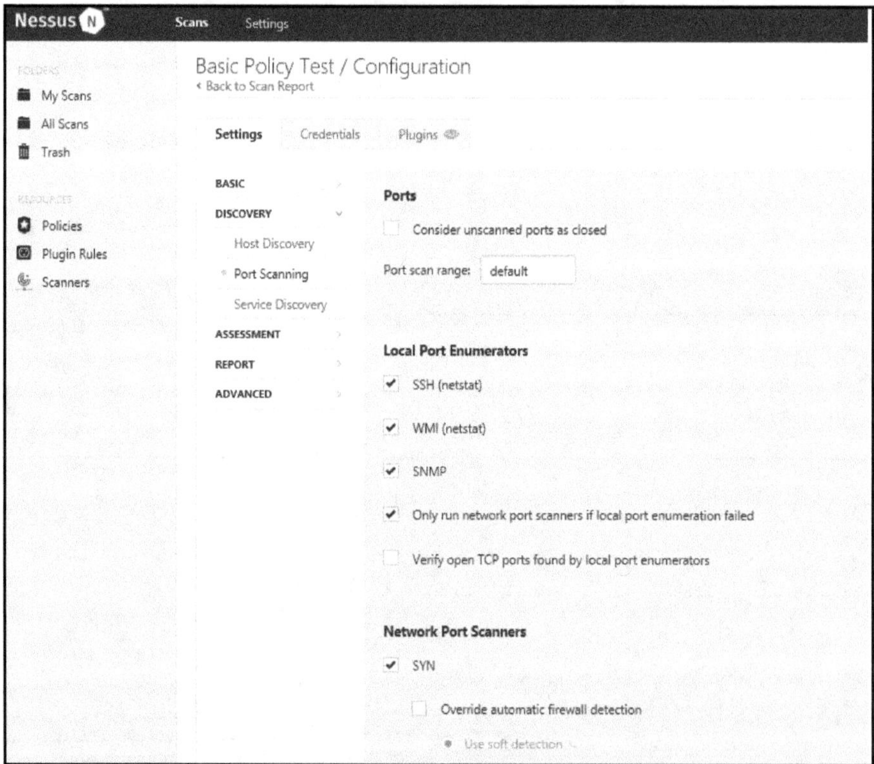

A **Simple Network Management Protocol** (**SNMP**) test is meant for devices like routers, switches, firewalls and other networking devices. The type of device can be predicted by looking at the SNMP walk reply. Make sure you provide a SNMP community string before you launch a scan:

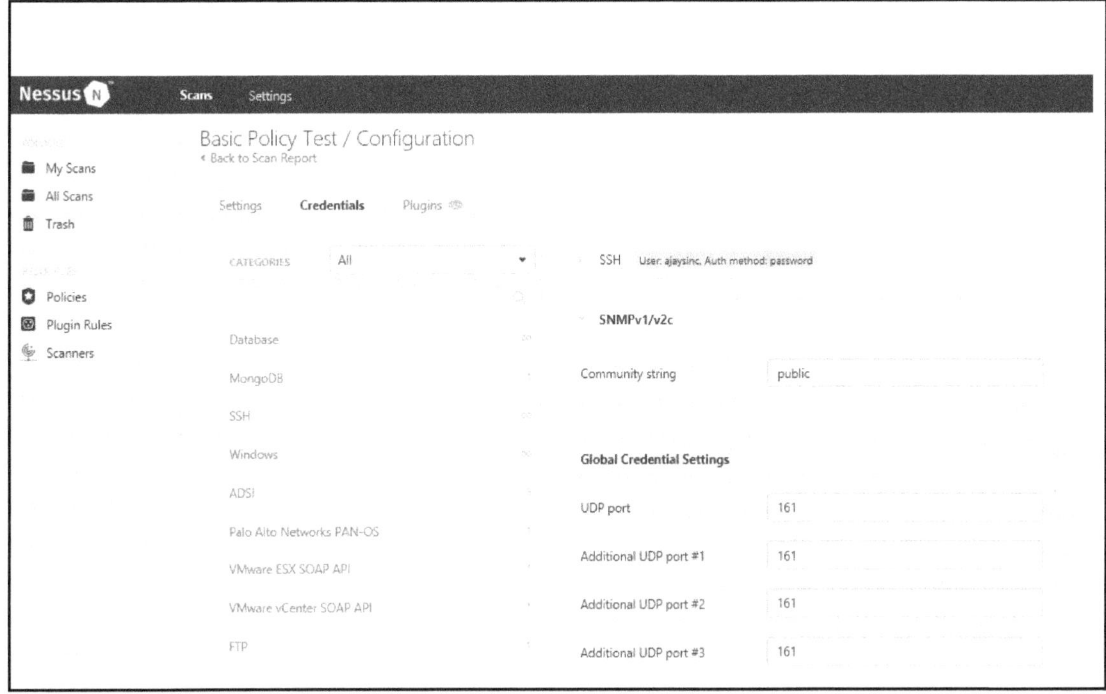

- **Service Discovery**: This is a Nessus setting designed to find the services associated with port numbers. It probes all ports to find the services running on all of them. **Enabling CRL checking (which connects to the Internet)** will check the certificates' revocation:

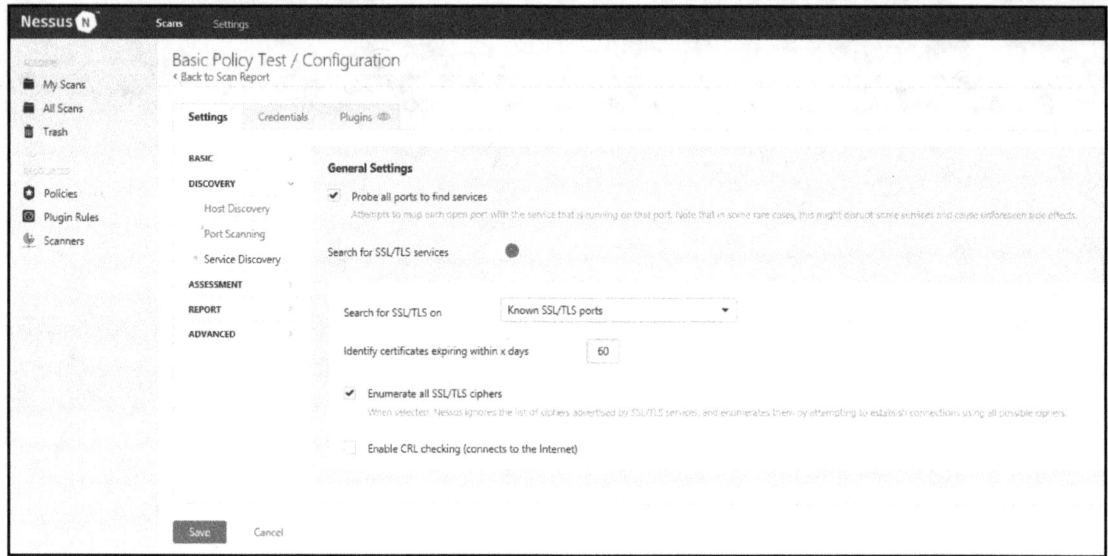

- **ASSESSMENT**: The assessment setting can be divided into different categories:
    - **General**
    - **Brute Force**
    - **Web Applications**
    - **Windows**:

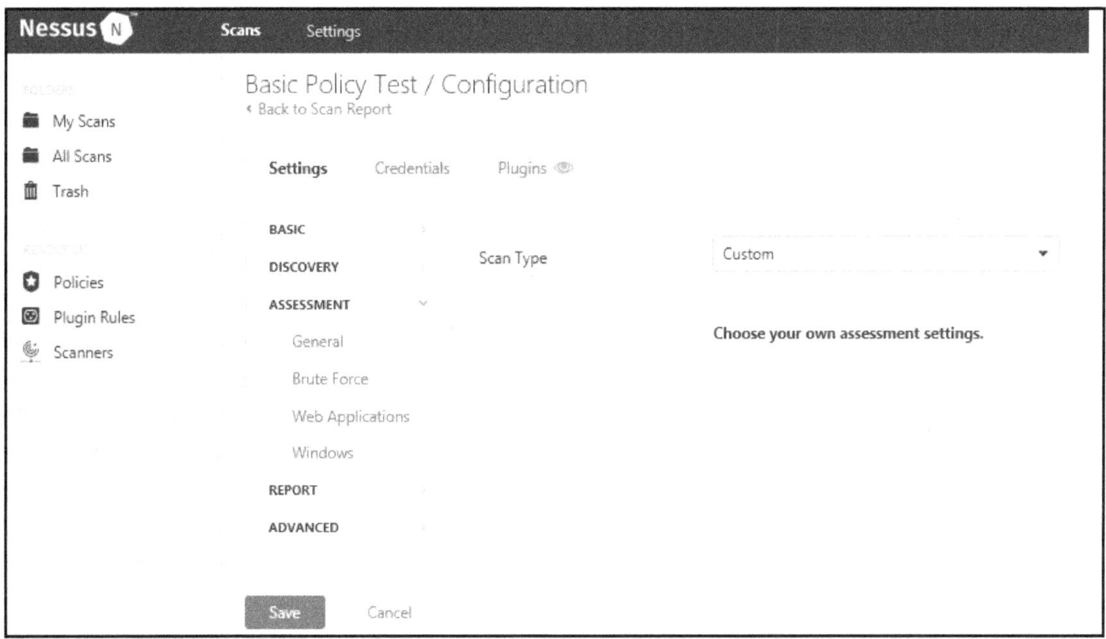

- **General**: The **General** tab represents accuracy in a result based on response. If you want Nessus to not report the vulnerabilities due to any uncertainty, then select **Avoid potential false alarms**:

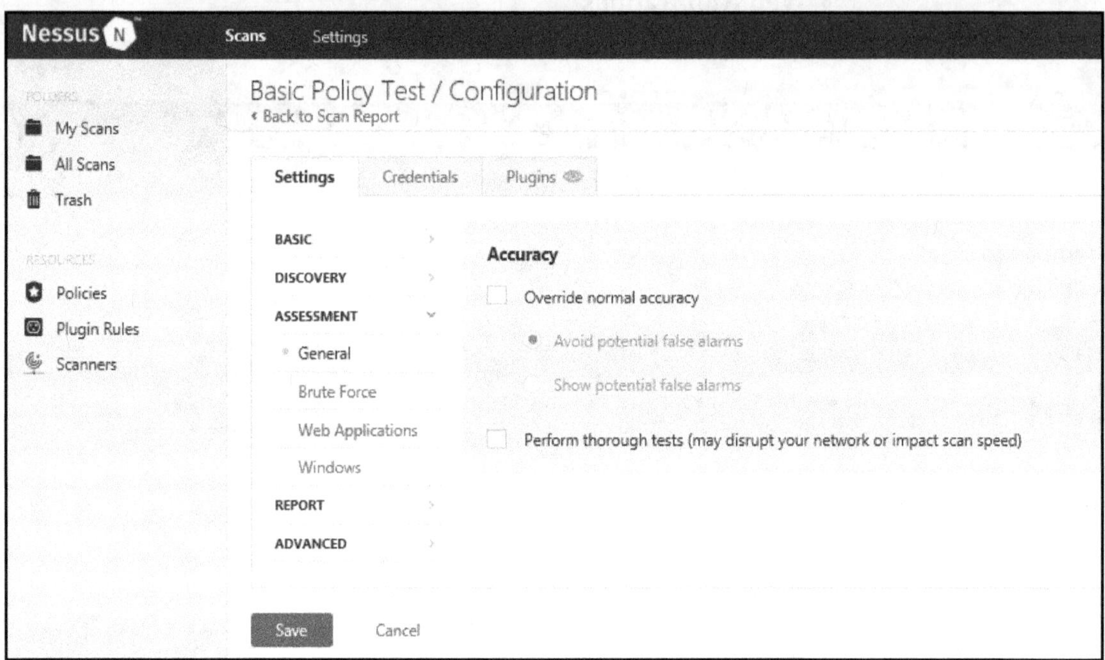

- **Brute Force**: On the first attempt, Nessus will try to login by using the credentials provided by a Nessus administrator. If you also want to test system security, then you may select the second option of using the default accounts stored with Nessus:

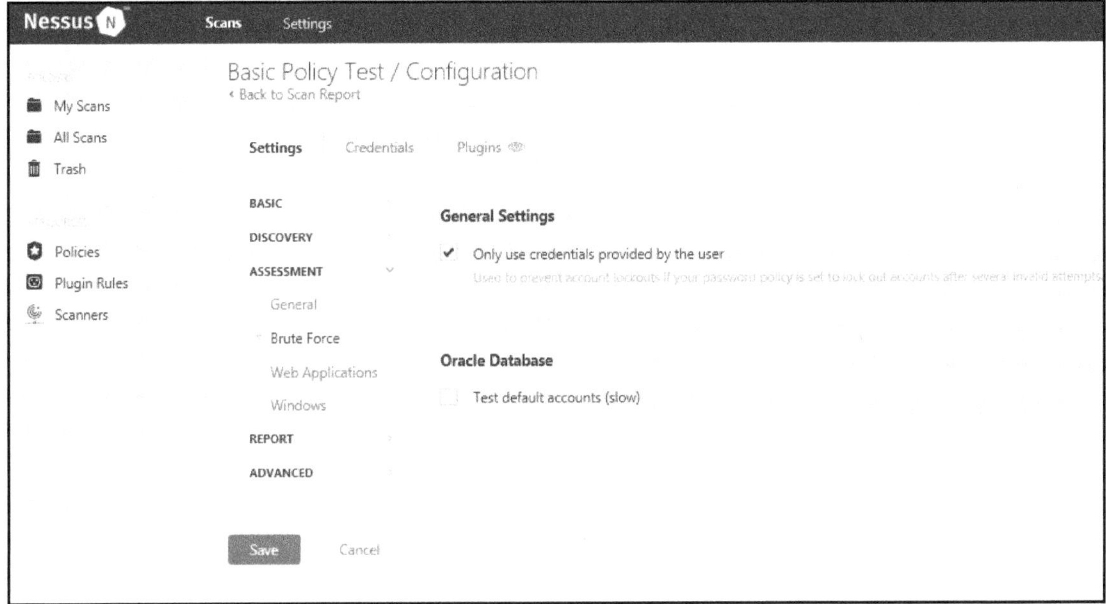

- **Web Applications**: If you want Nessus to perform the web app test, you can enable the web application scanning option:

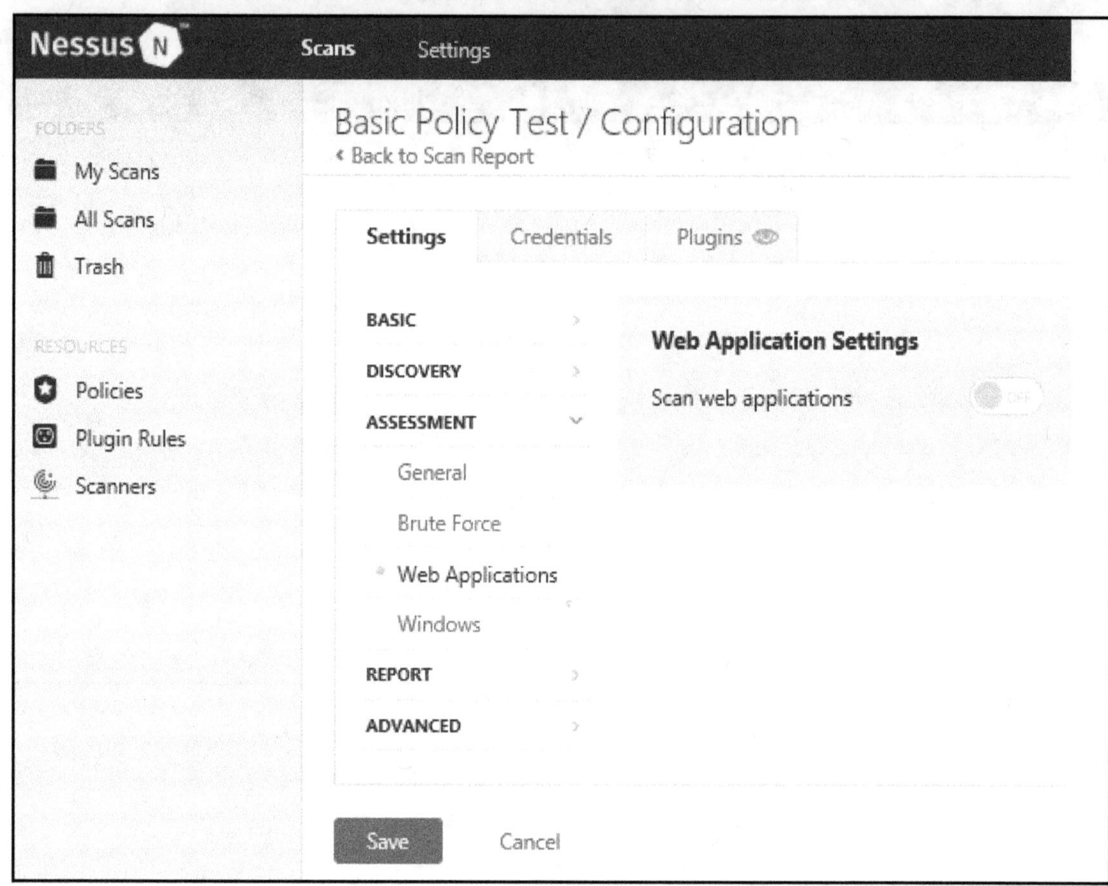

- **Windows**: In the Nessus Windows option tab, you can configure the domain user's enumeration values. Configure the UID values for a reverse domain lookup:

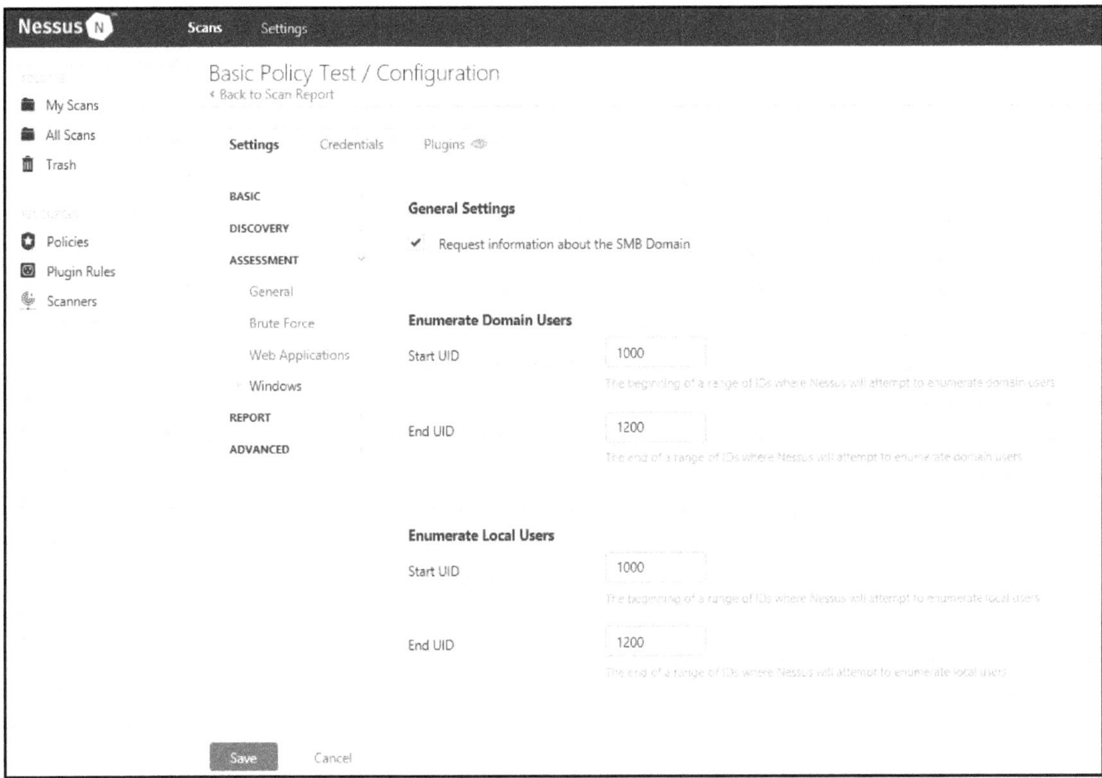

- **Report**: By default, overriding normal verbosity is disabled and you have two options. First, if you have limited disk space then choose to report as little (or as much) information as possible. For report output, use the host name rather than the IP address and report hosts that successfully respond to a Ping. These are also self-explanatory options based on what you want to see in the reporting pattern:

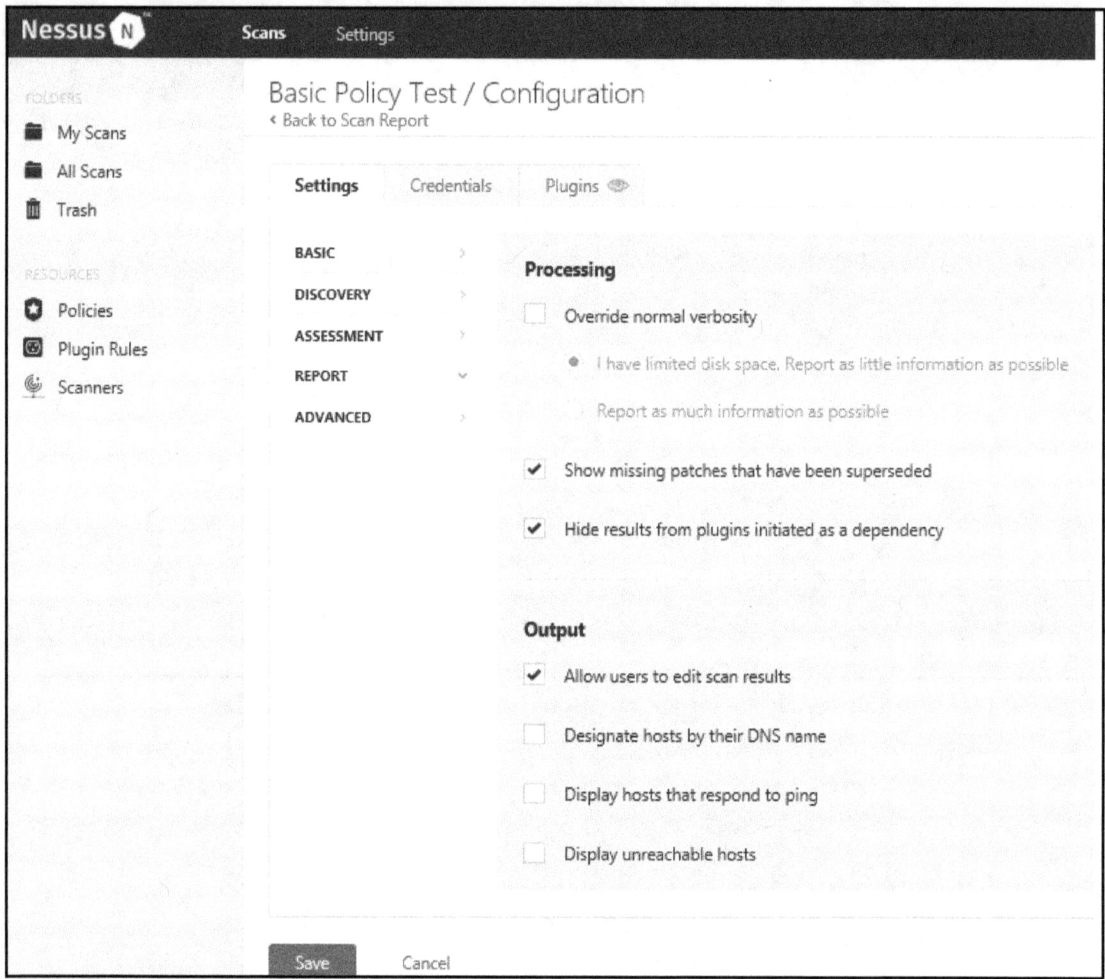

Once you are done with the credentials, save and launch the scanner.

Sample report

Let's take a look at a sample report based on my Azure-hosted website app. This report was generated by a scan with a default web scan policy to scan URLs `myapptestsec.azurewebsites.net`:

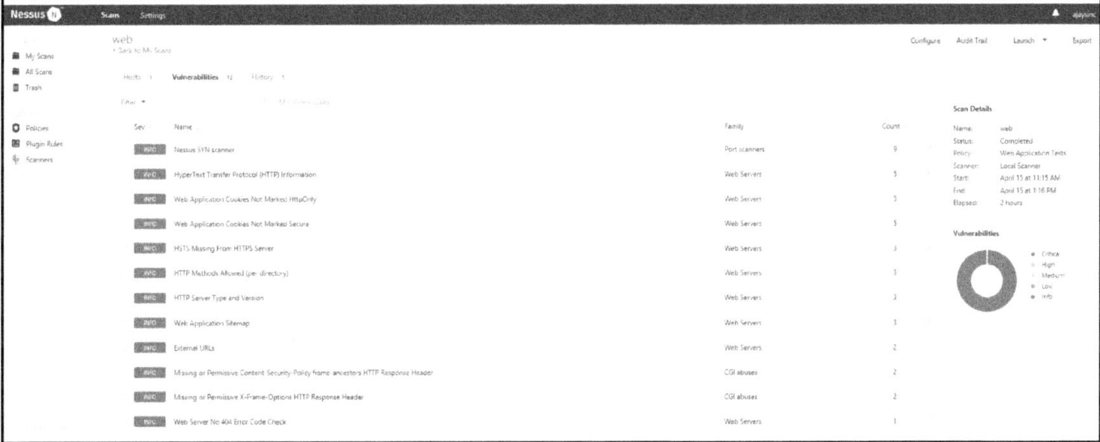

Nessus categorized the levels of vulnerabilities into five different parts (from low to high):

- Info
- Low
- Medium
- High
- Critical:

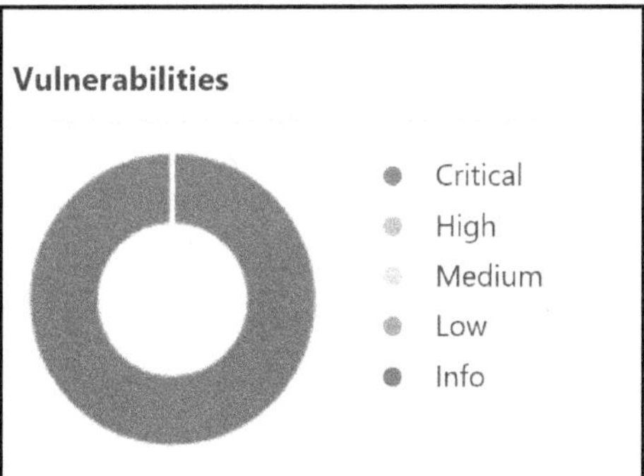

In the following screenshot, you can see that Nessus did not find any critical vulnerabilites but has listed twelve INFOs. For further details, you can click on the INFO tab to expand and view detailed information:

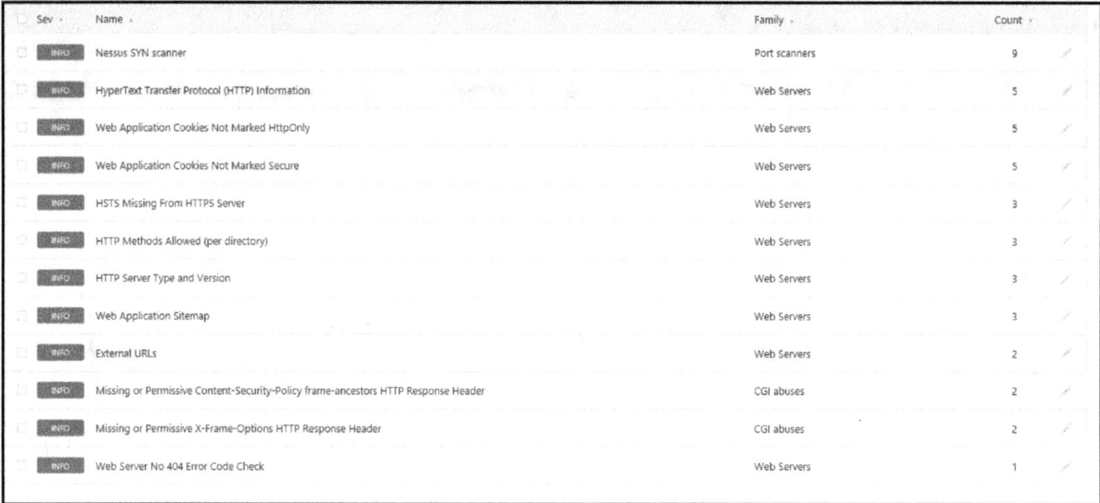

Sev	Name	Family	Count
INFO	Nessus SYN scanner	Port scanners	9
INFO	HyperText Transfer Protocol (HTTP) Information	Web Servers	5
INFO	Web Application Cookies Not Marked HttpOnly	Web Servers	5
INFO	Web Application Cookies Not Marked Secure	Web Servers	5
INFO	HSTS Missing From HTTPS Server	Web Servers	3
INFO	HTTP Methods Allowed (per directory)	Web Servers	3
INFO	HTTP Server Type and Version	Web Servers	3
INFO	Web Application Sitemap	Web Servers	3
INFO	External URLs	Web Servers	2
INFO	Missing or Permissive Content-Security-Policy frame-ancestors HTTP Response Header	CGI abuses	2
INFO	Missing or Permissive X-Frame-Options HTTP Response Header	CGI abuses	2
INFO	Web Server No 404 Error Code Check	Web Servers	1

Summary

Vulnerabilities are increasing by the day, and networks are becoming increasingly difficult to secure. Vulnerability assessments have become the preferred, mandatory method for managing security flaws for many organizations who care about their reputation. Network vulnerability assessments provide quick identification and a 360-degree view of security weaknesses on a given network, supplemented by host assessment. There are many automated tools that are available to detect and report all critical vulnerabilities. The approach, the way these systems are designed and the techniques they use for vulnerability tests may vary widely. As vulnerability scanning usually targets specific hosts or a range of hosts, it often conducts a deeper inspection than network scanners, identifying software versions, operating systems, specific software applications and services, and system configuration attributes.

In this chapter, we have explored how to install the Nessus VA tool and different settings that you should know about before you launch, scan and generate reports.

In the next chapter, we will discuss remote OS-detection techniques using NMAP.

Questions

1. How many levels of vulnerability have Nessus categorised?
    1. 1
    2. 3
    3. 5
    4. 7

2. Which of the following is not a part of system security hardening?
    1. Shutting down unused services
    2. Implementing an IDS
    3. Patching the operating system
    4. Logging analytics

3. What is the most important reason to run the system utility, `NetStat` ?
    1. To mitigate DDoS attempts
    2. To edit system registry
    3. To check passwords
    4. To determine open ports on host

4. What is the best approach when using scanners?
    1. Use an external scanner
    2. Use multiple scanners
    3. Use one scanner to scan all remote network
    4. To get the best results, use one scanner per network segment of an asset

5. Which is not a network scanner?
    1. Qualys
    2. Openvas
    3. Nessus
    4. Radware

Further reading

There are many tools, articles, guides and online resources available to help you to build a better understanding of Vulnerability Assessment. For more information, I would recommend exploring the following three famous tools:

- `www.tenable.com`
- `www.openvas.org`
- `www.qualys.com`

8
Remote OS Detection

In this chapter, we will look at the techniques and methods that can be used to detect remote OSes. The vulnerabilities of operating systems are specific and inevitable. Consequently, it becomes important for network administrators to know about the operating system installed on all running hosts inside the network. For a small network, it might be easy to identify operating systems for all hosts. However, it becomes a challenging job for large-scale cloud organizations to maintain a database where thousands of hosts are being deleted and created every minute and are therefore constantly changing.

There are many scanning tools available on the market, but Nmap and Wireshark are the most popular and widely used tools. You should also have done some background reading in order to successfully use the Wireshark capture feature. In this chapter, we will use Nmap and Wireshark to run a scan and to capture packets. In the next chapter, we will discuss SSL, fundamental security and technical issues, along with the implementation for web-based services.

In this chapter, you will learn about the following topics:

- Reasons for OS detection
- Determining the vulnerability of target hosts
- Tailoring exploits
- OS detection technique with Nmap
- TCP/IP fingerprinting methods supported by Nmap
- Understanding an Nmap fingerprint
- OS matching algorithms

Reasons for OS detection

Before we discuss the reasons for detecting an OS, let's understand what an operating system actually is. An operating system is a set of programs compiled to manage multiple hardware resources associated with a computer, and designed to provide a resource platform pool to run other application programs:

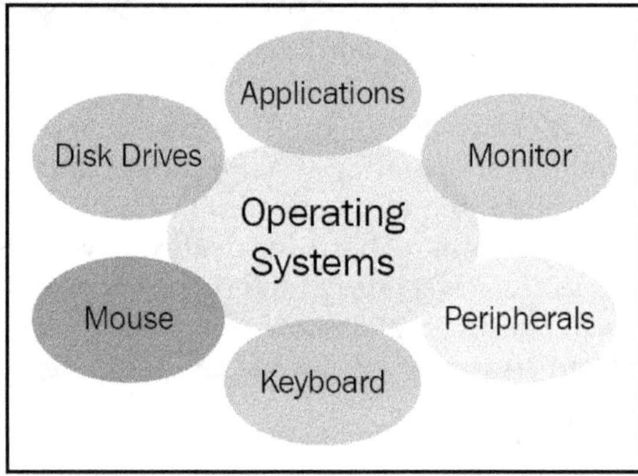

The following are the most common operating systems available on the market:

- Linux
- Windows
- Red Hat
- FreeBSD
- Solaris
- macOS

Let us now discuss why we need to detect an operating system. You can see what operating system is installed on your computer at the following, fun website: `http://whatsmyos.com/` . As a system administrator, you will want to keep track of IT resources. In the same way, attackers will want to have access to your inventory. This will help them to find resources and launch attacks against vulnerabilities.

Network operating system inventory – trace your infrastructure

As a system administrator, it is very important to know what is running on your network and there are multiple tools available for creating an inventory. An inventory can help you to determine operating system's end-of-life, licensing cost, budgeting, and patch management. Most importantly, it gives you the visibility and analysis of the OS running on your infrastructure. The only similarity between system administrators and attackers is that they both use a similar set of methods for fixing or exploiting a system. System administrators need to run a scan and fix problems before an attacker exploits any vulnerabilities found.

Determining vulnerability of target hosts

A vulnerability scan (often referred to as a network-based scan) can be done remotely. The method for running a scan directly on a host is named a host-based scan. Only determining the application version does not always help us to find vulnerabilities to crack the system. It is also very important to detect an OS version to combine results. From time to time, operating system updates are released, and they do patching for an application without even changing the application version. Finding a vulnerability with a remote scan is a bit difficult, as results might become false positive.

Tailoring exploits

Buffer overflow is one of the most famous, powerful and frequently used attacks used to exploit applications. Buffer overflow attacks can provide attackers access to execute commands or customize shell codes in a system. Once you have access to a targeted machine, you could add accounts, access a command prompt, remotely control the GUI, and alter the system's configuration.

When I say *buffer memory*, I am referring to **random-access memory** (**RAM**) used to hold data temporarily before it passes to a desired application. Every application on the system has a fixed size data buffer (memory allocated from a common pool). Attackers use techniques to fill a buffer with data until there is no buffer space left—this is known as **buffer overflow**. It is important to know or detect the actual operating system before you try to execute such scripts to exploit vulnerabilities. Use OS detection first, or you may end up sending Linux shellcode to a FreeBSD server.

OS detection technique with Nmap

Before we talk about remote operating system detection, let's discuss what Nmap is and what it can do. I will also walk you through different flags and nobs that can be used with the Nmap tool in general.

Nmap tool

Network Mapper (**Nmap**) is a freely available open source tool for systems and network administrators, allowing them to perform tasks such as collecting enterprise network inventory, managing service upgrade schedules, basic security audits, and monitoring hosts or service up-time. Nmap is officially available for major computer operating system platforms such as Linux, Windows and macOS X.

Nmap binaries can be downloaded from `https://nmap.org/download.html`. After successful installation, you can check the version simply by passing the `nmap -V` command:

- **Windows**: Output on Windows shows that the program currently installed is `Nmap version 7.60`:

```
C:\Program Files (x86)\Nmap>nmap -V

Nmap version 7.60 ( https://nmap.org )
Platform: i686-pc-windows-windows
Compiled with: nmap-liblua-5.3.3 openssl-1.0.2l nmap-libssh2-1.8.0 nmap-libz-1.2.8 nmap-libpcre-7.6 Npcap-0.93 nmap-libc
net-1.12 ipv6
Compiled without:
Available nsock engines: iocp poll select

C:\Program Files (x86)\Nmap>_
```

- **Linux**: Output on Linux shows that the program currently installed here is `Nmap version 6.40`:

```
ajaysinc@ajaysinclinux:~$ nmap -V

Nmap version 6.40 ( http://nmap.org )
Platform: x86_64-pc-linux-gnu
Compiled with: liblua-5.2.3 openssl-1.0.1f libpcre-8.31 libpcap-1.5.3 nmap-libdn
et-1.12 ipv6
Compiled without:
Available nsock engines: epoll poll select
ajaysinc@ajaysinclinux:~$
```

Nmap can be run using the Linux/Unix shell or Windows Command Prompt interface with root or administrator privileges.

The base syntax of Nmap is as follows:

```
# nmap [scan type] [options] [target]
```

A very simple scan can be performed just by inputting the target IP address without any other options. The target field can be IPv4 `address:1.1.1.1`, IPv6 `address :2001:db8:0:0:0:5678:d334:8af`, hostname `www.xyz.com`, IP address range `192.168.0.1 - 192.168.0.10` and **Classless Inter Domain Routing** (**CIDR**) block `10.10.10.0/24`:

- **Example 1**: Scan with host name `myapptestsec.azurewebsites.net`. By default, it will scan for one thousand ports. A total of nine hundred and ninety-eight ports are filtered, and two ports are open, as shown in the screenshot.

  Please only mention the host name of the website:

```
ajaysinc@ajaysinclinux:~$ sudo nmap https://myapptestsec.azurewebsites.net

Starting Nmap 6.40 ( http://nmap.org ) at 2018-05-07 14:18 UTC
Unable to split netmask from target expression: "https://myapptestsec.azurewebsi
tes.net"
WARNING: No targets were specified, so 0 hosts scanned.
Nmap done: 0 IP addresses (0 hosts up) scanned in 0.24 seconds
ajaysinc@ajaysinclinux:~$ sudo nmap myapptestsec.azurewebsites.net

Starting Nmap 6.40 ( http://nmap.org ) at 2018-05-07 14:18 UTC
Nmap scan report for myapptestsec.azurewebsites.net (52.176.6.0)
Host is up (0.036s latency).
Not shown: 998 filtered ports
PORT    STATE SERVICE
80/tcp  open  http
443/tcp open  https

Nmap done: 1 IP address (1 host up) scanned in 12.60 seconds
ajaysinc@ajaysinclinux:~$
```

Please refer to the help option for further information:

```
TARGET SPECIFICATION:
  Can pass hostnames, IP addresses, networks, etc.
  Ex: scanme.nmap.org, microsoft.com/24, 192.168.0.1; 10.0.0-255.1-254
  -iL <inputfilename>: Input from list of hosts/networks
  -iR <num hosts>: Choose random targets
  --exclude <host1[,host2][,host3],...>: Exclude hosts/networks
  --excludefile <exclude_file>: Exclude list from file
```

- **Example 2**: Scan host with specified port number. As we have seen, only one thousand ports are scanned by default, but Nmap gives you the flexibility to define port options by inputting the flag `-p` and then options such as port range `-p <Port 1>-<Port 2>`, port list `-p <Port 1>,<Port 2>`, and more:

```
ajaysinc@ajaysinclinux:~$ sudo nmap -p 22 myapptestsec.azurewebsites.net

Starting Nmap 6.40 ( http://nmap.org ) at 2018-05-07 14:23 UTC
Nmap scan report for myapptestsec.azurewebsites.net (52.176.6.0)
Host is up (0.041s latency).
PORT    STATE    SERVICE
22/tcp filtered ssh

Nmap done: 1 IP address (1 host up) scanned in 0.93 seconds
ajaysinc@ajaysinclinux:~$ sudo nmap -p 80 myapptestsec.azurewebsites.net

Starting Nmap 6.40 ( http://nmap.org ) at 2018-05-07 14:23 UTC
Nmap scan report for myapptestsec.azurewebsites.net (52.176.6.0)
Host is up (0.040s latency).
PORT    STATE SERVICE
80/tcp open  http

Nmap done: 1 IP address (1 host up) scanned in 0.43 seconds
ajaysinc@ajaysinclinux:~$
```

Please refer to **help** options for more information:

```
PORT SPECIFICATION AND SCAN ORDER:
  -p <port ranges>: Only scan specified ports
    Ex: -p22; -p1-65535; -p U:53,111,137,T:21-25,80,139,8080,S:9
  -F: Fast mode - Scan fewer ports than the default scan
  -r: Scan ports consecutively - don't randomize
  --top-ports <number>: Scan <number> most common ports
  --port-ratio <ratio>: Scan ports more common than <ratio>
```

- **Example 3**: Scan hosts with different scan types. You have options to specify multiple flags to do different types of scan. This includes syn scan `-sS`, host discovery without a port scan `-sN`, Version scan `-sV`, TCP connect scan `-sT`, and OS detection `-O`:

```
ajaysinc@ajaysinclinux:~$ sudo nmap -O myapptestsec.azurewebsites.net

Starting Nmap 6.40 ( http://nmap.org ) at 2018-05-07 14:26 UTC
Nmap scan report for myapptestsec.azurewebsites.net (52.176.6.0)
Host is up (0.036s latency).
Not shown: 998 filtered ports
PORT    STATE SERVICE
80/tcp  open  http
443/tcp open  https
Warning: OSScan results may be unreliable because we could not find at least 1 o
pen and 1 closed port
OS fingerprint not ideal because: Missing a closed TCP port so results incomplet
e
No OS matches for host

OS detection performed. Please report any incorrect results at http://nmap.org/s
ubmit/ .
Nmap done: 1 IP address (1 host up) scanned in 23.82 seconds
```

Please refer to **help** options for more information:

```
SCAN TECHNIQUES:
  -sS/sT/sA/sW/sM: TCP SYN/Connect()/ACK/Window/Maimon scans
  -sU: UDP Scan
  -sN/sF/sX: TCP Null, FIN, and Xmas scans
  --scanflags <flags>: Customize TCP scan flags
  -sI <zombie host[:probeport]>: Idle scan
  -sY/sZ: SCTP INIT/COOKIE-ECHO scans
  -sO: IP protocol scan
  -b <FTP relay host>: FTP bounce scan
```

Operating system detection

OS detection is valuable information about a targeted host on what OS is currently installed and running. Let's discuss the logic behind discovery and how Nmap guesses the operating system.

Nmap decodes attributes and patterns of response of standard probes, and sends it to a remote host to determine the operating system. This process is named TCP/IP fingerprinting. In the following output, you can see a number of services running on targeted host IP `23.100.21.174`. Folllowing is my Linux box. For testing purposes, I installed Apache2 web server. In the following screenshot, we can see that the default page appears when the browser is launched:

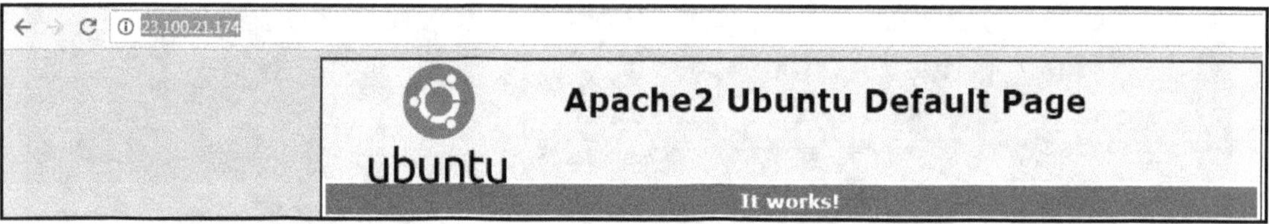

The best guess by Nmap (aggressive OS guess) is that there is an 86% chance that it is running on the Linux 3.5 or Linux 2.6.32 system, and this is true. If you find that this information is incorrect, the output can be uploaded to the Nmap portal. This will help Nmap developers to improve the next release:

```
ajaysinc@ajaysinclinux:~$ sudo nmap -O 23.100.21.174

Starting Nmap 6.40 ( http://nmap.org ) at 2018-05-07 14:51 UTC
Nmap scan report for 23.100.21.174
Host is up (0.0013s latency).
Not shown: 997 filtered ports
PORT     STATE  SERVICE
22/tcp   open   ssh
80/tcp   open   http
443/tcp closed https
Device type: general purpose
Running (JUST GUESSING): Linux 3.X|2.6.X (86%)
OS CPE: cpe:/o:linux:linux_kernel:3 cpe:/o:linux:linux_kernel:2.6
Aggressive OS guesses: Linux 3.5 (86%), Linux 2.6.32 (86%), Linux 2.6.35 (85%),
Linux 3.4 (85%), Linux 2.6.39 (85%)
No exact OS matches for host (test conditions non-ideal).

OS detection performed. Please report any incorrect results at http://nmap.org/s
ubmit/ .
Nmap done: 1 IP address (1 host up) scanned in 14.98 seconds
```

Using Nmap, let's try to dig more for a service version. This scans for a slightly longer time, completing in 26.4 seconds as opposed to the 14.98 seconds it takes for a normal scan to complete. The output shows you different versions for different services running on this host machine, along with their software version:

```
ajaysinc@ajaysinclinux:~$ sudo nmap -sV 23.100.21.174

Starting Nmap 6.40 ( http://nmap.org ) at 2018-05-07 14:58 UTC
Nmap scan report for 23.100.21.174
Host is up (0.0015s latency).
Not shown: 997 filtered ports
PORT    STATE  SERVICE VERSION
22/tcp  open   ssh     (protocol 2.0)
80/tcp  open   http    Apache httpd 2.4.18 ((Ubuntu))
443/tcp closed https
1 service unrecognized despite returning data. If you know the service/version,
please submit the following fingerprint at http://www.insecure.org/cgi-bin/servi
cefp-submit.cgi :
SF-Port22-TCP:V=6.40%I=7%D=5/7%Time=5AF069A2%P=x86_64-pc-linux-gnu%r(NULL,
SF:29,"SSH-2\.0-OpenSSH_7\.2p2\x20Ubuntu-4ubuntu2\.4\r\n");

Service detection performed. Please report any incorrect results at http://nmap.
org/submit/ .
Nmap done: 1 IP address (1 host up) scanned in 26.44 seconds
ajaysinc@ajaysinclinux:~$
```

TCP/IP fingerprinting requires collecting detailed information about the target's IP stack. Here is the link for Nmap current database signatures `https://svn.nmap.org/nmap/nmap-os-db`.

In the current Nmap database (6.47), there are 4485 fingerprints for 5009 CPE (platform) names, over 800 of which match various versions of MS-Windows, and over 1000 of which match various Linux systems (including appliances).

TCP/IP fingerprinting methods supported by Nmap

In the past, the banner grabbing method was used to detect remote operating systems. Telnet Connect used to be sent to a targeted system and the system would display a banner of the operating system running on a host. This was not a very accurate method as the system admin could also disable a banner or change the actual banner in order to misguide attackers.

The new method of remote OS detection is to analyze the packet between the source and destination. This detection technique detects OS platforms and OS versions as well.

TCP/UDP/IP basic

To use an analogy, if IPs are a building address, service ports are flat numbers. Both TCP and UDP uses incoming and outgoing ports for data communication. Most IP-based services use standard ports (HTTP `TCP:80`, SMTP `TCP:25`, and DNS `TCP-UDP:53`).

TCP stack has six flag message types to complete a three-way handshake:

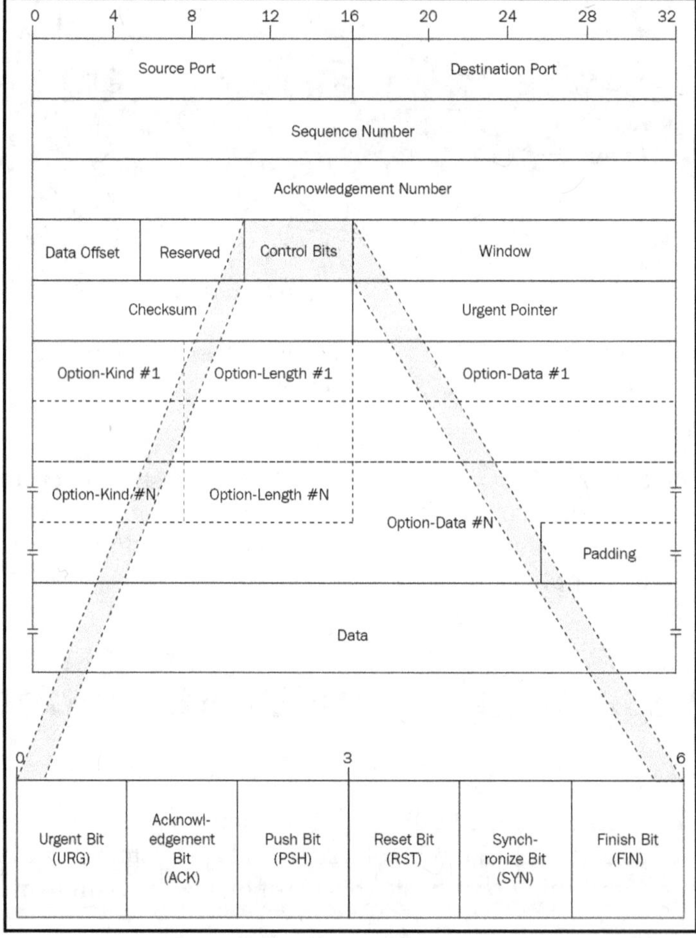

Here is a packet capture for one of the websites I opened on the web browser. This shows a three-way handshake with SYN-SYN-ACK. By default, Wireshark will keep track of all TCP sessions and convert all sequence numbers (SEQ numbers) and acknowledge numbers (ACK numbers) into relative numbers. This means that instead of displaying the real/absolute SEQ and ACK numbers in the display, Wireshark will display a SEQ and ACK number relative to the segment first seen in that conversation:

```
2420 28.310976   192.168.0.102   192.185.85.31   TCP   66 63045 → 80 [SYN] Seq=0 Win=65535 Len=0 MSS=1460 WS=8 SACK_PERM=1
2421 28.565106   192.185.85.31   192.168.0.102   TCP   66 80 → 63046 [SYN, ACK] Seq=0 Ack=1 Win=29200 Len=0 MSS=1452 SACK_PERM=1 WS=128
2422 28.565199   192.168.0.102   192.185.85.31   TCP   54 63046 → 80 [ACK] Seq=1 Ack=1 Win=262144 Len=0
```

If you are interested in knowing the exact, real number of the TCP sequence, then you have to tune Wireshark settings via the unchecked box relative to the sequence number:

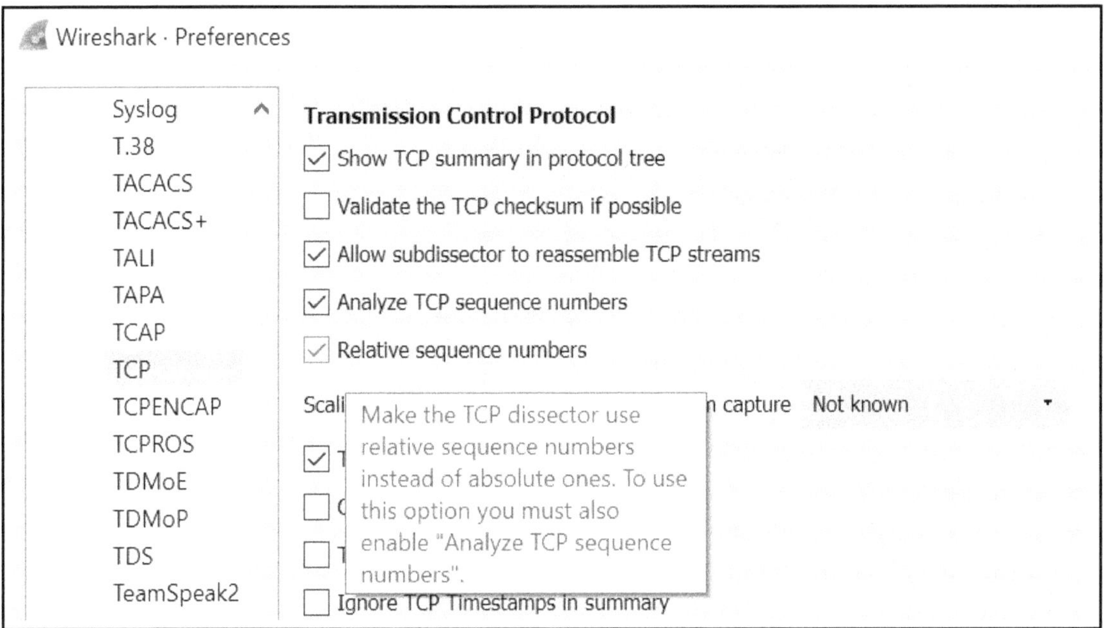

In Wireshark, I have extended the first connection to show that the SYN flag is set to `1`. Similarly, you can also extend the rest of the connection:

```
v Transmission Control Protocol, Src Port: 63045, Dst Port: 80, Seq: 0, Len: 0
    Source Port: 63045
    Destination Port: 80
    [Stream index: 133]
    [TCP Segment Len: 0]
    Sequence number: 0    (relative sequence number)
    Acknowledgment number: 0
    1000 .... = Header Length: 32 bytes (8)
  v Flags: 0x002 (SYN)
      000. .... .... = Reserved: Not set
      ...0 .... .... = Nonce: Not set
      .... 0... .... = Congestion Window Reduced (CWR): Not set
      .... .0.. .... = ECN-Echo: Not set
      .... ..0. .... = Urgent: Not set
      .... ...0 .... = Acknowledgment: Not set
      .... .... 0... = Push: Not set
      .... .... .0.. = Reset: Not set
    > .... .... ..1. = Syn: Set
      .... .... ...0 = Fin: Not set
```

- **SYN and SYN-ACK**: Any TCP communication will start with a SYN (synchronization) packet by setting the flag to `1`. A server responds with SYN-ACK, which means that a service port is listening and in an open state.
- **ACK**: After receiving SYN-ACK from a server, a client sends the final ACK to complete the three-way handshake by setting the ACK flag to `1`.
- **RST**: The reset flag means that the server is not accepting the connection on the service port where the connection was made, or it is rejecting the request.
- **FIN**: The finish flag is set to `1` when either party wants to finish the connection and this can be achieved by closing the browser.

The following techniques are used to determine the OS on the system.

The FIN probe

A FIN packet is used to close the TCP connection between client and server. Closing the connection is more complex than creating a connection because both sides have to release its resources. In the following diagram, you can see that a FIN packet works with the last ACK:

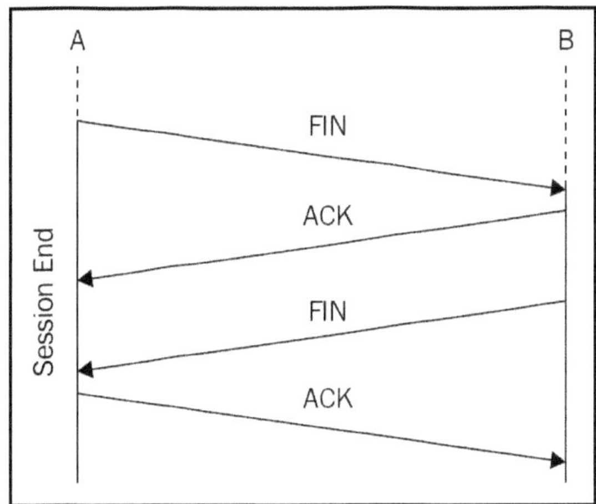

Tools like Nmap can generate a FIN packet without having the ACK set to `1`. An operating system might respond to this with RST, which gives you a clue about the remote operating system.

When designing their TCP/IP implementations, vendors have had different interpretations of RFC 793, Transmission Control Protocol. When a TCP segment arrives with the FIN flag set, but not the ACK flag, some implementations send RST segments, whereas others drop the packet without sending an RST.

Let's test a live environment with the packet capture. I tested FIN on my wireless router, and here are the results when I followed the TCP stream on Wireshark:

```
C:\Program Files (x86)\Nmap>nmap -sF 192.168.0.1

Starting Nmap 7.60 ( https://nmap.org ) at 2018-03-03 19:59 India Standard Time
Nmap scan report for dlink.router (192.168.0.1)
Host is up (0.014s latency).
Not shown: 996 closed ports
PORT    STATE         SERVICE
21/tcp open|filtered ftp
22/tcp open|filtered ssh
23/tcp open|filtered telnet
80/tcp open|filtered http
MAC Address: 78:32:1B:37:F2:EA (D-Link International)

Nmap done: 1 IP address (1 host up) scanned in 4.01 seconds

C:\Program Files (x86)\Nmap>
```

Let's test the result on Wireshark for port `80`, which I know is open on this box. You can see that only FIN was sent and no response was received from the router:

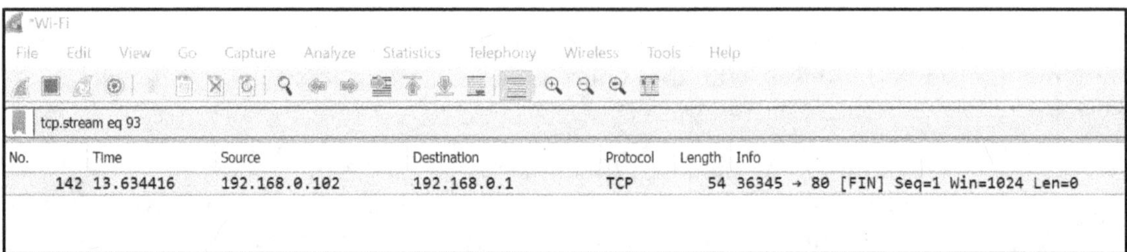

The FIN sent on port `443` gets a RST back because this port is not open on this router:

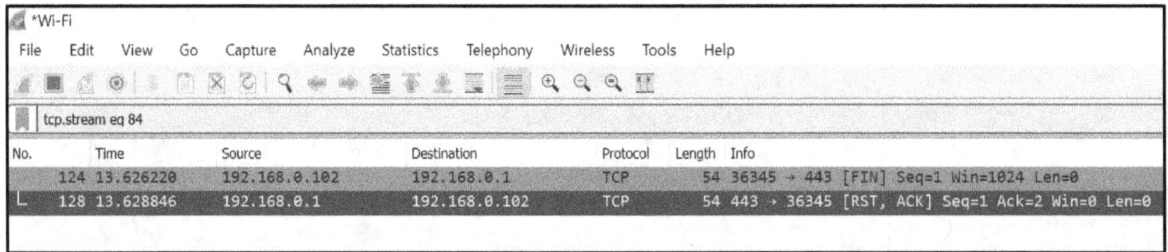

FIN scans only work on Linux machines, and do not work on the latest version of Windows. CISCO, HP/UX, MVS, and IRIX send an RST packet in return.

TCP ISN sampling

In a TCP stack sequence and acknowledgement, fields are 32 bit [4 Byte]. There are *2^32= 4,294,967,296* possibilities of generating a random number:

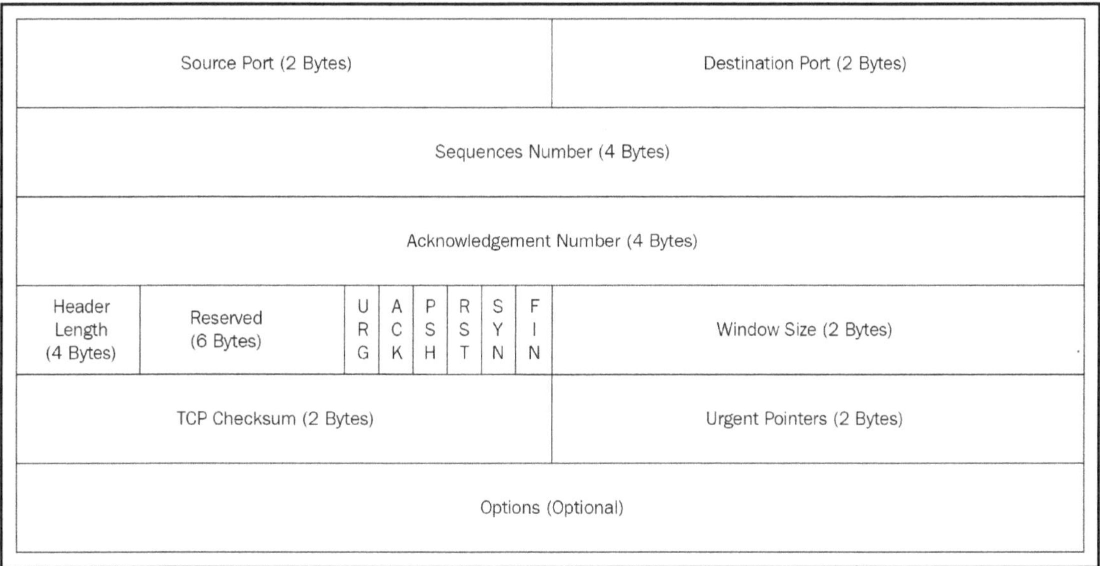

Between a client and a server, when a client initiates a connection it generates an **initial sequence number** (**ISN**). Every OS uses its own algorithm to generate an ISN, and this is pretty much predictable.

Windows NT 4.0 generates predictable random TCP ISN, which allows remote attackers to perform spoofing and session hijacking.

Random ISNs are good because they make it far harder to predict sequence numbers. In Windows 2003 onward, the ISN algorithm has been modified so that ISNs increase in random increments using an RC4-based random number generator initialized with a 2048-bit random key upon system startup.

RFC 6528 states that Initial Sequence Number Generation Algorithm TCP should generate its ISN using the following expression:

ISN = M + F(localip, localport, remoteip, remoteport, secretkey)

Here, *M* is the four microsecond timer, and *F()* is a **pseudo-random function** (**PRF**) of the connection-id. To summarize, ISN values are completely based on TCP/IP stack implementations and algorithms used by different operating systems, but there is always a common pattern that can help to predict operating systems.

TCP initial window

This is to check the window size on returned packets, and this value seems to be pretty constant for different types of OS.

Type of service

This field is usually set to zero for all OSs. Linux has the precedence bits of the ToS field set to 0xC0. ICMP error messages are always sent with the default ToS value of 0x0000. The ICMP echo reply message should have the same ToS value as the ICMP request message.

Time-to-live (TTL)

Based on network traffic between hosts, it is possible to predict what OS is running on a system. Every operating system has its own unique way to implement TCP/IP stack. A very simple but effective passive method is to inspect the initial **time-to-live** (**TTL**) in the IP header:

OS/Device	Version	Protocol	TTL
Cisco Nexus		ICMP	255
juniper		ICMP	64
Linux	4.4.0	ICMP	64
Windows	98	ICMP	32
Windows	98, 98 SE	ICMP	128
Windows	10 Family	ICMP	128

I am on a Windows 10 machine and tried the ICMP ping to host `4.2.2.2`. In the Wireshark capture attached below, you can see that the Windows 10 initial TTL value is `128`:

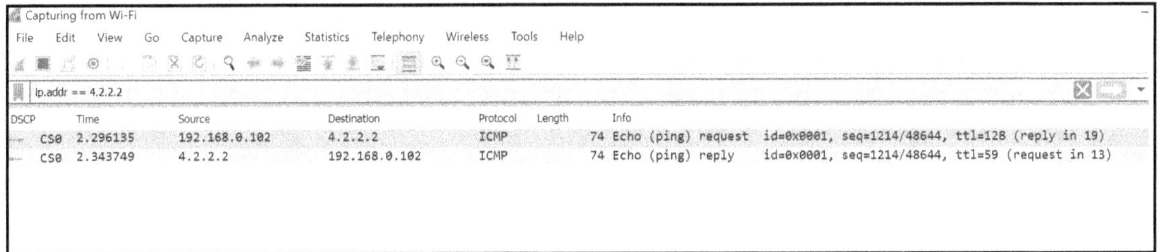

I expended the first packet from Wireshark, which confirms TTL `128`:

```
Wireshark · Packet 13 · wireshark_30E6EA4A-5FAA-4555-9766-47319BE3B41E_20180304100828_a23180

> Frame 13: 74 bytes on wire (592 bits), 74 bytes captured (592 bits) on interface 0
> Ethernet II, Src: IntelCor_08:56:6f (f8:59:71:08:56:6f), Dst: D-LinkIn_37:f2:ea (78:32:1b:37:f2:ea)
v Internet Protocol Version 4, Src: 192.168.0.102, Dst: 4.2.2.2
    0100 .... = Version: 4
    .... 0101 = Header Length: 20 bytes (5)
  > Differentiated Services Field: 0x00 (DSCP: CS0, ECN: Not-ECT)
    Total Length: 60
    Identification: 0x5fc3 (24515)
  > Flags: 0x00
    Fragment offset: 0
    Time to live: 128
```

Let's try to expend the return packet, allowing us to see that the TTL value is `59`:

```
Wireshark · Packet 19 · wireshark_30E6EA4A-5FAA-4555-9766-47319BE3B41E_20180304100828_a23180

> Frame 19: 74 bytes on wire (592 bits), 74 bytes captured (592 bits) on interface 0
> Ethernet II, Src: D-LinkIn_37:f2:ea (78:32:1b:37:f2:ea), Dst: IntelCor_08:56:6f (f8:59:71:08:56:6f)
v Internet Protocol Version 4, Src: 4.2.2.2, Dst: 192.168.0.102
    0100 .... = Version: 4
    .... 0101 = Header Length: 20 bytes (5)
  > Differentiated Services Field: 0x00 (DSCP: CS0, ECN: Not-ECT)
    Total Length: 60
    Identification: 0x95e3 (38371)
  > Flags: 0x00
    Fragment offset: 0
    Time to live: 59
```

You can now take match results with Nmap remote OS detection. There is a 90% chance that this system will be running a Linux operating system. This should match our reference table. The linux TTL value 64 and value 59 means that this host is five hops away from me.

Don't Fragment (DF) bit

Some OSs set this bit, whereas others don't.

There are many more tools and scanning techniques that can be used to detect remote OS. Please read `https://nmap.org/book/osdetect-methods.html` for more information.

Understanding an Nmap fingerprint

OS fingerprinting is a technique used to determine the type and version of the operating system running on a remote host. The `nmap-os-db` data file contains thousands of signatures. However, different remote operating systems respond to Nmap's specialized OS detection probes. A fingerprint contains an operating system's name, its general classification, and response data pattern.

A typical fingerprint format appears as shown in the following figure. During detection probe, attributes and results are compared against the Nmap `os-db` OS database. A simple command can be used for OS detection with the flag `-O`:

```
#sudo nmap --O <ip or ip subnet>
```

The following screenshot is specific to the Cisco 2820 device and shows that a number of tests will be performed before Nmap declares that device as Cisco 2820. This Nmap database will have similar fingerprints for most known devices, and this keeps growing:

```
# Cisco 2820 Switch w/ OS v5.37
Fingerprint Cisco Catalyst 2820 switch (CatOS 5.37)
Class Cisco | CatOS | 6.X | switch
CPE cpe:/h:cisco:catalyst_2820
CPE cpe:/o:cisco:catos:5.37
SEQ(SP=42-6A%GCD=1-6%ISR=46-5E%TI=I%II=I%SS=S%TS=U)
OPS(O1=M5B4%O2=M5B4%O3=M5B4%O4=M5B4%O5=M5B4%O6=M5B4)
WIN(W1=400%W2=400%W3=400%W4=400%W5=400%W6=400)
ECN(R=Y%DF=N%T=FA-104%TG=FF%W=400%O=M5B4%CC=N%Q=)
T1(R=Y%DF=N%T=FA-104%TG=FF%S=O%A=S+%F=AS%RD=0%Q=)
T2(R=Y%DF=N%T=FA-104%TG=FF%W=0%S=Z%A=S%F=AR%O=%RD=0%Q=U)
T3(R=Y%DF=N%T=FA-104%TG=FF%W=400%S=O%A=S+%F=AS%O=M5B4%RD=0%Q=)
T4(R=Y%DF=N%T=FA-104%TG=FF%W=0%S=A%A=Z%F=R%O=%RD=0%Q=U)
T5(R=Y%DF=N%T=FA-104%TG=FF%W=0%S=Z%A=S+%F=AR%O=%RD=0%Q=U)
T6(R=Y%DF=N%T=FA-104%TG=FF%W=0%S=A%A=Z%F=R%O=%RD=0%Q=U)
T7(R=Y%DF=N%T=FA-104%TG=FF%W=0%S=Z%A=S+%F=AR%O=%RD=0%Q=U)
U1(DF=N%T=FA-104%TG=FF%IPL=38%UN=0%RIPL=G%RID=G%RIPCK=G%RUCK=G%RUD=G)
IE(DFI=N%T=FA-104%TG=FF%CD=S)
```

We can see the following terms in the above snapshot:

- **SEQ test**: SEQ test returns information regarding sequence analysis
- **OPS test**: OPS test returns information regarding TCP options received for each of the 6 [01-06] probes
- **WIN test**: WIN test returns the TCP initial windows size information for each of the 6 [W1 -W6] probes
- **ECN test**: ECN test returns explicit congestion notification response
- **T1 to T7 test**: These are TCP probes:
    - T1 is a SYN packet with a bunch of TCP options for opening the port
    - T2 is a NULL packet with options to open the port
    - T3 is a SYN/FIN/URG/PSH packet with options to open the port
    - T4 is an ACK with options to open the port
    - T5 is a SYN with options to close the port
    - T6 is an ACK with options to close the port
    - T7 is a FIN/PSH/URG with options to close the port
- **PU test**: PU test is a UDP packet used to close a port

OS matching algorithms

Nmap's algorithm for detecting matches is a simple process which collects target fingerprints and tests it against every single reference fingerprint in `nmap-os-db`. After testing all the probes against a fingerprint, Nmap divides NumMatchPoints by possible points. The result of this is a confidence factor describing the probability that the subject fingerprint matches that particular reference fingerprint.

Defense against port scans

So far, we have learned how to use port scanning techniques to discover and detect information about remote hosts. Let's try to understand that any services/hosts will be vulnerable to port scans, which are exposed to users through some sort of connectivity. This might include an enterprise WAN or the internet. Port scanning is also not classed as illegal activity unless information is used to exploit systems.

The amount of information that should be exposed to the outside world is down to the system administrator. Any IP scanning starts with an ICMP, and you can block all incoming ICMPs on an enterprise edge device. This will make Ping ineffective and will filter ICMP unreachable messages to block Traceroute as part of the first line of defense. But does this solve all of the problem? No, port scan works on TCP/UDP ports as well.

Another way to limit information is to disable all unnecessary services on a system. Of course, you cannot block all services. For example, if you are running HTTPS services on a host, then only port `443` [HTTPS] should be exposed to the internet. One more simple method is to restrict services by source IP address. Scans from other IP addresses will then not detect them.

A final clever solution would be to configure policies on firewall/IPS/IDS for threat signature detection. Just like other applications, Nmap itself has its own signature.

Summary

In this chapter, we discussed the basics of TCP/IP and how its different attributes can be used for port scanning techniques as well as for remote OS detection. We also discussed how to operate an Nmap tool on different operating systems and how to carry out packet capture analysis using Wireshark. Good hackers know how to crack a system, but a great network administrator knows how to fend off those attacks.

> *"The best defense is a good offense"*

In the next chapter, we will discuss the fundamentals of SSL, why this is important for web-based applications, and what security considerations are required before we secure applications.

Questions

1. Port scan is a part of:
    1. Traceroute
    2. Nmap
    3. Route
    4. Ipconfig/all
2. What is the pattern of a TCP connection?
    1. SYN-ACK
    2. SYN-ACK-FIN
    3. SYN-RST-ACK
    4. SYN-SYN-ACK
3. What is the most important activity in system hacking?
    1. Information Gathering
    2. Brute force attack for cracking a password
    3. DDoS attack
    4. Vulnerability exploit

Further reading

- `https://nmap.org`

9
Public Key Infrastructure – SSL

In the previous chapter, we learned about network mapping tools and port scanning techniques used to detect the remote OS.

In today's digital era, more and more internet users are growing web businesses. Small to large businesses are coming up with higher numbers of marketing tools such as ads, web services, emails, social media, digital content, online banking, online cell phone apps and, of course, online shopping. However, no one wants to store or send information on the internet until information security is guaranteed.

Secure Socket Layer (**SSL**) provides transport layer security for web-based applications and also provides end users or customers with a secure browsing experience. In this chapter we are going to discuss what SSL is, how it works and who needs it. We will also discuss the evolution of SSL, focusing on what you need to know in order to implement it. This will include looking at current threats and verification methods.

We will be covering the following topics:

- Foundation of SSL
- TLS versus SSL
- **Public Key Infrastructure** (**PKI**)
- Attacks against PKI
- Microsoft Windows and IIS
- OpenSSL
- SSL Management tools

Foundation of SSL

In this section, we will learn the basics of SSL from the point of view of the end user, focusing on what users should know about SSL for the purpose of safe browsing. Having an SSL certificate stamp on your website is very important for security. In order to protect data from attackers, SSL technology is used to create an encrypted connection between an end user (typically a web browser) and the web server. SSL allows sensitive information such as credit card numbers, social security numbers, and login credentials to be transmitted securely in an encrypted format. Even if an attacker is able to intercept all of the data sent between a client and a web server, they still cannot read and use the information in encrypted data.

To understand where SSL fits into a TCP/IP or OSI model, let's take a look at the following diagram. For secure applications such as HTTPs, SSL/TLS comes in between the application and the Layer 4 transport layer:

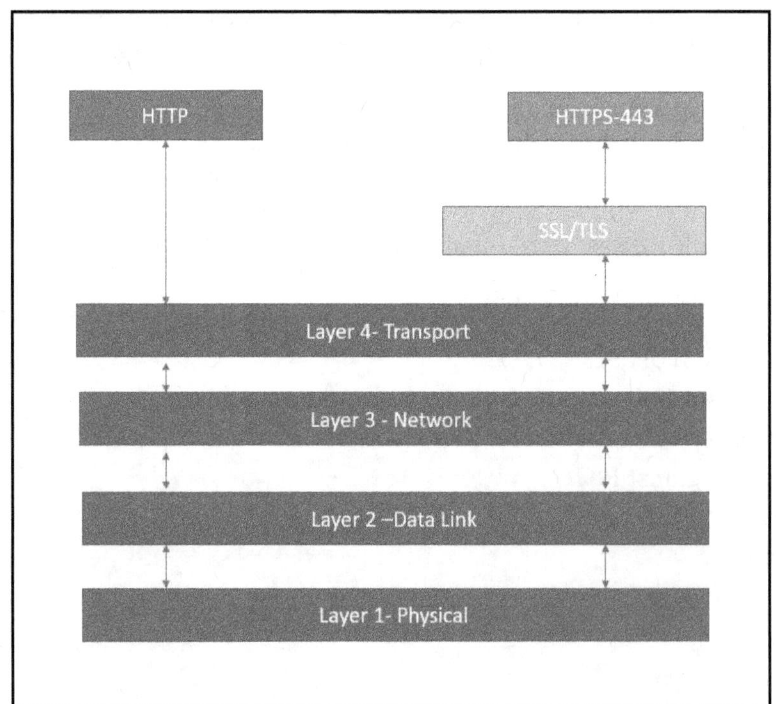

How do I know that SSL is working?

Before exchanging any information, it is very important for users to know that the area of a website they are on is safe and secure. Different browsers have different ways of showing SSL status but you can usually find it by checking the address bar at the top of the browser. Let's take a look at a few browsers:

Microsoft Edge:

Microsoft IE:

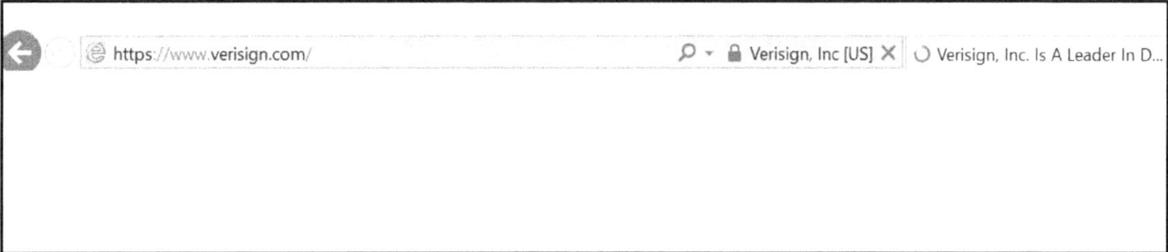

Google Chrome:

We can clearly observe that each is similar in the sense that they all have a green accent color, a padlock symbol and the information is displayed in the status bar, which tells you that this is a secure site.

Why no PadLock?

Browsers are smart enough nowadays. Let's take a look at the alarming error message I was getting when accessing a banking website. In this situation, you should not share your information:

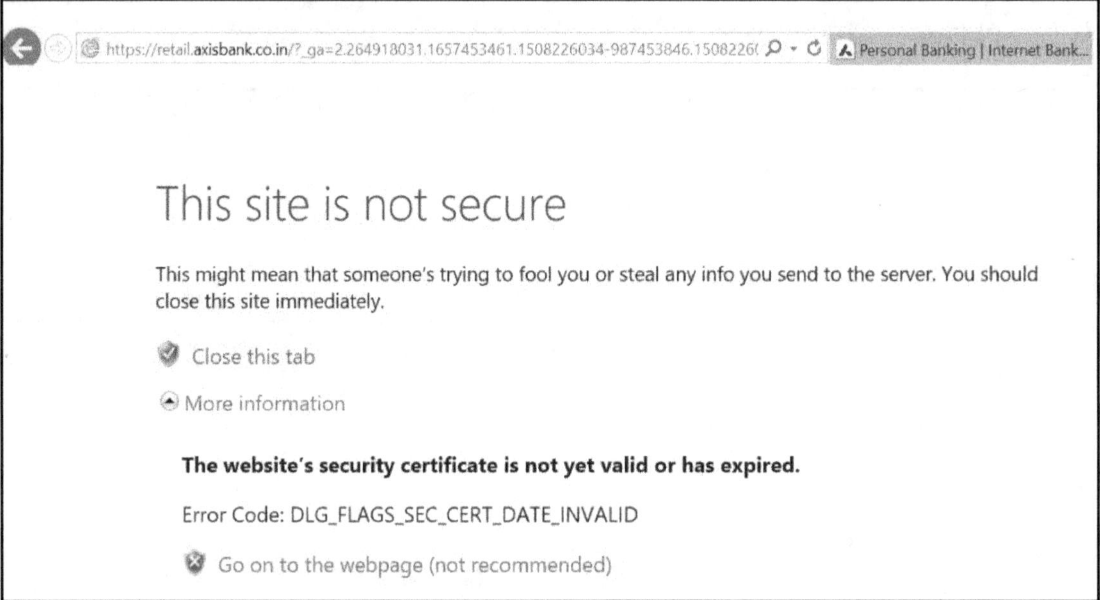

Here, you can clearly see that there is no green color and no padlock sign on the status bar. The browser also indicates a reason why this site is not secure.

SSL certificate

An SSL certificate is a digital public document that binds a cryptographic key to the details of an owner or organization such as through domain name, host name or location. This verifies that a legitimate company owns the website which is being accessed.

An SSL certificate has three specific functions:

- Authentication
- Verification
- Data Encryption

In other words, the SSL certificate will have information about who has issued the certificate and to whom it is issued. This is not limited to web servers, it can also be used for end user machines, mobile phones and many more applications. Every SSL certificate will have an expiry date attached to it, which is similar to how an exam certificate cannot be used after its expiry date. Consequently, to extend the validity of the certificate, it must be renewed. An SSL certificate will also have a public key and digital signatures. As the name suggests, a public key is incorporated into the SSL certificate shared with web browsers and a digital certificate is a process that guarantees that the contents of a message have not been altered in transit.

The evolution of SSL and TLS

Transport Layer Security (**TLS**) protocol is the most widely used protocol on the internet today. SSL was originally developed by Netscape in 1993. Let's take a look at the history of the SSL protocol:

- **SSL 1.0**: This was the first specification by Netscape in early 1994, which was never released for public use. This is because it was heavily criticized by the cryptographic community for the implementation of weak cryptographic algorithms.
- **SSL 2.0**: In early 1995, Netscape released SSL 2.0, an improved version of the original. However, this also did not succeed. In this version, message authentication used MD5, which most security-aware users had already moved away from. Handshake messages are not protected. This permits a MITM attack to trick the client into picking a weaker cipher suite than it would normally choose.

- **SSL 3.0**: SSL version 3 was released by Netscape in 1996 to enhance SSL version 2 and to support more algorithms. Many SSL version 2 platforms were already deployed at the time so there was no clean way to cut over to SSL version 3. This forced SSL version 3 to allow the backward compatibility to SSL version 2. Therefore, unless you definitely know which SSL versions the server supports, your SSL application should run in both SSL version 2 and SSL version 3 mode. This enables a client to communicate with both SSL version 2 and SSL version 3 servers. This also allows the server to have connections with SSL version 2 and SSL version 3 clients. However, if either the client or the server supports only SSL version 2, only that version will be used.

SSL 3.0 was vulnerable to the POODLE attack, marking the end to the SSL 3.0 era. This was discovered by the Google security team and disclosed to the public on October 14, 2014.

- **TLS 1.0**: The TLS protocol itself is based on the SSL 3.0 specification as published by Netscape in January 1999. The differences between this protocol and SSL 3.0 are not dramatic, but they are significant enough that TLS 1.0 and SSL 3.0 do not inter-operate.
- **TLS 1.1, TLS 1.2 and TLS 1.3**: RFC 4346 was released in April 2006 and TLS 1.1 is an update to TLS 1.0. The changes that were brought about included replacing the implicit **initialization vector** (**IV**) with an explicit IV to protect against **Cipher block chaining** (**CBC**) attacks. In August 2008, TLS 1.2 was based on TLS 1.1.

  As of January 2018, TLS 1.3 is the latest protocol, though it is a working draft. Let's take a look on a browser (Internet Explorer) for current supported version of SSL and TLS.

Current Supported Standard

For Microsoft Internet Explorer, follow these steps: **Tools** | **Internet Options** | **Advance**. In the following screenshot, we can see that TLS 1.o to TLS 1.2 options are checked while SSL 3.0 is disabled or unchecked:

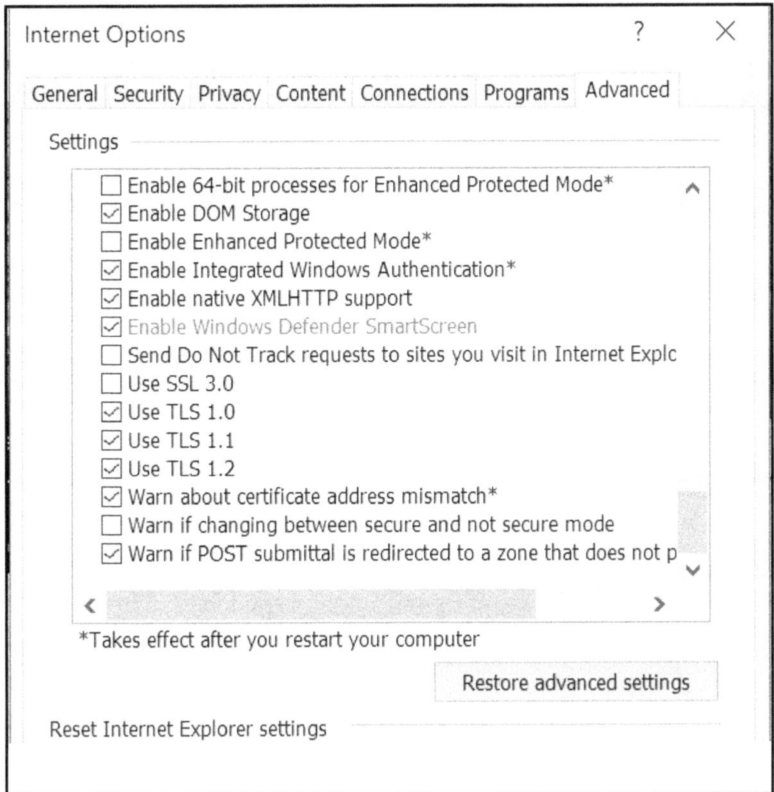

Why hasn't TLS 1.3 been implemented yet?

Such security upgrades are complex in nature. In a multi-vendor internet environment, you need to update both client and servers to support a new security standard. So far, no major browsers have TLS 1.3 enabled by default. It cannot be assumed that by a specific date, every server and end user device will support all new security standards. Furthermore, TLS 1.3 is not an extension but a major change with complete revamping. The way TLS or SSL version negotiation works is that an end user device sends the latest version of a supported protocol to a server, which responds with the latest version and chooses something which is supported by both of them.

Time to say goodbye to SSL and early TLS

According to **PCI Data Security Standard** (**PCI DSS**) for safeguarding payment data, 30 June 2018 is the deadline for disabling SSL/early TLS and implementing a more secure encryption protocol of TLS 1.1 or higher. There are many vulnerabilities in SSL and early TLS that, left unaddressed, put organizations at risk of being breached. The widespread POODLE and BEAST exploits are just a couple of examples of how attackers have taken advantage of weaknesses in SSL and early TLS to compromise organizations.

Visit the following website for more information:

`https://blog.pcisecuritystandards.org/are-you-ready-for-30-june-2018-sayin-goodbye-to-ssl-early-tls`

SSL certificate component

Let's first discuss client side SSL, and then we will focus on server side. Your browser comes pre-installed with trusted CAs. Every time we visit a website, your browser verifies a trust chain and, during handshake, ends with one of the locally trusted root certificates.

Root certificate

Let's take a look at Microsoft IE pre-installed CAs. You can check this in the browsing directory through **Tools** | **Internet Options** | **Content** | **Certificates** | **Trusted Root Certification Authorities**:

Root certificates do have an expiry date, but they tend to have exceptionally long validity times (often between 10-20 years). As part of a browser or operating system update patch, you will get fresh root certificates before the old ones expire. Lacking a CAs root certificate, no browser would know whether to accept an SSL certificate issued by that CA. These SSL certificates are known as *single root* certificates.

Intermediate certificate

From a security point of view, the private key of the root certificate is critical and should be kept in the certificate provider's secure data center. Furthermore, the public key of the root certificate is given to browsers such as Microsoft and Google to be added to their list of trusted roots. Any compromise of the root certificate's key would deem the complete certificate chain built by the certificate provider as untrustworthy.

An intermediate certificate authority is an entity that is authorized to sign certificates. Logically, the root CA must sign all certificates. For security reasons, the intermediate CA signs certificates on behalf of the root CA, but intermediate certificates are signed by the root CA.

Let's browse a few sites and look at an intermediate certificate. In this example, I have opened `www.google.com` in IE. I have mentioned that **GeoTrust Global CA [Root]** reflects root signing authority, **Google Internet Authority G2 [Intermediate]** reflects Intermediate Certificate and, finally, ***.google.com [End Host]** is the End host identity:

Let's take another example. This time we have `www.flipkart.com`. Here, there are two intermediate certificates and, by logic, there can be multiple since these are a subset of a main certificate. The confusing aspect comes in when you try to relate different classes and groups associated with a certificate:

These classes are vendors defined but pretty much consistent across all top level certificate authorities. Let's take a look at the different possible classes of certificates that CAs will offer to their clients and what these classes mean to the client.

SSL certificates classes

CA uses the concept of classes for different types of digital certificates, but these classes are not specified in any SSL/TLS RFC. Let's try to understand what different classes mean to SSL end users.

- **Class 1**: Class 1 certificates are delivered without any prior verification. This is also known as a **Domain Validation** (**DV**) certificate and relies on the `WHOIS` information database (you must prove you own the domain). A DV certificate is a low authentication product which does not guarantee the identity of the website's owner nor the actual existence of the organization. This simply refers to two entities talking over an encrypted channel without knowing each other.

Note: This can be heavily misused by attackers by launching phishing sites. Users assume that the website has a valid certificate issued by a major certificate authority.

Never use low—authentication certificates for web based applications.

- **Class 2**: For Class 2 certificates, (Medium Security Level) a background check is required which includes looking at the organization, business, or person who owns the domain, and confirming its existence. These are typically called the organization validated certs.
- **Class 3**: These are client certificates (Extended validation High Security) that are delivered after an audit. They check details of the organization, including verifying the physical address using multiple sources of truth and the certificate's owner.
- **Class 4**: Class 4 certificates are intended for online business transactions between companies.
- **Class 5**: Class 5 certificates are intended for private organizations or governmental security.

TLS versus SSL

Both TLS and SSL are security frameworks that provide data encryption and authentication for web based applications to ensure data protection. An SSL and TLS handshake is a mechanism for web based applications which takes place just after the TCP handshake occurs between a client and a server. The handshake doesn't encrypt anything on its own, but actually negotiates for a shared secret and encryption type which both sides agree on.

In the diagram below, we can see that just after the TCP and SSL handshake starts, a secure client sends a 'hello' message to the server with a supported set of ciphers. The server responds with a top support cipher and also shares its certificate with the public key:

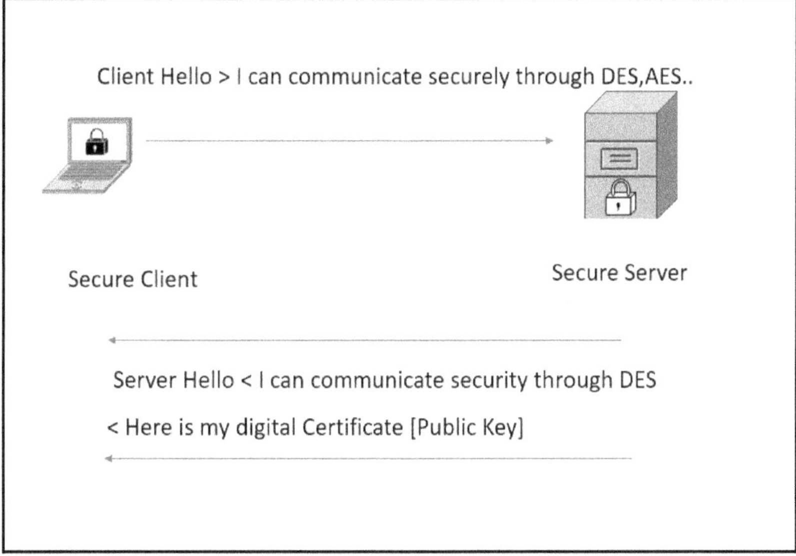

Let's take a look at Wireshark to validate. A client sends all available cipher suits to a server marked in the black box:

```
Wireshark · Packet 844 · wireshark_30E6EA4A-5FAA-4555-9766-47319BE3B41E_20180318193137_a08488

> Internet Protocol Version 4, Src: 192.168.0.102, Dst: 151.101.1.136
> Transmission Control Protocol, Src Port: 1997, Dst Port: 443, Seq: 2786289989, Ack: 684383354, Len: 517
v Secure Sockets Layer
  v TLSv1.2 Record Layer: Handshake Protocol: Client Hello
      Content Type: Handshake (22)
      Version: TLS 1.0 (0x0301)
      Length: 512
    v Handshake Protocol: Client Hello
        Handshake Type: Client Hello (1)
        Length: 508
        Version: TLS 1.2 (0x0303)
      > Random: 33e56fd8569393ea6e46c8427fb1279140c9b62833277cb3...
        Session ID Length: 32
        Session ID: 0a1b17038f6430d06c3beea01490b5c3c608fe699d78b5f1...
        Cipher Suites Length: 34
      v Cipher Suites (17 suites)
          Cipher Suite: Reserved (GREASE) (0x3a3a)
          Cipher Suite: TLS_AES_128_GCM_SHA256 (0x1301)
          Cipher Suite: TLS_AES_256_GCM_SHA384 (0x1302)
          Cipher Suite: TLS_CHACHA20_POLY1305_SHA256 (0x1303)
          Cipher Suite: TLS_ECDHE_ECDSA_WITH_AES_128_GCM_SHA256 (0xc02b)
          Cipher Suite: TLS_ECDHE_RSA_WITH_AES_128_GCM_SHA256 (0xc02f)
          Cipher Suite: TLS_ECDHE_ECDSA_WITH_AES_256_GCM_SHA384 (0xc02c)
          Cipher Suite: TLS_ECDHE_RSA_WITH_AES_256_GCM_SHA384 (0xc030)
```

In server hello, the sever sends the top cipher it can use for security, shown in the black box:

```
Wireshark · Packet 888 · wireshark_30E6EA4A-5FAA-4555-9766-47319BE3B41E_20180318193137_a08488

> Frame 888: 1494 bytes on wire (11952 bits), 1494 bytes captured (11952 bits) on interface 0
> Ethernet II, Src: D-LinkIn_37:f2:ea (78:32:1b:37:f2:ea), Dst: IntelCor_08:56:6f (f8:59:71:08:56:6f)
> Internet Protocol Version 4, Src: 151.101.1.136, Dst: 192.168.0.102
> Transmission Control Protocol, Src Port: 443, Dst Port: 1996, Seq: 660387694, Ack: 3671505136, Len: 1440
v Secure Sockets Layer
  v TLSv1.2 Record Layer: Handshake Protocol: Server Hello
      Content Type: Handshake (22)
      Version: TLS 1.2 (0x0303)
      Length: 88
    v Handshake Protocol: Server Hello
        Handshake Type: Server Hello (2)
        Length: 84
        Version: TLS 1.2 (0x0303)
      > Random: 5f380dae145743879c960b8a5e76d8469c6dc7daa9470443...
        Session ID Length: 0
        Cipher Suite: TLS_ECDHE_RSA_WITH_AES_128_GCM_SHA256 (0xc02f)
        Compression Method: null (0)
```

Public Key Infrastructure

PKI refers to processes and technologies which provide a secure data exchange between two nodes over unsecured infrastructure. It uses private and public key pairs to achieve the underlying security service.

There are three types of cryptography algorithms:

- Symmetric
- Asymmetric
- Hash function.

Symmetric encryption

In symmetric encryption, a single key is used both to encrypt and decrypt traffic. Symmetric encryptions are fast, simple and easy to implement. However, some easy ciphers are vulnerable to brute-force attacks, making management a complex job. If the key is compromised, then the whole system becomes vulnerable. **Data encryption standard** (**DES**) and **Advance encryption standard** (**AES**) are symmetric systems, but AES is much more reliable than DES.

The symmetric encryption scheme has five elements:

- **Plain-text**: Refers to the original data that needs to be encrypted
- **Encryption Algorithm**: Refers to a combination of ciphers used to encrypt data
- **Secure Key**: Refers to input in the encryption algorithm
- **Cipher-text**: Refers to output and format, which is dependent upon plain-text and key input

- **Decryption Algorithm**: This works in reverse of encryption - the cipher test becomes input data and the output becomes plain-text original input:

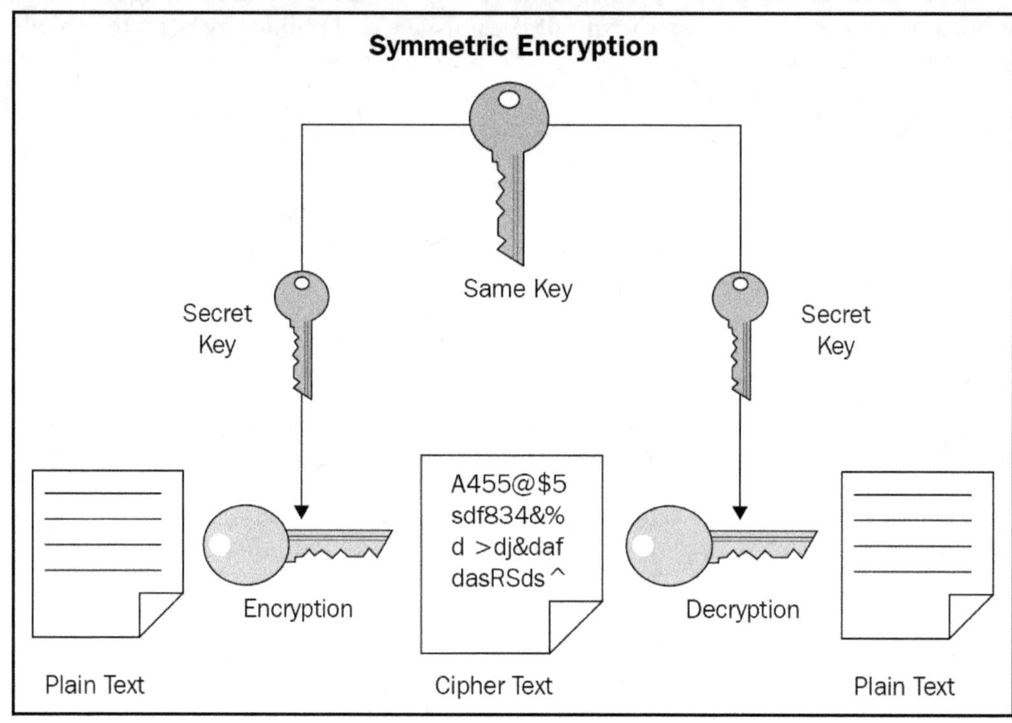

Asymmetric encryption

Asymmetrical encryption is also known as public key cryptography, which is a relatively secure method compared to symmetric encryption. In this method, two keys are used. One key is used for encryption and the other key is used for decryption. The public key is what its name suggests— public. It is made available to a browser when accessing the web server during the SSL handshake process. On the other hand, the private key must remain confidential and secure to its respective owner. Let's assume that the client generates the secret, encrypts it using the server's RSA public key and sends it to the server, which decrypts it using its private key. It is very important to protect the private key, because if the key is lost, then the system becomes void:

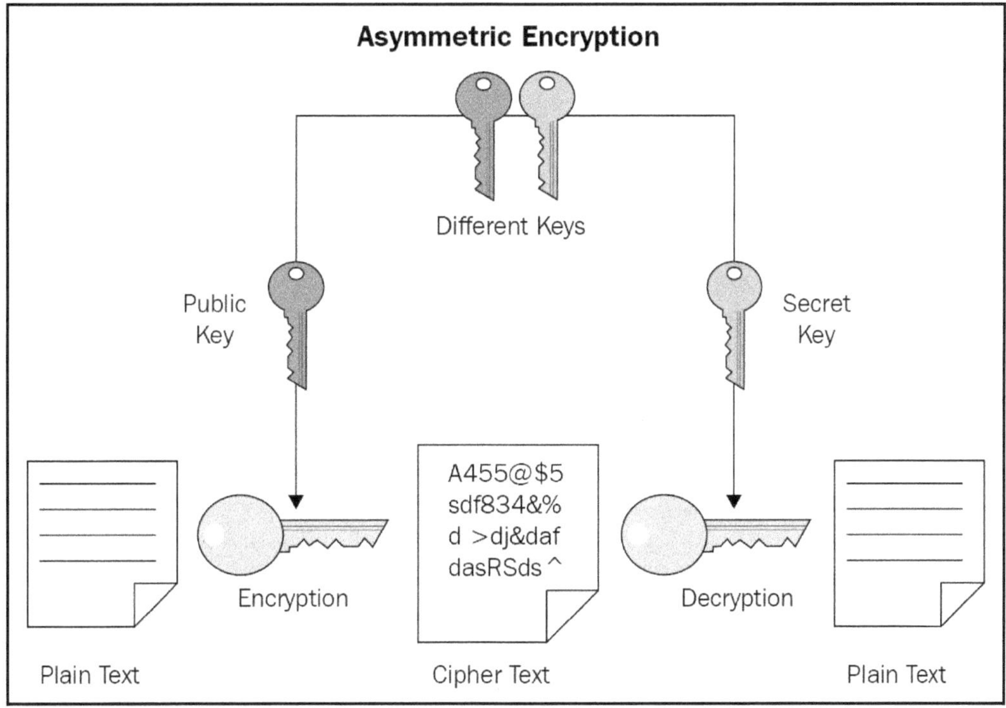

Two of the most popular Asymmetric Encryption Algorithms are:

- **Rivest-Shamir-Adleman (RSA)**: This is the most widely used asymmetric algorithm. Let's take a look at the SSL certificate to verify what algorithm is being used. Under certificate details, you can see that the Public Key value is RSA (2048) and this indicates RSA encryption:

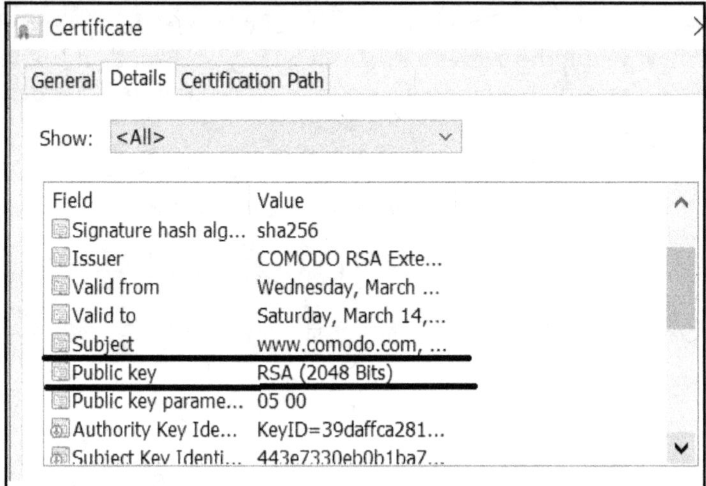

- **Elliptic Curve Cryptography (ECC)**: In the second example, you can see that the Public Key value is ECC by viewing certificate details. ECC is gaining fame within the industry as an alternative to RSA:

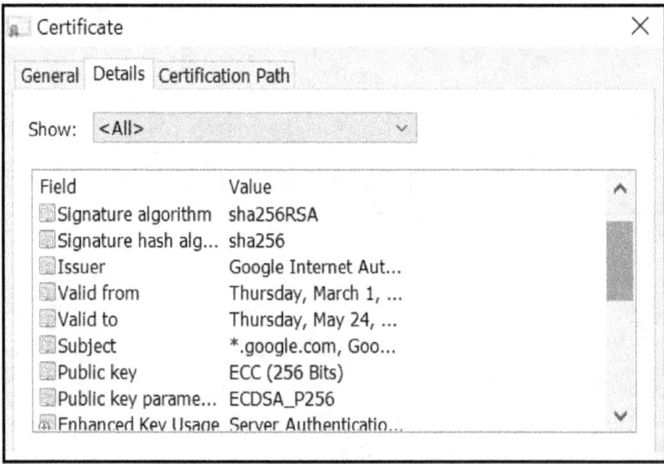

Hash function

A hash is a number generated from the information inside a file, maybe a clear text file. The resulting string is a fixed length, and will vary widely with small variations in input. Hashing differs from encryption and does not use a process to encrypt and decrypt data. Hashing, however, is a one-way function that scrambles plain text to produce a unique message digest. With a properly designed algorithm, it works in a one-way direction, hence there is no way to reverse the hashing process to reveal the original password:

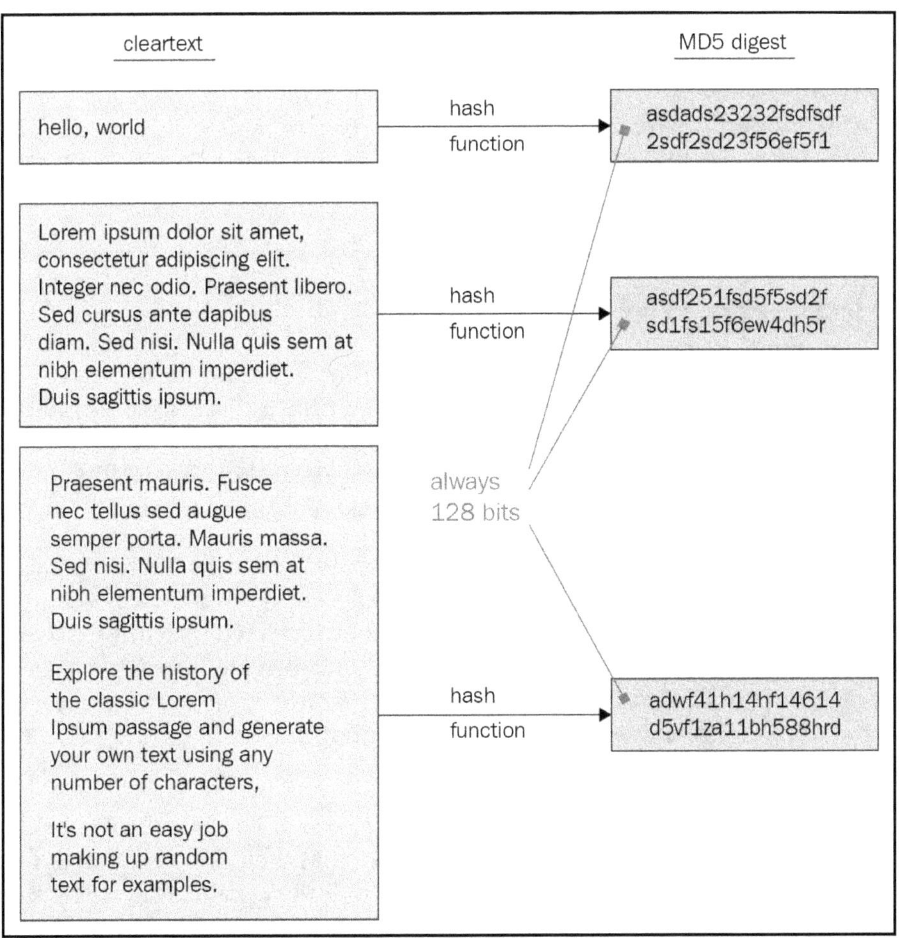

Let's understand the working.

A user enters a password and a User ID in a browser and sends it to the authentication server over a secure channel. The server uses the User ID to look up the associated message digest. The password submitted by the user is then hashed with the same algorithm, and if the resulting message digest matches the one stored on the server, it is then authenticated.

Some of the popular Hashing Algorithms are:

- **MD Family**: MD2, MD4 and MD5 (1989 -1992). All of these were 128 bit hash functions. MD5 is the most famous hash algorithm. MD6 also came into the industry but never gained popularity and was replaced by SHA3.
- **SHA Family**: There are four versions of SHA. This includes SHA0 (most vulnerable), SHA1 (most popular), SHA2 (widely deployed) and SHA3, which was introduced in 2012.
- **AES Family**: AES comes with three block ciphers. This includes AES-128, AES-192 and AES-256. Each cipher encrypts and decrypts data in blocks of 128 bits using cryptographic keys of 128, 192 and 256 bits.

Attacks against PKI

If you ask any security expert if PKI is 100% safe, the answer would be a big *NO* - there are a few concerns that are raised by security experts from time to time. I will begin by looking at the management of CA certificates and private keys. The internet is full of billions of websites and services, and so there are multiple certificate authorities. Rolling out new standards takes many years since this affects the whole security ecosystem.

As a system, PKI is nothing but mathematics. Once someone cracks the formula, a new formula will be introduced to the industry, which looks stronger and more secure. But for how long would this be the case? Another major issue comes with securing private keys. The normal scenario is that you, as a client, generate your private key pair on your own machine, then send the CSR to the CA as part of a certificate request. In some cases, it is a good idea to let the CA generate the key pair and send it to you. In case of private key loss, your CA can provide you with a private key.

Let's take a look at a recent incident in which this happened. Thousands of customers received emails from the security firm DigiCert to say that their SSL certificates were being revoked because of a security compromise at Trustico. If the certificate is currently in an active state, this would mean that customers would begin receiving untrusted certificate warnings. According to an official statement, 23,000 private keys were compromised. This mainly affected customers who used Trustico's website to generate both their private/public keys and their CSRs.

You should never trust anyone with your private keys. They should be generated and kept safe only on the servers upon which you wish to install the certificates.
You can also visit `https://www.ssllabs.com/ssl-pulse.` SSL pulse is a continuous and global dashboard for monitoring the quality of SSL/TLS support over time across 150,000 SSL and TLS-enabled websites, based on Alexa's list of the most popular sites in the world.

Microsoft Windows and IIS

In this section, we will discuss SSL certificate installation with Microsoft IIS:

1. Start IIS manager and double click server certificate.
2. Select **Actions** menu (on the right) and click on **Create Certificate Request**:

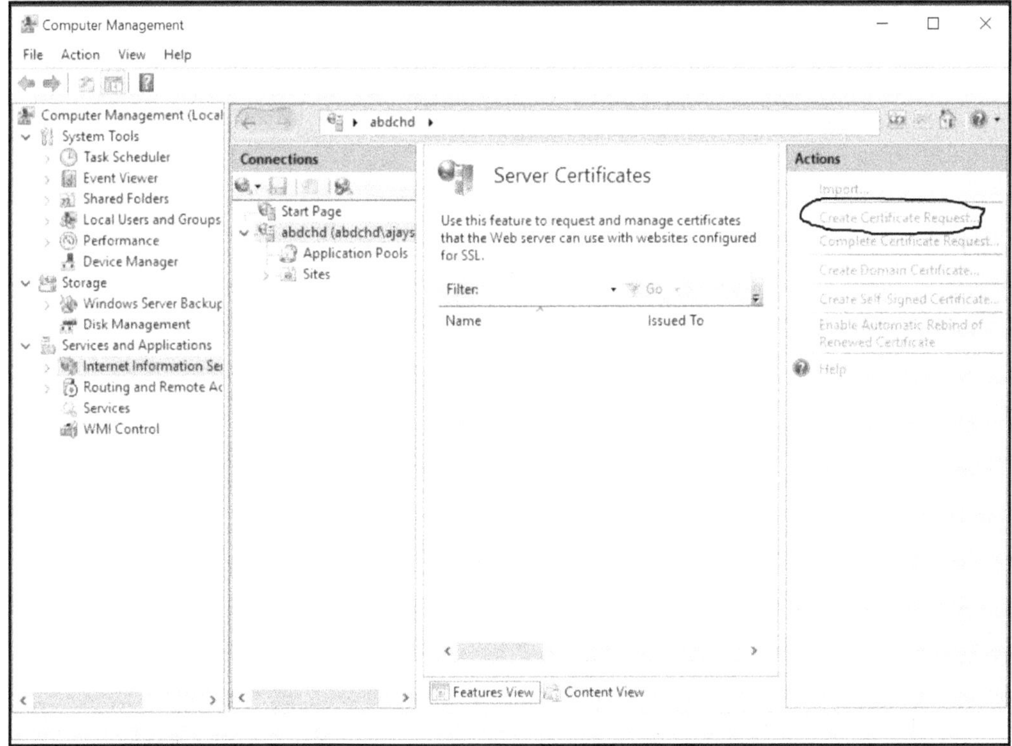

This will open the Request Certificate wizard:

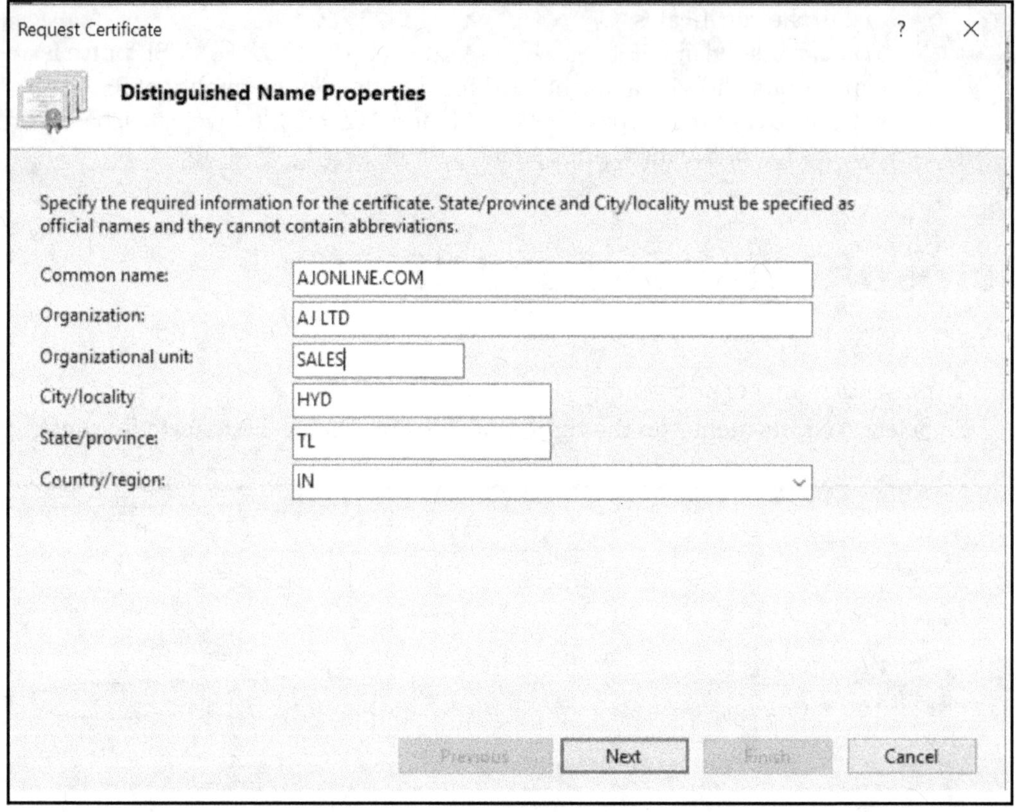

In the **Cryptographic Service Provider Properties** window, leave both settings at their default values (Microsoft RSA SChannel and 2048) and then click **Next**:

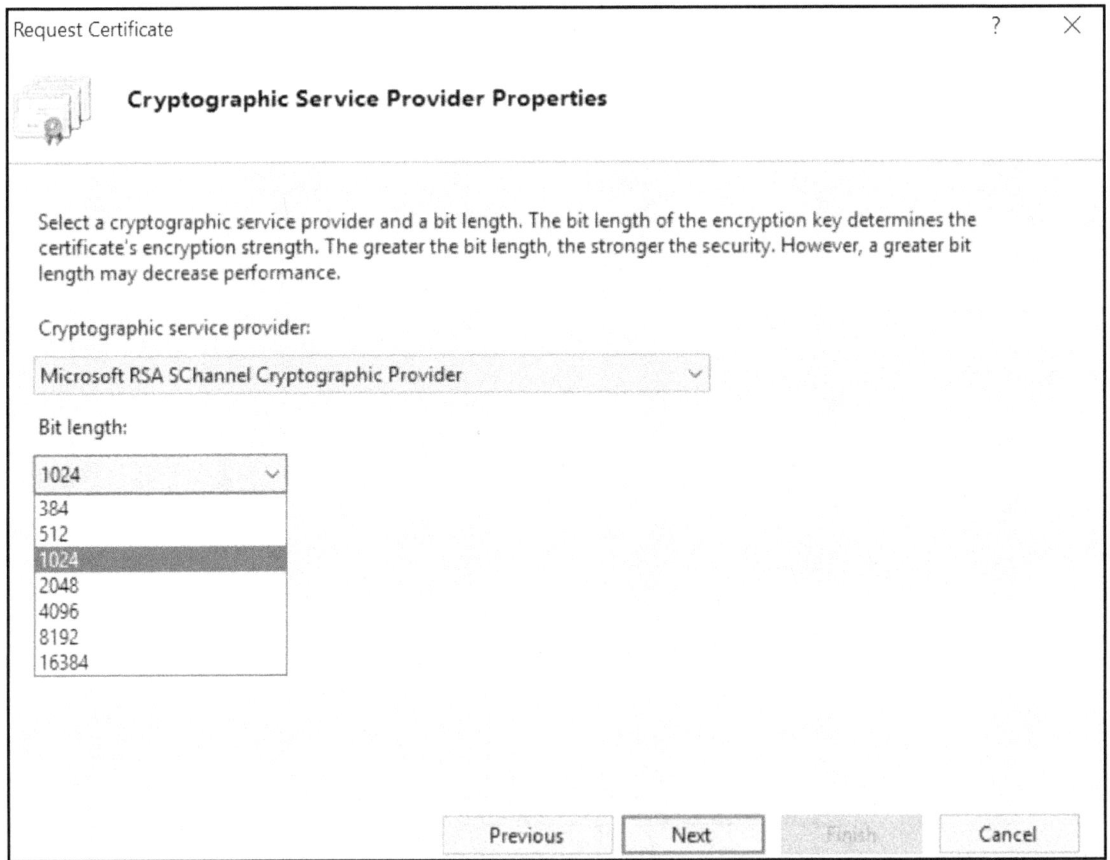

Enter a filename and location to save your CSR:

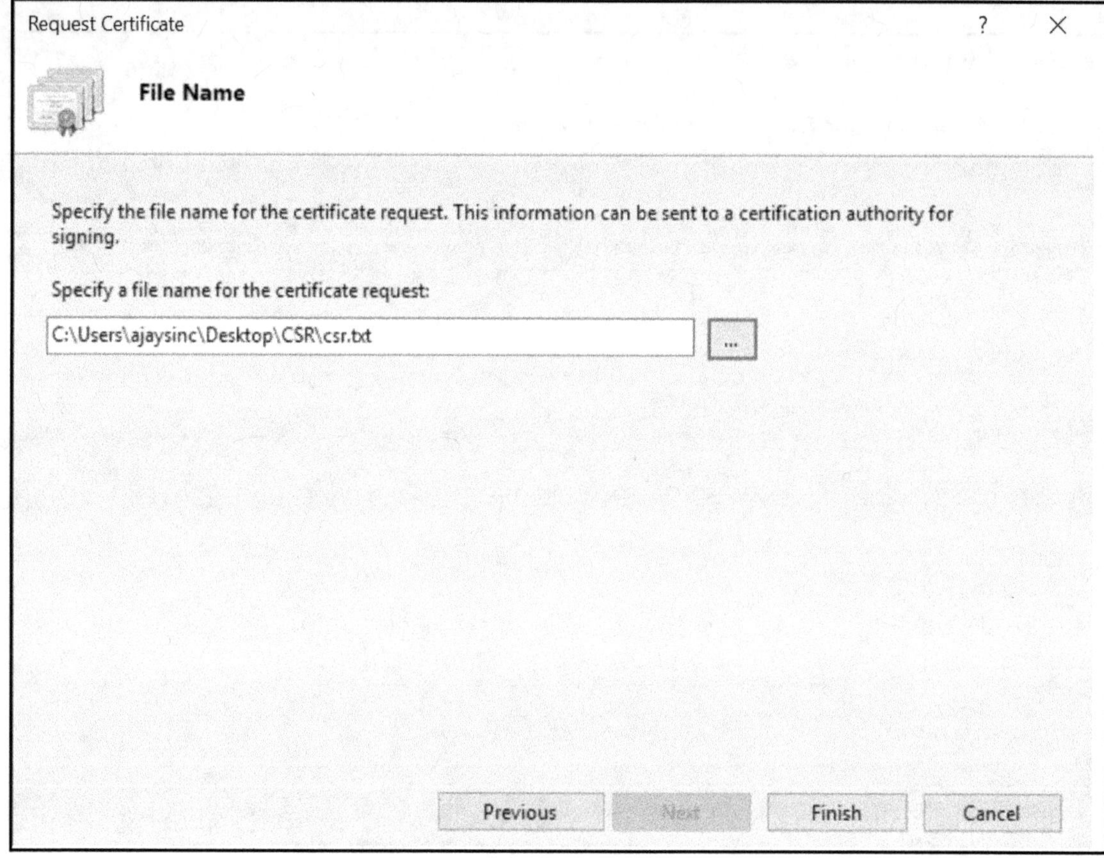

You can now open the text file to check the CSR request. This file should go to CA to receive a signature:

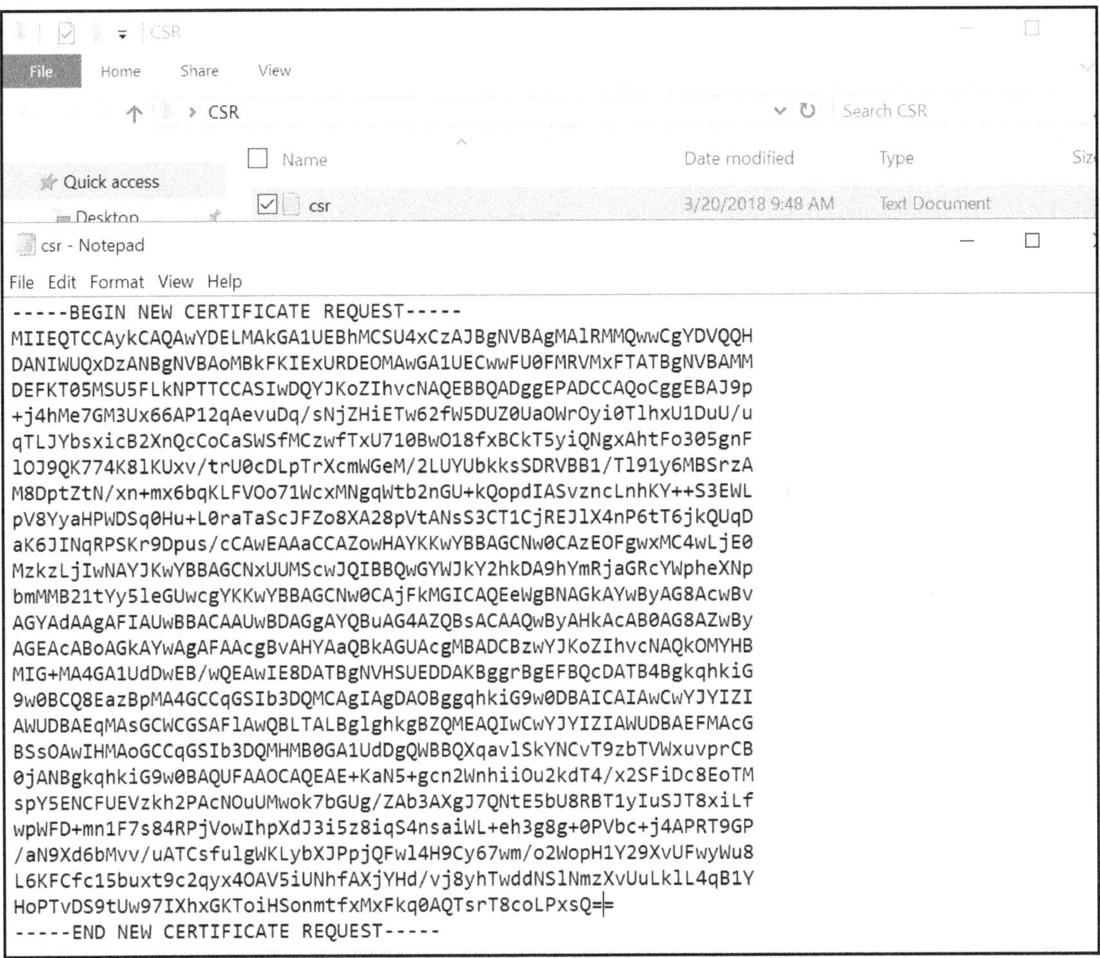

OpenSSL

OpenSSL is an open source project that consists of a cryptographic library and an SSL toolkit.

According to the project's website itself, the OpenSSL Project is:

> *"A collaborative effort to develop a robust, commercial-grade, full-featured, and Open Source toolkit implementing the* ***Secure Sockets Layer*** *(SSL) and* ***Transport Layer Security*** *(TLS) protocols as well as a full-strength general purpose cryptography library. The project is managed by a worldwide community of volunteers that use the Internet to communicate, plan, and develop the OpenSSL toolkit and its related documentation."*

OpenSSL libraries can be used to create a certificate request (CSR), a self-signed certificate and even to issue a certificate as a CA. If you are running a small or corporate organization and have the ability to import a root trust certificate to all computer systems, you can become your own CA and issue certificates yourself.

For example, I will be using my Ubuntu server. This is an old release but of course you have the choice to upgrade it:

```
ajaysinc@ubuntu-lin:~$
ajaysinc@ubuntu-lin:~$ openssl version
OpenSSL 1.0.2g  1 Mar 2016
ajaysinc@ubuntu-lin:~$ openssl
OpenSSL> version
OpenSSL 1.0.2g  1 Mar 2016
OpenSSL>
```

The latest version can be downloaded from the OpenSSL official website: `https://www.openssl.org/source/`:

KBytes	Date	File
6333	2018-Feb-27 13:50:44	openssl-1.1.1-pre2.tar.gz (SHA256) (PGP sign) (SHA1)
5249	2017-Dec-07 13:47:59	openssl-1.0.2n.tar.gz (SHA256) (PGP sign) (SHA1)
5278	2017-Nov-02 14:51:59	openssl-1.1.0g.tar.gz (SHA256) (PGP sign) (SHA1)
1457	2017-May-24 18:01:01	openssl-fips-2.0.16.tar.gz (SHA256) (PGP sign) (SHA1)
1437	2017-May-24 18:01:01	openssl-fips-ecp-2.0.16.tar.gz (SHA256) (PGP sign) (SHA1)

On the Ubuntu server, you can locate files under the `/usr/lib/ssl` path:

```
ajaysinc@ubuntu-lin:/usr/lib/ssl$ ls
certs  misc  openssl.cnf  private
ajaysinc@ubuntu-lin:/usr/lib/ssl$
```

Let's take a look at how to generate a private key and the CSR:

1. First we will generate the private key. This will be an RSA 2048 key. However, you have the option to choose DSA or EC keys. The fields which ask for your email address, optional company name and challenge password can be left blank:

```
ajaysinc@ubuntu-lin:/usr/lib/ssl$ sudo openssl req -nodes -newkey rsa:2048 -keyout ajay_private.key
 -out ajay.csr
Generating a 2048 bit RSA private key
................................+++
.............................+++
writing new private key to 'ajay_private.key'
-----
You are about to be asked to enter information that will be incorporated
into your certificate request.
What you are about to enter is what is called a Distinguished Name or a DN.
There are quite a few fields but you can leave some blank
For some fields there will be a default value,
If you enter '.', the field will be left blank.
-----
Country Name (2 letter code) [AU]:
```

2. In step two you will be asked for the information required for the certificate, organization, state, organization name, FQDN and email address:

```
-----
Country Name (2 letter code) [AU]:IN
State or Province Name (full name) [Some-State]:TL
Locality Name (eg, city) []:HYD
Organization Name (eg, company) [Internet Widgits Pty Ltd]:AJ LTD
Organizational Unit Name (eg, section) []:IT
Common Name (e.g. server FQDN or YOUR name) []:ajay.in
Email Address []:

Please enter the following 'extra' attributes
to be sent with your certificate request
A challenge password []:123
string is too short, it needs to be at least 4 bytes long
A challenge password []:1234
An optional company name []:
ajaysinc@ubuntu-lin:/usr/lib/ssl$
ajaysinc@ubuntu-lin:/usr/lib/ssl$
```

The private key and CSR can now be located in same folder:

```
ajaysinc@ubuntu-lin:/usr/lib/ssl$ ls
ajay.csr  ajay_private.key  certs  misc  openssl.cnf  private
ajaysinc@ubuntu-lin:/usr/lib/ssl$ cat ajay.csr
-----BEGIN CERTIFICATE REQUEST-----
MIICsjCCAZoCAQAwWDELMAkGA1UEBhMCSU4xCzAJBgNVBAgMAlRMMQwwCgYDVQQH
DANIWUQxDzANBgNVBAoMBkFKIExURDELMAkGA1UECwwCSVQxEDAOBgNVBAMMB2Fq
YXkuaW4wggEiMA0GCSqGSIb3DQEBAQUAA4IBDwAwggEKAoIBAQCtxUsp1yQjEqRv
H3bggaAbo8+q8Th1KseEqHzUTfqcDiHogjISclTPrfVUaiSRJ+NoZ7Wo+NASfrN6
mLPAZ+N1BVnDv9WsfVvYLyYw8iHjTWr6oSnVjEqQ8OeRdUtyAhhhS1/mDB8pgkky
Tgw8XFbI9UEFSjdsWegFFGEqwzm4wcM1P4qClNHZz+4USsmS6G5F/OQkOoY1pxkP
CVCwSajevtMedaizbdjqYHgHJtrXH4sUBWnfQ9J2bPxkGYIfeLrEWXSdByEwOOtH
8+ge3sU+vdACOb92SMpgiTo3GQ7qzPg2vx9BR91OtGxW9yURtSRZr+fx5Sc5yMki
OT4J0UO7AgMBAAGgFTATBgkqhkiG9w0BCQcxBgwEMTIzNDANBgkqhkiG9w0BAQsF
AAOCAQEAaMQhcqQF+ubM3q3S1UPl0UuBczjOOcgn+VOtdBsITZmjDHXJPHD4a9jc
kiSTyHO9alIXPTNQHXLfhXsBRsTv3PDel23NtoVpOsm7LKMqGmik5m7Xuv05a7pF
wwrncNn5eEEg8Bm1h/SiZKKifN1OH7cV1yBj+/8W2Jym1d84hipR+joI8Zrkcpdm
F/EEY3Z2Xutc3nFPk8Y0sOdegOetWOx6RjuV20TvzjFC+n0cGQ9y35FyrebczPHx
0Iy0W0oR6c2KeZaLoDOtJrSBX3I1cPURSWzj3280+77NPd+1U65JVLnstA7QBiq7
v7KBy2/x39wI4Z4olph5App+OwRjfw==
-----END CERTIFICATE REQUEST-----
ajaysinc@ubuntu-lin:/usr/lib/ssl$
```

This is just an overview. For more information, you can visit `https://www.openssl.org/` or main pages.

SSL Management tools

In my personal experience, the most common issue with managing certificates is the certificate expiry. For small organizations, manual tracking is possible, but this would be a strenuous exercise. It is better to have an automated framework to monitor the certificate expiry/renewal across all service assets.

A few of the very famous SSL management tools include:

- **SolarWinds SSL Certificate Management**
- **Qualys CertView**

Summary

This chapter served as an introduction to understanding the world of PKI. The chapter began with the basic fundamentals of SSL from a user's point of view and discussed how SSL works for web-based applications. We also covered what functions and algorithms are available for us to generate a strong certificate. In addition, we have seen how certificates are generated for Windows IIS and looked at how to use the OpenSSL tool. This chapter also gave you an insight into the threats to PKI and how to safeguard against them for a better user experience.

In the next chapter, we will discuss firewall as a security appliance and explore its place in network infrastructure.

Questions

1. The full form of SSL is:
    1. Serial Session Layer
    2. Secure Socket Layer
    3. Session Secure Layer
    4. Series Socket Layer

2. What provides security at the transport layer?
    1. SSL
    2. TLS
    3. either (1) or (2)
    4. both (1) and (2)

3. What is the standard TCP port for an SSL supported application?
    1. `420`
    2. `1032`
    3. `443`
    4. `322`

4. How do you identify a secure site? Select all correct answers.
    1. `http`
    2. `https`
    3. the open padlock
    4. the locked padlock

Further reading

For more information, refer to the following links:

- `https://tools.ietf.org/html/rfc6101`
- `https://tools.ietf.org/html/rfc5246`
- `https://www.ssllabs.com/`
- `https://blog.pcisecuritystandards.org/are-you-ready-for-30-june-2018-sayin-goodbye-to-ssl-early-tls`
- `https://www.openssl.org/`

10
Firewall Placement and Detection Techniques

In the previous chapter, we learned all about SSL. We also explored how SSL provides the authentication, confidentiality, and integrity to achieve transport layer security.

This chapter provides a brief overview of firewall technology, looking at its placement in a network and the services it offers. In this chapter, you will explore a different generation of firewalls and use cases. You will also learn where a firewall fits into a network and what it can and cannot do. Furthermore, the chapter covers the basics of TCP/IP, Traceroute, scanner tools, setting up firewalls, testing, the best practices to maintain firewalls, and much more. We will be covering the following topics:

- Firewall and design considerations
- DMZ secure design
- TCP/IP & OSI model
- Firewall performance, capabilities, and functions

Technical requirements

You will need a Unix or Linux machine with hping installation, as well as a basic knowledge of TCP/IP, firewalls and IP communication.

Firewall and design considerations

Security is the most important consideration for any secure network design. There are many ways to secure the network, and firewall techniques are one of the most important ways to implement network security.

The term *firewall* was in use as early as 1764 to describe walls that isolate the parts of a building most likely to have a fire (for example, a kitchen) from the rest of a structure. There are two types of firewalls: one is based on hardware, and the second is based on software. Hardware-based firewalls are dedicated hardware units used to protect a piece of network or segment, while software-based firewalls run on top of the operating system to protect host machines.

A firewall protection strategy totally depends on the expertise of a firewall administrator and the efficiency of firewall hardware. Security rules and management policies are the most critical tasks for access control policies. IP communication is based on five basic tuples, and for each firewall rule you need a valid source address, destination address, source port, destination port, and transport protocol TCP or UDP, along with action or rejection permits.

The most commonly implemented solution for enterprise is based on the combination of firewall technologies such as packet filtering, **Virtual Private Network** (**VPN**) and **Network Address Translation** (**NAT**).

Firewall terminology

Before we discuss firewalls in detail, you must understand the basic terminology:

- **IP Address**: An IP address is a host identity on the internet through which reachability is achieved via a routing protocol between networks. There are two types of IP address available—IPv4 (32 bit with class A, B, C, or D) and IPv6 (128 bit with unicast address, any cast address, or multicast address). For example, IPv4: `200.10.20.1` and IPv6: `2001:0db8:85a3:0000:0000:8a2e:0370:7334`
- **Ports**: Any application that is hosted on an operating system makes its service available on a network using standard ports. When accessing any application on the internet, a dynamic port is opened on source and a standard known port for destination. For example, HTTP uses port `80`, FTP uses port `22`, and Telnet uses port `23`.

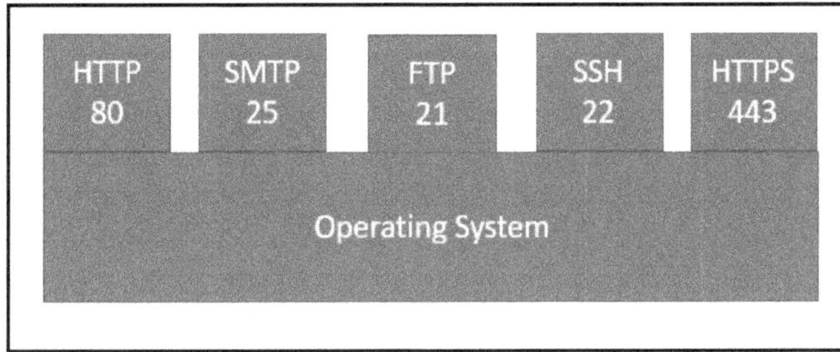

- **Protocol**: A protocol is a standard method and mutual agreement for exchanging data over a network host on a local area network, internet, intranet, and WAN.
- **Tuples**: The term 5-tuple refers to the five items (source and destination IP, source and destination port, and protocol) in any given IP packet. The firewall policy uses these tuples to define the firewall rule of whether to block or allow traffic.

Firewall generations

A firewall is a network security device that monitors and controls all incoming and outgoing network traffic based on a defined and advanced set of security rules. Let's discuss the evolution of firewalls and their capabilities.

- **Packet filtering:** First-generation firewalls—these are relatively less expensive with a simple filter function called static packet filtering, also referred to as stateless firewalls. In firewall terminology, *stateless* refers to rule inspection in both directions in and out; hence, the firewall unit does not maintain any session or connection state.

  Basically, packet filtering is performed at Layer 3 (IP) and Layer 4 (Transport) by matching the header fields of the packet against four tuples: source and destination IP address, and ports and transport protocol (TCP/UDP). A good example would be to relate this to a router and an access control list to control traffic going in and out.

  In 1988, the **Digital Equipment Corporation** (**DEC**) developed the first firewall systems, known as packet filter firewalls. Basic packet filtering firewalls are vulnerable to IP spoofing as they do not maintain a connection state and can be exploited by attackers.

- **Stateful firewalls :** Second-generation firewalls—these firewalls have the same capabilities as the first generation, but with the added ability to monitor and store the session along with the connection state. For any connection, packet matching works bidirectionally, which means that a packet being sent is matched with the attribute of a returning packet, confirming that it belongs to the same packet flow. Unlike putting an access control list in a stateless device in both directions, the firewall allows the return packet based on the packet flow. It looks at the TCP header information for SYN, RST, ACK, and FIN to determine the state of the connection.
- **Application Gateway**: Third-generation firewalls—an application gateway firewall works based on deep packet inspection to understand the application (Layer 7) and to act as a proxy between the server and client. Suspicious data and connections are dropped by these proxies. Since they are application aware, they can handle more complex protocols like web, H.323, SIP, FTP, SQL Net, and so on. The disadvantage of an application gateway is establishing proxy connectivity, which requires two steps to connect to either an inbound or outbound connection. In simple terms, the user needs to connect to the application firewall, rather than connecting directly with the host.
- **Next-Generation Firewalls (NGFW)**: The core and backbone function for next-generation firewalls is **Deep Packet Inspection** (**DPI**), which comes with standard features like NAT, VPN, and content filtering. The DPI function allows the firewall to look deeply into the packet using protocol identification methods. These identifications are based on specific parameters of an application, rather than a port-based identification of applications. This can also block sophisticated cyberattacks based on IPS engines and signatures. Security policies or rules can be implemented based on application and network protocol.

A very similar approach is being followed by SDN implementation, a controlled policy to block or allow traffic across multiple gateways installed in multiple locations. These policies are based on applications rather than being IP and port based. The flexibility we get means that we can centralize controllers and applications routed on the network.

The different security services of the NGFW offering can work together to provide a higher level of security than **Stateful Packet Inspection** (**SPI**) firewalls, due to DPI capability:

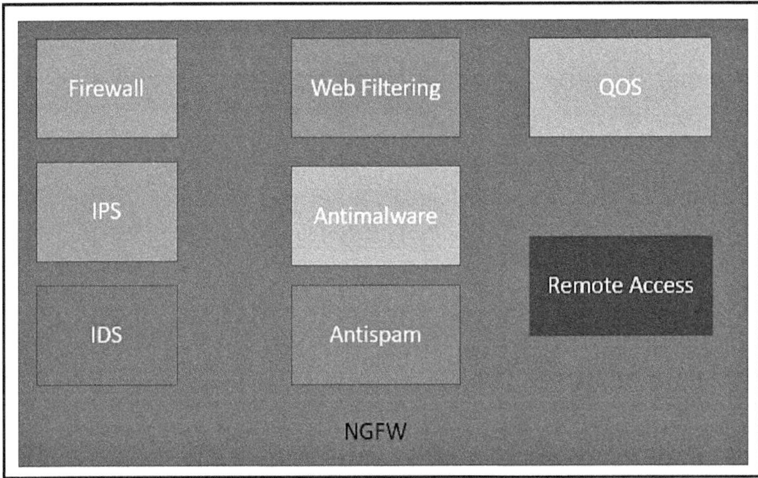

Let's take a look at how to choose a firewall fit for business and performance criteria.

Firewall performance

The performance of a firewall is tested under different traffic loads when considering different metrics to evaluate the firewall performance. The metrics are as follows:

- **Throughput**: This is the actual payload that is received per unit of time
- **Delay**: This is the transit time for a packet to be transmitted from the source to the destination
- **Jitter**: This measures the variation in delay of the received packets
- **Packet-loss-rate (PLR)**: This is the ratio of the lost packets to the total transmitted packets

If you're upgrading your firewall or buying a new next-generation firewall, how do you select one that's appropriate for your business? Vendors will always tell you how great their firewall product is and downplay others, so it would be difficult to approach them directly for advice.

You should first determine a list of features and a level of performance, then decide what extended functionality or feature you would like to have on top of that. Of course, you should also consider budget.

Security consideration questions:

- Is traffic always being scanned in both directions?
- Are all ports left open by default?
- Is deep packet inspection turned on by default?
- Can IPS and application control run together?

Management consideration question:

- Is an event analysis dashboard provided?

Performance consideration questions:

- Is the performance claimed by a vendor based on real traffic?
- Is testing performed with a large number of security policies?

Feature consideration question:

- Do I need a VPN?
- What would be the throughput for my network?
- Which license and size do I need for my network—SOHO or Enterprise?
- Do I need high availability?
- Should I use a software appliance or a hardware appliance?
- Does the firewall support virtualization and routing?
- What is the total number of sessions?
- Is the SSL throughput and remote access connection provided by Firewall?

These are a few sample questions. Based on the answers to these, you can choose the best firewall for your network.

Firewall placement and design network topology

When we talk about firewall placement architecture, you have two options: a single firewall or a multilayer firewall.

Single firewall architecture

The placement of a single firewall on a network depends upon a number of factors such as the number of IP subnets and services offered and hosted behind firewall. Let's take a look at a few scenarios.

Single firewall architecture with a single IP subnet

In the following diagram, a single firewall is placed under a WAN router and all traffic travels via this firewall. All servers are hosted on a single subnet and given equal security protection provided by the firewall, which provides isolation from the internet. A firewall having a single subnet may be justified when further isolation is not required between the servers and does not cause a significant risk:

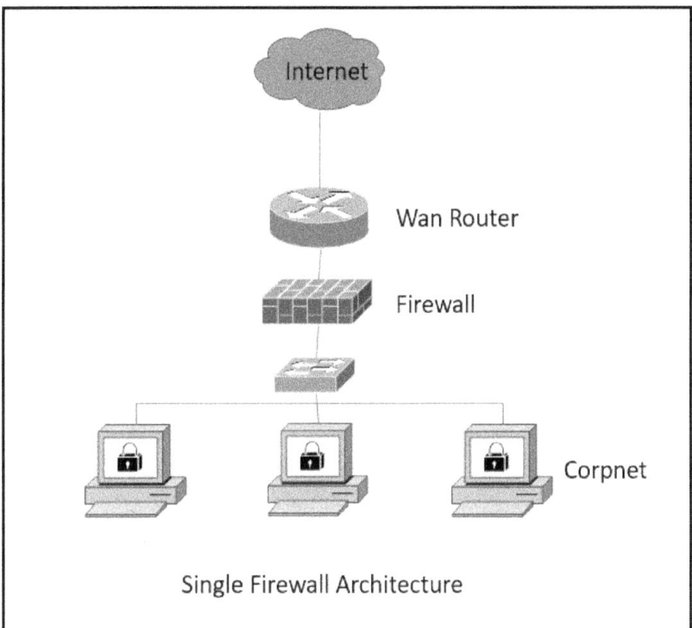

Single Firewall Architecture

Single firewall architecture with multiple IP subnets

As shown in the diagram below, a simple way to isolate the network resources without introducing another set of firewalls is to use multiple interfaces configured with multiple subnets. In the design, the web, application and database servers are placed in different subnets using different IP subnets with different security levels configured on interfaces. Let's assume that only one web server has to be exposed to the internet and the rest of the server will talk to the web server internally. This can be easily configured and controlled by inputting firewall rules. This can be achieved by exposing the web server to the internet and allowing an internet subnet policy. An attacker could only gain access to all subnets if a firewall is compromised due to a missed configuration:

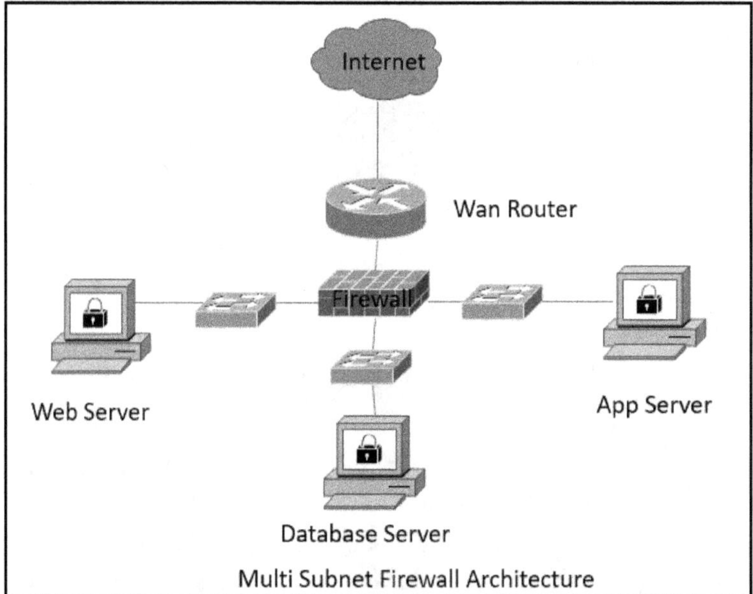

Multi Subnet Firewall Architecture

Multilayer firewall architecture

The placement of multilayer firewall security is part of the network security strategy. Keeping everything behind one firewall that offers all services can be risky and a single point of failure. Let's take a look at the firewall sandwich security design to protect highly critical assets behind the multilayer security:

Firewall sandwich design

You will often see a multi-tier firewall or sandwich design topology deployed by an enterprise network. Instead of interfaces being dedicated to different subnets, a separate firewall can also be dedicated to server roles. In such a design, applications based on roles are *sandwiched* between firewalls, and a dedicated firewall moderates communications between adjacent subnets according to the application's architecture and security policy. The basic idea behind this architecture is to dedicate firewall roles for simple management and to look for the best size of hardware to support the amount of traffic expected on different application segments:

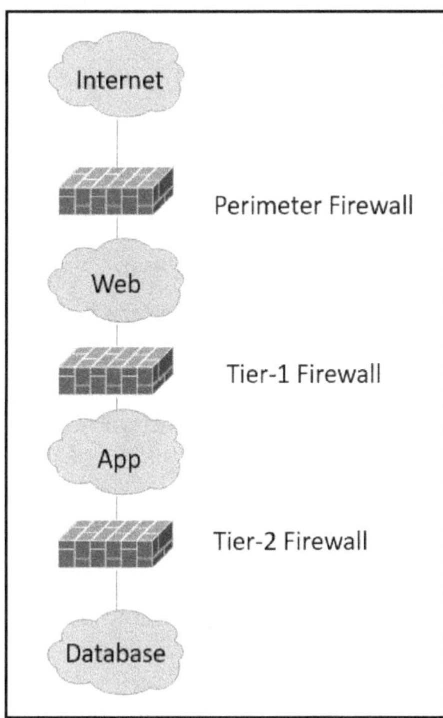

Demilitarized Zone

Demilitarized Zone (**DMZ**) is your front line, which protects valuables from direct exposure to an untrusted environment. In other words, a DMZ is generally a secure network segment that is exposed to the internet, where you keep valuable resources like a web server (the most common internet application) to enhance application security by adding an extra layer of security. It's very important to carefully plan and design a DMZ because it may not be easy task to fix loopholes when handling production traffic.

So how do you design a DMZ? Most of the time, an administrator puts the energy into securing and concentrating on DMZ security only and forgets about the rest of the internal data communications designed to access valuable information. Access to the DMZ from an internal application should be locked down as tightly as possible.

DMZ to Internal Access Policy

Internal systems hold valuable data and are not exposed directly to the internet, but a DMZ plays a proxy role in between. Just imagine that a DMZ server is compromised and the internal LAN is wide open. In this situation, attackers could find a way into your network.

Let's take a look at the example for setting up a web server in DMZ.

You must set a baseline for what you want to protect and consider scalability, availability, and agility. You have the freedom to choose the number of firewalls for setting up a DMZ, but two firewalls would be a good start. With two firewalls, you can put front-line servers behind a perimeter firewall (DMZ) and internal resources under a different firewall.

You can also have multiple scenarios in this design. I will try to cover those as well. A web server can be configured using a private IP and further natted with public IP for internet readability. However, you can also configure public IP directly on a server. Web servers can be configured with dual NIC , FE NIC and BE NIC. A connection coming from the internet will be terminated on FE NIC, and a new connection will be made to access app and database servers. Since this is a web server, the only rule for port `80` or `443` is required on DMZ firewall. Port `1433` on Tier-1 firewall will allow a connection from web to app and database servers, assuming it is a SQL server.

In this diagram, you can see that a new connection has been made for a web server on port `80` on public IP `2.2.2.2`. Once this connection hits the front-line firewall, the NAT rule will translate this connection to the real IP of the web server, which is `10.10.10.1`. The decision of whether single or dual interface IPs should be used in order to connect further to database servers will now depend upon the NIC design:

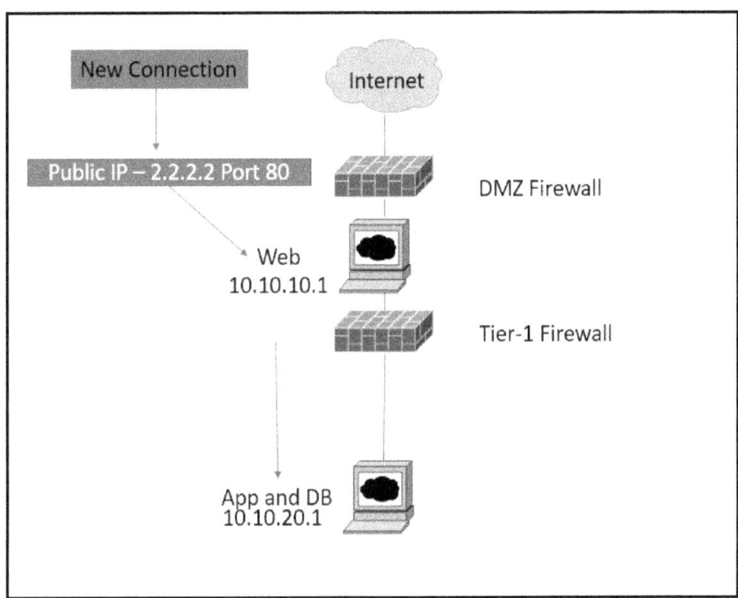

Do I really need dual NIC? This design is also possible when based on single or dual NIC. A dual NIC design is more secure, considering the fact that with a single NIC you might need to adjust the routing, switching, and NAT statement in order to talk between a private IP space. Dual NICs give an extra physical layer of separation to achieve higher security.

Having said that, a DMZ is an important part of your network security architecture. You need a way to expose services to the internet world, but in a controlled and secure manner. To create a DMZ successfully, a proper understanding of access policies and configuration is required for firewall detection.

OSI model versus TCP/IP model

Before discussing how a firewall works, we must first understand how the different layers of a network interact. Network communication is based on a seven-layer model, and each layer has its own set of responsibilities in order to make the communication happen. Firewalls can operate on different layers in order to use different criteria to block or permit the traffic.

In general, a firewall is going to have to operate at the network layer (L3) and transport layer (L4). The upper layers are more like scanning for viruses in data payloads and doing deep packet inspection. The Layer-1 physical layer is basically just a network connectivity requirement.

TCP/IP, also known as the internet model developed by the **Department of Defense** (**DoD**), is a simplified and practical version of the **Open System Interconnection** (**OSI**) model (1984), which is based on a theoretical concept.

The OSI model is based on server layers and its specific function. The following diagram shows layers along with their functions:

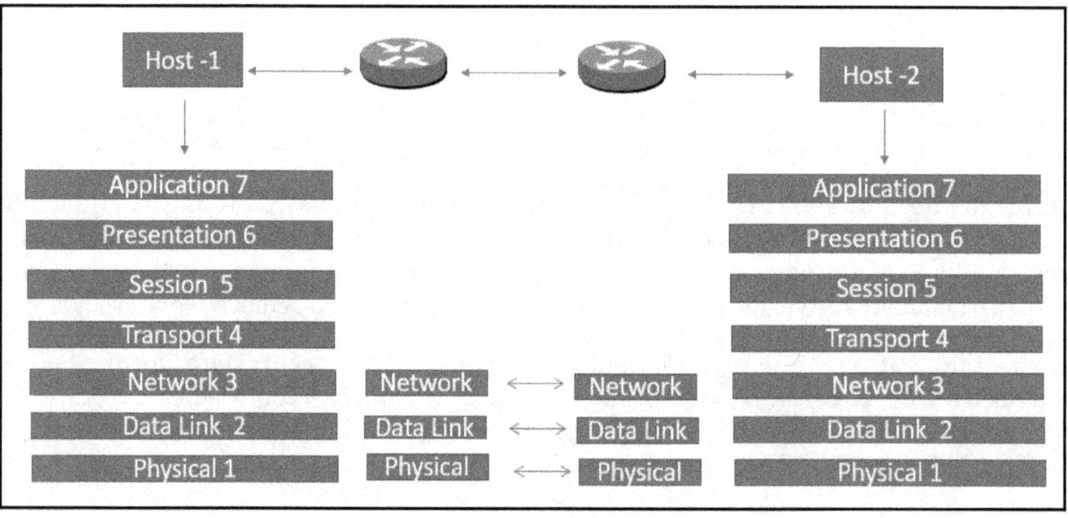

The layers in the preceding diagram are as follows:

- **Physical layer**: This layer connects networking nodes over physical media and encodes bits into electrical signals
- **Data Link layer**: This layer is responsible for error detection and flow control over physical media
- **Network layer**: This layer is responsible for IP routing, switching, and network IP addressing
- **Transport layer**: This layer is responsible for transport protocol TCP/UDP and error handling
- **Session layer**: This layer is responsible for connection establishment and data flow
- **Presentation layer**: This layer is responsible for the standard format of data as well as encryption and decryption
- **Application layer**: This layer provides services directly to user application over the network to end users.

Let's take a look at the difference between OSI and TCP/IP models. On the right hand side of the diagram, we can see that the TCP/IP model has four layers, including the network interface, internet, transport, and application layers. TCP/IP follows a top-to-bottom approach, and the OSI model follows a bottom-up approach. Of course, it appears simple due to a smaller number of layers:

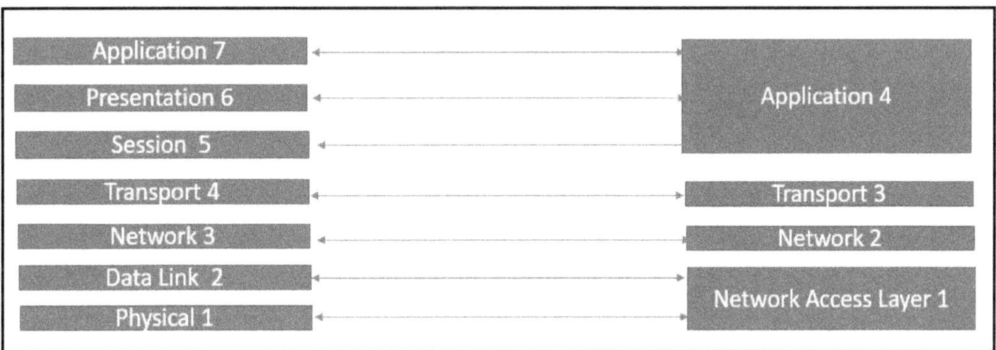

Firewall performance, capabilities, and function

So far, we have discussed the basic features of a firewall. There are many more functions that can be used for multiple purposes. Let's list these below:

- **URL filtering**: Random web surfing may expose your network to malware that can cause security risks to your organization. URL filtering is a way to limit access by comparing web traffic in a database to prevent employees from accessing unproductive URLs or contents.
- **Antivirus and malware protection**: NGFW comes with an inbuilt antivirus engine and malware protection, which is capable of inspecting traffic along with malicious infected files.
- **Integrated IPS/IDS**: In a traditional enterprise network, the deployment of IPS/IDS is very common as a separate appliance. A next-generation firewall comes with an IPS/IDS module and can be enabled or disabled according to requirements. The biggest thing to consider is how much traffic we want to pass through the IPS/IDS device and that should be supported by these modules.
- **Quality of Service (QoS)**: QoS is a framework on a network to guarantee bandwidth ability for high-priority applications. Traffic can be classified based on DSCP packet marking, application port, source and destination IP, and deep packet detection to detect application based approaches.
- **Remote Access (VPN)**: Instead of going to a separate unit for terminating a VPN, a firewall can be used for the same purpose. There are multiple versions of VPN— corporate HQ networks connectivity to their remote location is often built on site-to-site VPNs. Remote access VPNs such as SSL, web VPN, and IPsec VPN Client allow individual users to connect to the corporate network remotely.
- **High Availability (HA)**: This is a deployment in which two or more firewalls are placed into a group and their configuration is synchronized to prevent a single point of failure on a network. High availability can be achieved by putting firewall in active-passive mode or active-active mode by sharing traffic.
- **Virtualization**: This is another important function or feature of a firewall to operate in a virtual context mode. Topology can be formed based on requirements, and context can operate in active-passive or active-active. This works best in a hosting environment where separation between customers is required. Please refer to the product documentation to check which features are supported in a virtualized environment.

Firewall management

Firewall protects the enterprise network and plays a critical role on perimeter defense. The majority of data breaches take place due to misconfiguration. Consequently, it becomes very important for enterprises to leave admin access in the hands of experts and not to leave security in auto-pilot mode. A real-time dashboard is absolutely required to monitor network firewall traffic continuously to identify and respond to threats before the damage is done.

There are couple of best practices that must be implemented to operate firewall properly:

- **Change control policy**: Firewall rules or policy changes are very dynamic in nature and are mostly inevitable when it comes to accommodating new changes in the infrastructure environment and responding to new threats or vulnerabilities.
- **Perform periodic audit of the configurations**: Auditing is a requirement to keep firewall patches up to date and to make sure that a device is compliant with standards like SOX, PCI-DSS, and HIPAA.
- **Firewall rule consolidation and optimization**: Over time your firewalls will accumulate thousands of rules and policies, and many of these rules will become out of date or obsolete. This adds complexity to daily tasks, troubleshooting, and auditing, and may also cause performance issues to firewall appliances. It's always recommended to consolidate rules in a group based on application and remove unused rules from policies.
- **Threat detection signature updates**: Threat detection is based on patterns found in an attack. In an ever growing internet environment, new threats are detected every day. Because of this, it becomes important to update signatures and fine tune policies to avoid false alarms.

Application proxies

An application proxy (sometimes called an application-level gateway) often acts as a middle layer. These proxy applications are run on top of the firewall. The users connect the gateway using applications like Telnet, FTP, or web connect. Users are prompted to enter resources they want to access and are also asked to validate their credentials. After successful authentication, the gateway will establish a connection to a remote application and relay data between the application and end user. Since application gateways are application aware, it becomes very easy from a gateway management point of view. In a typical firewall, either ports will be closed or open, and policies are defined by the administrator.

In the following diagram, you can see that Tom will be authenticated against the rule configured as ALG firewall, which allows Tom to access an application running on `20.20.20.1`. All other connections will be denied:

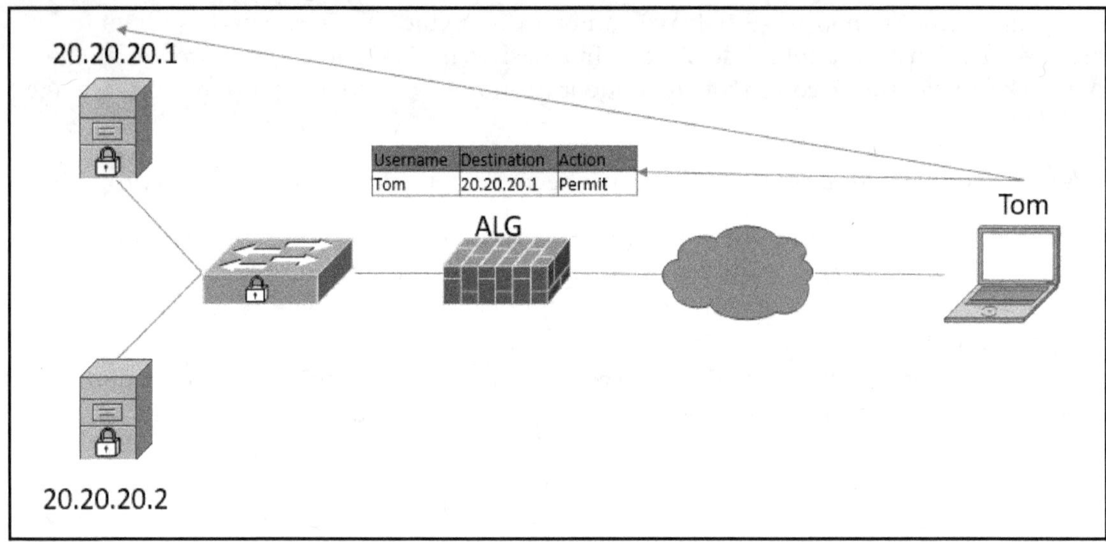

One of the biggest limitations of an application gateway is that it requires a separate application for each network service. Consequently, it is mandatory to check which services are supported with the firewall vendor. Another disadvantage of ALG is an additional processing overhead on each connection.

Detecting firewalls

Firewalls secure small to large infrastructure networks from malicious attacks and unwanted traffic. But it would be wrong to assume that inputting a firewall will solve everything. Vulnerabilities are part of any hardware and software appliance. The biggest vulnerability is a misconfiguration of the firewall. A well-configured, architecturally designed, updated, and well-maintained firewall is almost impossible to penetrate.

There are several methods available that can help you to detect the location of the firewall. A very easy method to locate a firewall is through `traceroute` (Unix utility) or `tracert` (Windows utility).

Let's take a brief look at the background of `traceroute` and how it works. People commonly say that traceroute uses ICMP, and this is partially true because ICMP is used for error message reporting. ICMP, UDP, and TCP are all Layer 4 protocols, and IP packets contain a field **Time To Live** (**TTL**). The TTL field is 8 bit and can reach a maximum of 255 hops. Different operating systems use different values. For example, Windows 10 uses 128 by default. Here is quick way to find a default value and ping localhosts from a command prompt. Every time a packet passes via a router or L3 device, the TTL value decrements by 1.

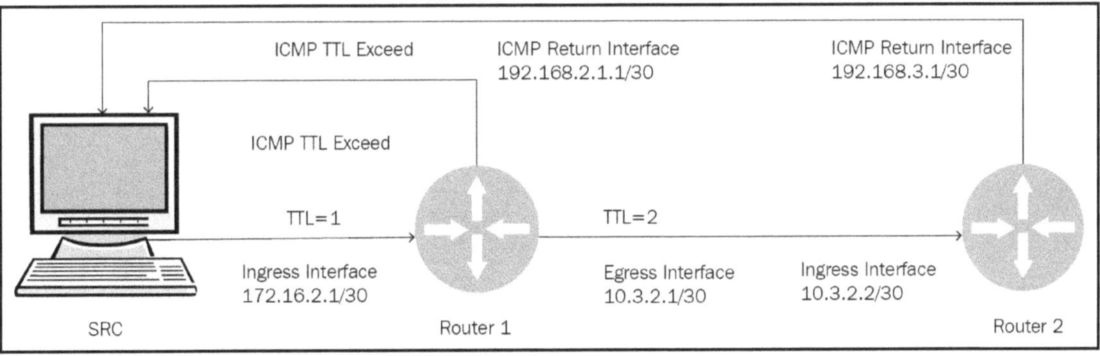

Here is a quick way to find the default value and ping localhosts from a command prompt. I did this on my Windows 10 machine. You can also get or adjust the value from a Windows registry:

```
C:\Users\ajaysinc>ping 127.0.0.1

Pinging 127.0.0.1 with 32 bytes of data:
Reply from 127.0.0.1: bytes=32 time<1ms TTL=128
Reply from 127.0.0.1: bytes=32 time<1ms TTL=128
```

Let's assume ICMP is open: take a look at traceroute results. I have taken this from an online trace portal, which shows that the last hop is `182.168.6.81`. After that, ICMP seems to be blocked by a firewall:

Traceroute online - Start **traceroute online**, the results you should see below. **This should take up to 30seconds.**

```
traceroute to 107.180.0.209 (107.180.0.209), 30 hops max, 60 byte packets
 1  praha-4d-c1-vl55.masterinter.net (77.93.199.253)  0.581 ms  0.622 ms  0.717 ms
 2  vl1391.cr2.c16.127.cecolo.prg.masterinter.net (83.167.254.142)  0.194 ms  0.208 ms  0.381 ms
 3  prag-b3-link.telia.net (62.115.147.38)  1.004 ms  1.015 ms  1.006 ms
 4  win-bb2-link.telia.net (62.115.137.40)  5.764 ms prag-bb1-link.telia.net (62.115.136.218)  0.317 ms  0.290 ms
 5  win-b4-link.telia.net (62.115.136.231)  6.196 ms win-b4-link.telia.net (62.115.139.29)  6.300 ms win-b4-link.telia.net (80.91.247.1)  6.188 ms
 6  level-ic-1573273-wien-b4.c.telia.net (80.239.128.178)  20.351 ms  20.392 ms  20.463 ms
 7  * * *
 8  4.14.98.38 (4.14.98.38)  100.918 ms  100.904 ms  100.865 ms
 9  ip-184-168-6-81.ip.secureserver.net (184.168.6.81)  101.235 ms  101.607 ms  101.551 ms
10  ip-184-168-6-81.ip.secureserver.net (184.168.6.81)  102.436 ms  100.935 ms  102.394 ms
11  * * *
12  * * *
13  * * *
```

This is another trace which is not based on ICMP but TCP on port `80` and reaches the end server. When you compare both you can see that ICMP is being filtered by a firewall:

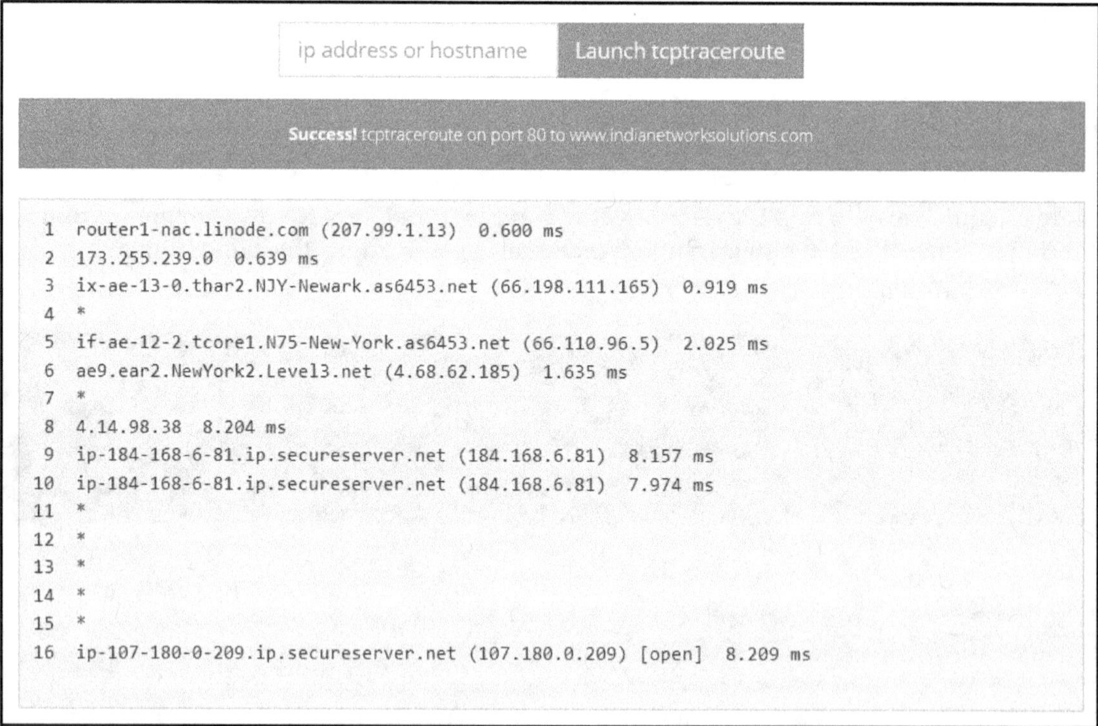

ip address or hostname | Launch tcptraceroute

Success! tcptraceroute on port 80 to www.indianetworksolutions.com

```
 1  router1-nac.linode.com (207.99.1.13)  0.600 ms
 2  173.255.239.0  0.639 ms
 3  ix-ae-13-0.thar2.NJY-Newark.as6453.net (66.198.111.165)  0.919 ms
 4  *
 5  if-ae-12-2.tcore1.N75-New-York.as6453.net (66.110.96.5)  2.025 ms
 6  ae9.ear2.NewYork2.Level3.net (4.68.62.185)  1.635 ms
 7  *
 8  4.14.98.38  8.204 ms
 9  ip-184-168-6-81.ip.secureserver.net (184.168.6.81)  8.157 ms
10  ip-184-168-6-81.ip.secureserver.net (184.168.6.81)  7.974 ms
11  *
12  *
13  *
14  *
15  *
16  ip-107-180-0-209.ip.secureserver.net (107.180.0.209) [open]  8.209 ms
```

In fact, no method is 100% accurate. They just provide you with more information so that you can guess which machine is filtering packets more accurately.

A very popular firewall Cisco ASA does not do TTL decrements by default, we have to do them manually to see the interfaces of ASA when doing traceroutes.

Firewalking is a technique used to discover information about a remote network protected by a firewall. Firewalking uses a traceroute analysis in backend to determine whether or not a data packet can pass a destination host via a packet filtering appliance.

The firewall fulfils a NAT/PAT function, and multiple applications can be served over one single public IP from the internet. You can see one public `20.20.20.10`, which is mapped with internal IPs on different port numbers. This is called a NAT operation and is performed by a firewall. This way you can create a network topology of remote networks:

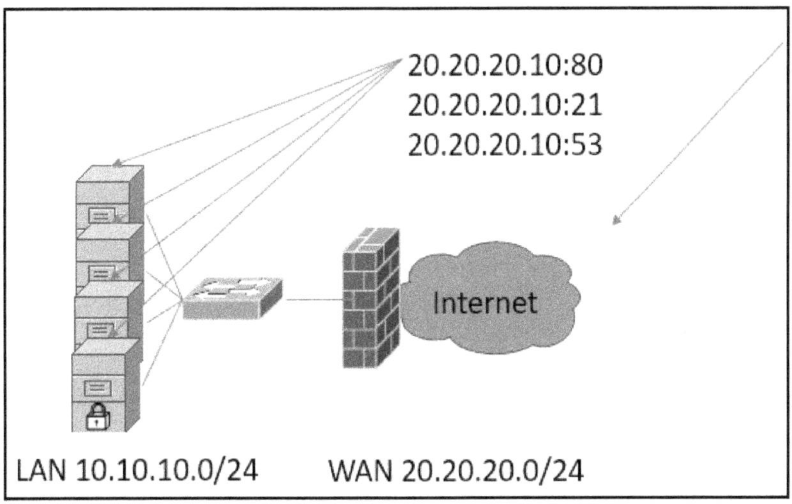

Debugging tools

The following debugging tools are used:

- **ICMP ping scan**: When checking any device on a network, the first thing that comes to mind is to test ICMP-based scanning. The way it works is that you send an ICMP request packet and expect ICMP echo to reply. The basic idea behind this is to get the live host on the network and then launch a port scanner against those live hosts. Angry IP Scanner is a very popular tool used for network scanning. The problem with ICMP is a network administrator can block ICMP on the network or host layers. You can also easily create a script for an IP scanner which can scan IPs for their defined range.
- **TCP ping scan**: We have learned that ICMP can be blocked and is therefore not very reliable nowadays. However, instead of using ICMP, a ping probe can be sent by a remote host to a specific port by sending TCP syn. You will then get a reply as a TCP syn-ack. If you want to keep your application alive, this cannot be be blocked by the network administrator.
- **Arp ping**: You can use utilities like NMAP for ping sweep, and if you use it on a local subnet, it uses an ARP Ping instead of ICMP. NMAP does this by default.
- **NAMP**: NAMP can do multiple things for you, starting with scanning a host. It can even detect the operating system of a remote host using the light capability of vulnerability scanning.
- **Hping**: Hping was mainly used as a security tool and can be used for firewall testing, port scanning, network testing, MTU discovery, advance traceroute,and OS fingerprinting. This tool gives you the ability to craft a packet. I am using the Ubuntu server, and you need to install the hping package:

```
ajaysinc@ajaysinclinux:~$ hping3
The program 'hping3' is currently not installed. You can install it by typing:
sudo apt-get install hping3
ajaysinc@ajaysinclinux:~$ sudo apt-get install hping3
Reading package lists... Done
```

Let's look at how to run this tool in port scan mode. Syntax has an argument of 0-100 (port range to be scanned), -S (Send Syn Packet) and `4.2.2.2` (IP address for host) to be scanned. Results show that one port is opened for DNS and this is true, `4.2.2.2` is a DNS server and hence the result is as expected:

```
ajaysinc@ajaysinclinux:~$ sudo hping3 --scan 0-100 -S 4.2.2.2
Scanning 4.2.2.2 (4.2.2.2), port 0-100
101 ports to scan, use -V to see all the replies
+----+-----------+---------+---+-----+-----+-----+
|port| serv name |  flags  |ttl| id  | win | len |
+----+-----------+---------+---+-----+-----+-----+
   53 domain     : .S..A...  51     0 14600    46
All replies received. Done.
Not responding ports: (0 ) (1 tcpmux) (2 nbp) (3 ) (4 echo) (5 ) (6 zip) (7 echo
) (8 ) (9 discard) (10 ) (11 systat) (12 ) (13 daytime) (14 ) (15 netstat) (16 )
 (17 qotd) (18 msp) (19 chargen) (20 ftp-data) (21 ftp) (22 ssh) (23 telnet) (24
 ) (25 smtp) (26 ) (27 ) (28 ) (29 ) (30 ) (31 ) (32 ) (33 ) (34 ) (35 ) (36 ) (
37 time) (38 ) (39 rlp) (40 ) (41 ) (42 nameserver) (43 whois) (44 ) (45 ) (46 )
 (47 ) (48 ) (49 tacacs) (50 re-mail-ck) (51 ) (52 ) (54 ) (55 ) (56 ) (57 mtp)
(58 ) (59 ) (60 ) (61 ) (62 ) (63 ) (64 ) (65 tacacs-ds) (66 ) (67 bootps) (68 b
ootpc) (69 tftp) (70 gopher) (71 ) (72 ) (73 ) (74 ) (75 ) (76 ) (77 rje) (78 )
(79 finger) (80 http) (81 ) (82 ) (83 ) (84 ) (85 ) (86 ) (87 link) (88 kerberos
) (89 ) (90 ) (91 ) (92 ) (93 ) (94 ) (95 supdup) (96 ) (97 ) (98 linuxconf) (99
 ) (100 )
ajaysinc@ajaysinclinux:~$
```

- **TCP connect scan**: TCP connect can be used as port scanning, a simpler form of probing a remote host. This involves a full TCP/IP connection, which is established with all TCP ports and one of the target hosts in an incremental manner. A TCP/IP is reliable as a protocol and such port scanning is a very reliable way to determine which TCP services are accessible on a given target host.

In this example, the `nmap` tool will try to connect to the remote host in two ways. The first way is through a syntax argument (`-sS`) , which means that a 3-way handshake will be completed. With the other method, an (`-sT`) tool will use an application like a browser in the backend to connect to a remote host:

```
ajaysinc@ajaysinclinux:~$ sudo nmap -sS 13.228.162.84

Starting Nmap 6.40 ( http://nmap.org ) at 2018-02-24 19:21 UTC
Nmap scan report for ec2-13-228-162-84.ap-southeast-1.compute.amazonaws.com (13.228.162.84)
Host is up (0.25s latency).
Not shown: 998 filtered ports
PORT    STATE SERVICE
80/tcp  open  http
443/tcp open  https

Nmap done: 1 IP address (1 host up) scanned in 15.98 seconds
ajaysinc@ajaysinclinux:~$ nmap  -sT 13.228.162.84

Starting Nmap 6.40 ( http://nmap.org ) at 2018-02-24 19:22 UTC
Nmap scan report for ec2-13-228-162-84.ap-southeast-1.compute.amazonaws.com (13.228.162.84)
Host is up (0.25s latency).
Not shown: 998 filtered ports
PORT    STATE SERVICE
80/tcp  open  http
443/tcp open  https

Nmap done: 1 IP address (1 host up) scanned in 13.92 seconds
ajaysinc@ajaysinclinux:~$ 
```

In case the target port is closed, the source receives an RST/ACK packet directly.

Summary

This chapter showed you the basics of firewalls and design considerations in firewall systems. You were introduced to different generations of firewalls and their functions, and you learned how to design a good firewall system. This can be something as simple as setting up a basic packet filtering firewall, to something as complex as using a stateful firewall with DMZs, ALG authenticated user connections, authenticating user connections, using different scanning techniques to probe host behind firewalls, and making use of many other features.

In the next chapter, we will discuss VPNs in a public internet infrastructure, as well as different attributes within an IPsec framework.

Questions

1. Which of the following are firewall types?
    1. Packet filtering firewall
    2. Application-layer gateway
    3. Screen Host Firewall
    4. All of the mentioned

2. An application proxy firewall filters at:
    1. Physical layer 1
    2. Data link layer 2
    3. Network layer 3
    4. Application layer 7
3. This 8-bit value identifies the maximum time the packet can remain in the system before it is dropped:
    1. Fragment
    2. Time to live
    3. Protocol
    4. Checksum

Further Reading

For more information, visit the following links:

- `https://www.juniper.net/documentation/en_US/learn-about/LA_FIrewallEvolution.pdf`
- `https://www.ietf.org/rfc/rfc1122.txt`
- `https://www.sans.org/reading-room/whitepapers/firewalls/intrusion-detection-response-leveraging-generation-firewall-technology-33053`

11
VPN and WAN Encryption

In the previous chapter, we discussed data protection and security techniques by looking at firewalls and firewall network design, as well as its placement. In this chapter, we will focus on protecting data before transmitting it over a public internet infrastructure or a network infrastructure shared by a service provider.

We are going to cover the following topics in this chapter:

- Overview
- Classes of VPN
- Type of VPN protocol
- VPN design
- IKE V1 versus IKE V2
- WAN encryption technique

Overview

Data is the new currency or oil. It can be found in your shopping pattern, emails, online banking, food ordering and in many places besides. Every year, we continue to encounter issues such as cyber threats, illegal surveillance (Wikileaks), and anti-privacy advocacy that targets these areas. In a connected world like the internet, security and privacy is a must when it comes to protecting data. As an end user, it's impossible to have an end-to-end visibility on public internet infrastructure that we use day to day. Fortunately, we have **virtual private networks** (**VPN**), a type of shield which forms a secure tunnel between two or more VPN supported devices. VPN helps to protect data traffic from snooping or man-in-the-middle attacks. However, to pick the best VPN service out there, we first need to understand the different VPN types and their use cases.

There are many use cases for VPNs. One very common reason why a VPN might be used for secure communication for mobile users or between branches and head offices is because it provides secure access for corporate IT resources:

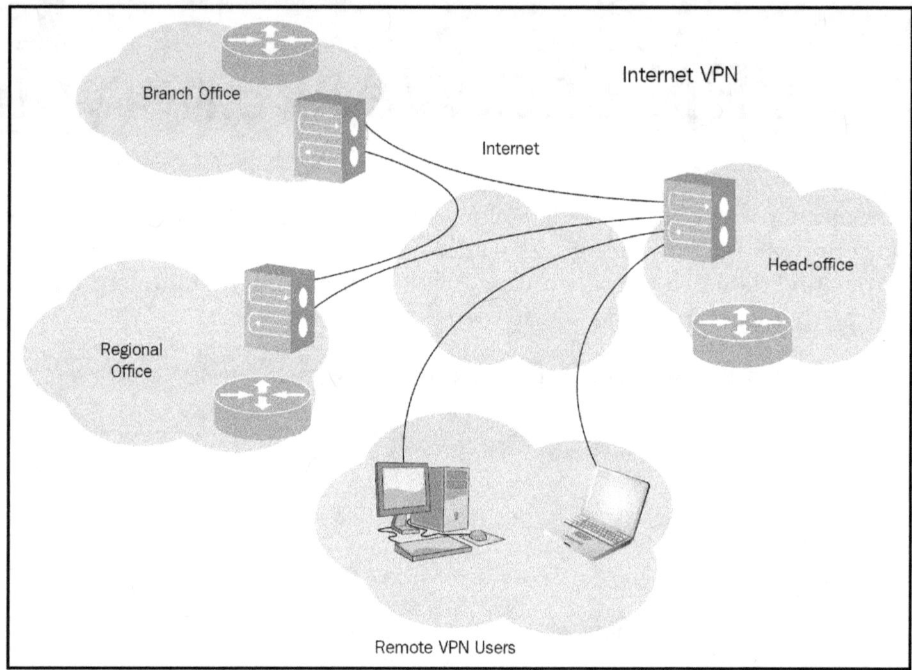

Your local ISP acts as a gateway for internet access and your activity can be tracked via this. In the same way as when you attempt to access any resources, the resource provider can also track your location based on your IP address. This is going to be another use case where you hide your identity by using third-party VPNs. In the following diagram, you can see that a user sitting in Manila can connect to a global resource, that might be blocked for the local ISP in Manila:

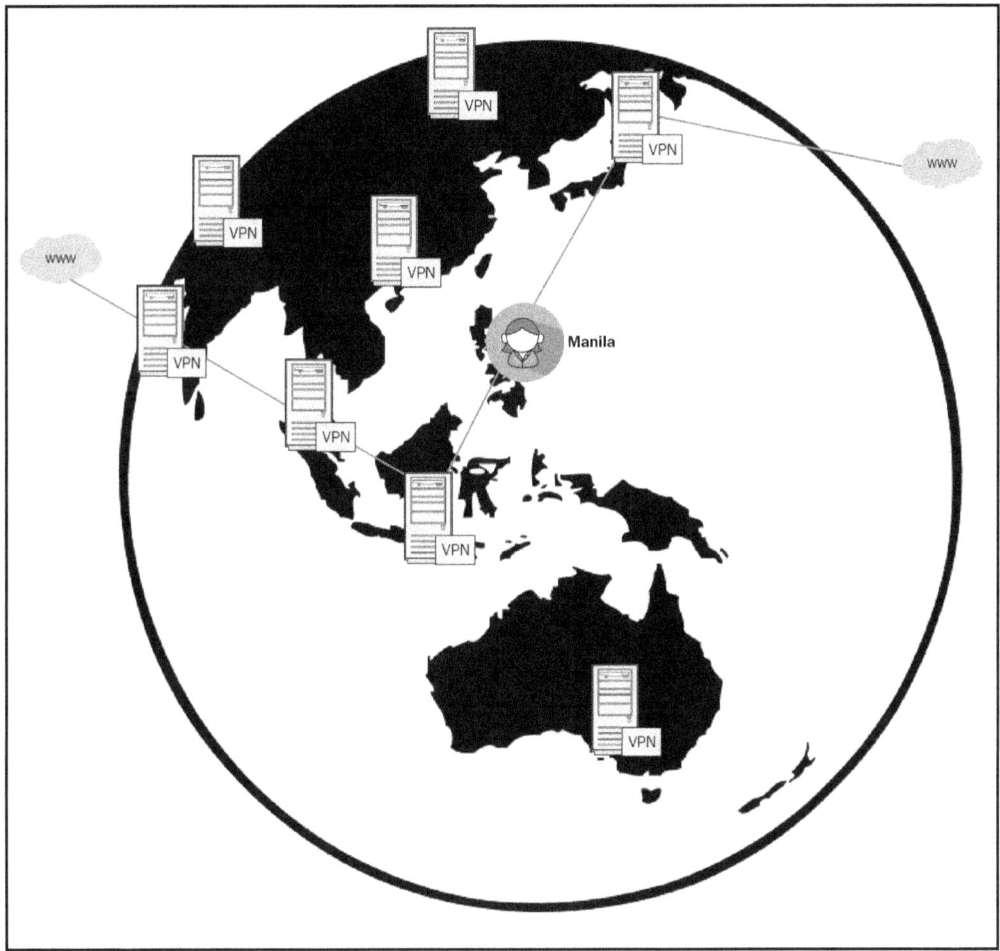

These VPNs are available either in app format or are inbuilt within the browser. Some organizations also provide full tunnel capabilities. Here, once you are connected to a corporate VPN, your exit point to the internet would be your organization's internet gateway.

Classes of VPN

VPN trusts a user to connect to private resources securely over public infrastructure networks that we don't trust. VPN creates an encrypted connection (known as a secure VPN tunnel) and all data traffic passes through this secure tunnel.

Let's consider several different VPNs and think about where they fit. We'll look at two main classes of VPN, which I will refer to as remote access VPNs and network-based site-to-site VPNs:

- **Remote access VPN**: This is a perfect solution for users who need to connect to a corporate network to gain access to IT resources remotely. For example, telecommuters, mobile users, and extranet users. The connection between the user and the corp network happens through the internet. VPNs might require users to install the VPN client firewall vendors' specific software, or they may be required to use a web-based client. The VPN client software forms a secure tunnel with the VPN server and encapsulates and encrypts the information before sending it over the internet to the VPN server. IPSec or tunnelling protocols can be used to establish a tunnel between endpoints on a network. VPN technology offers IPSec and SSL, two of the most famous and widely deployed methods to deploy remote VPNs.

A remote access VPN user must have an AAA profile to control access and authorization.

- **Site–to–Site VPN**: Site-to-site VPNs (often known as point-to-point VPNs) are mostly used in the corporate sector to provide IT resource access to branch offices and partners' offices in different geographic locations. When remote offices of the same organization are connected using site-to-site VPNs, it is known as an intranet based VPN. If the purpose was to provide connectivity to a partner's domain, then it would be known as an extranet VPN.

Type of VPN protocol

VPN types are distinguished by the various tunnelling protocols, such as PPTP, and L2TP with IPSec. Each of these VPN protocols offer different features and levels of security.

Point-to-Point tunneling protocol

PPTP remains a popular network protocol – especially on Windows computers - and it is one of the oldest protocols still in use. This has been developed by Microsoft to encapsulate another protocol called point-to-point. PPTP uses underlying authentication protocols such as MS-CHAP (**Challenge Handshake Authentication Protocol** (**CHAP**))—v1/v2, which are subject to serious security vulnerabilities. PPTP VPN encrypts data using 128-bit encryption, which makes it the fastest, but the weakest in terms of security.

Layer 2 Tunneling Protocol

L2TP is developed by combining characteristics of the **Layer 2 Forwarding Protocol** (**L2F**), designed by Cisco, with those of PPTP, designed by Microsoft. As L2TP does not offer confidentiality and encryption features on its own, another protocol called IPSec is used along with it to secure the connection. For end host clients, software installation is not required since almost all operating systems offer inbuilt VPN clients. 256 bit encryption is a mandatory addition to the L2TP VPN. L2TP is a CPU processor that is intensive due to double encapsulation. The first encapsulation takes place when the L2TP VPN functions and it is then topped off with the second IPSec encapsulation.

Let's look at Windows 10 inbuilt VPN options: You have the option to use L2TP with pre-shared keys and certificates:

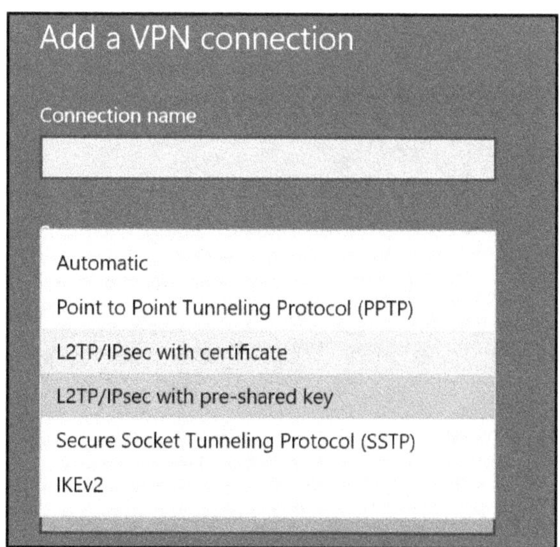

Secure Socket Tunneling protocol

Based on VPN, **Secure Socket Tunneling protocol** (**SSTP**) is best suited to VPN for highly confidential online activities, such as banking transactions, e-commerce transactions or business communications. SSTP VPN is Microsoft's SSL VPN, which worked on port `443`, and this port is likely not blocked by any ISP. SSTP comes with Integrated **Network Access Protection** (**NAP**) support for client health checks, including antivirus and firewall. Unlike other VPN protocols, SSTP establishes a single HTTPS channel from client to server, and also supports strong authentication smartcards, RSA secureID, and so on.

The NAP platform is not available from Windows 10 onwards.

Internet Protocol Security

Internet Protocol Security (**IPsec**) is a widely deployed open standard,multi-vendor supported framework design based on cryptography to achieve security and data protection for IPv4 and IPv6. IPsec does support symmetric and asymmetric cryptography to secure communications. The asymmetric cryptography always requires more CPU processing power and higher performance. This is because the implementation uses asymmetric cryptography to share a shared secret and it then performs symmetric encryption.

The main components of IPSec are mentioned below:

- **Authentication Header** (AH)
- **Encapsulating Security Payload** (ESP)
- **Internet Key Exchange Protocols** (IKE)

AH only provides message authentication. In other words, AH only lets the receiver verify that the message is intact and unaltered; it doesn't encrypt data. The following diagram shows the packet format before and after AH encapsulation:

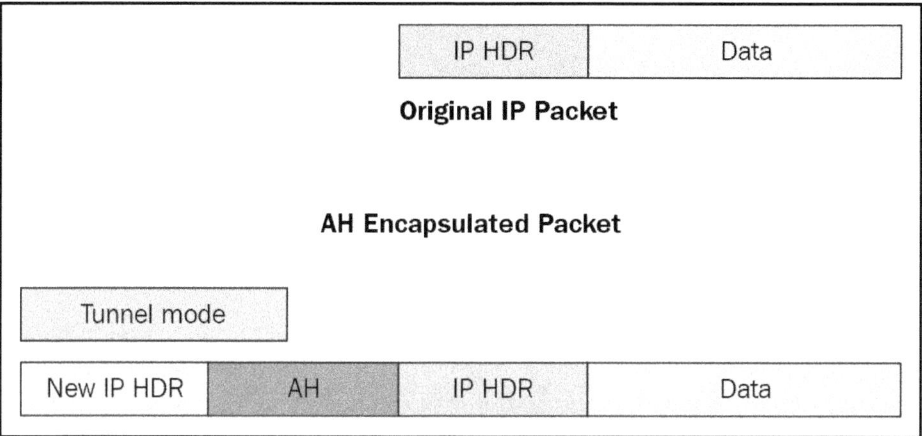

The basic difference is that ESP provides actual encryption. It encrypts the payload of the packet and protects it from snooping and replay. The following diagram shows the packet

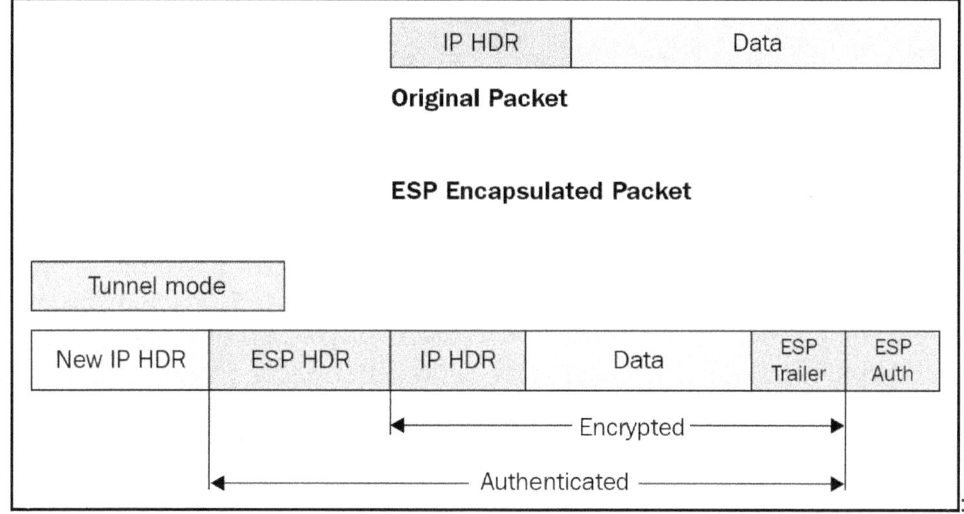

:

No current deployment of IPsec uses AH.

There are two phases for IPsec communication:

In the first phase (marked in blue), IKE establishes a secure channel. In the second phase (marked in green), encrypted data is transmitted.

There are two versions of IKE: IKE V1 and IKE V2. We will discuss the benefits of V2 in an upcoming section. For more details, you can refer to `https://tools.ietf.org/html/rfc6311`:

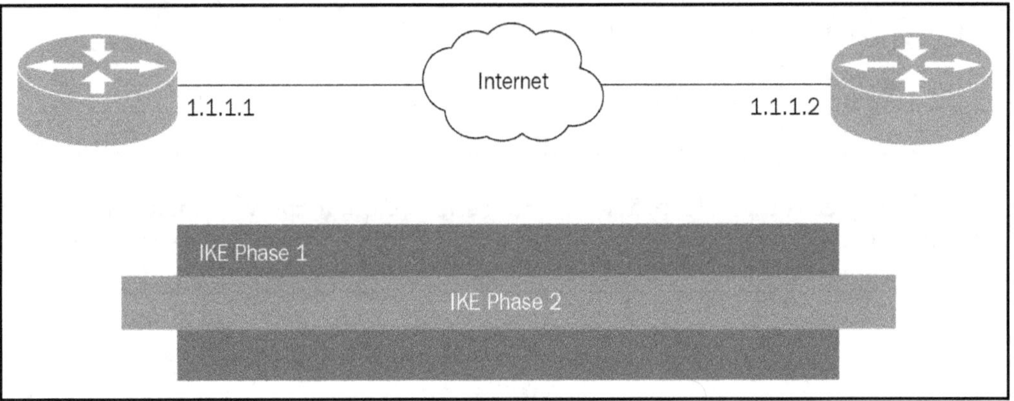

SSL VPN

For remote access roaming users, SSL VPN is the best solution. The SSL protocol provides confidentiality and authenticity over the public internet. SSL uses TCP `443`, which is a non-blocking port for any ISP. To connect VPN, users need to type SSL VPN FQDN in the browser, for example, `https://vpn.corp.com`. Upon successful authentication, users can communicate with corporate IT resources. SSL VPN doesn't require installation and configuration of client software at the user end.

Let's try to understand the security of SSL VPN. Having VPN does not mean that everything is good and that data transmission is safe. SSL VPN relies on SSL PKI cryptography. Using insecure or outdated weak encryption simply translates into putting corporate data at risk. Please refer to Chapter 9 for the latest SSL/TLS standard.

Please keep in mind that an SSL secure channel is always built between a host and gateway, not to the end resources.

MPLS VPN

MPLS VPNs are the best use case for multi-site global connectivity to Enterprise Networks. Enterprises connect to the same MPLS service provider with two or more sites to form a VPN. MPLS L3VPN is the most commonly deployed application over **multi-protocol label switched** (**MPLS**) networks. MPLS allows service providers to virtualize their network resources on the service provider Edge, so customers can share the physical network but still maintain logical isolation. Enterprise customers use service providers such as MPLS infrastructures to connect to multiple global sites. Alternatively, large enterprises may use MPLS internally for their own global infrastructures. The **Provider Edge** (**PE**) router terminates customers' circuit into a **virtual route forwarding** (**VRF**) instance that is unique to every customer, and then forwards it to a provider core router, using MPLS to tag the traffic and identify the VRF the traffic belongs to:

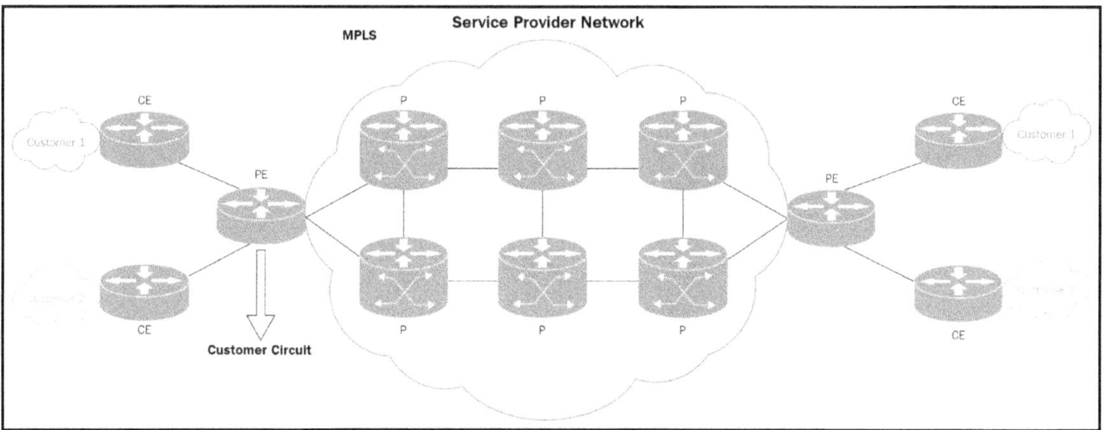

MPLS does not provide encryption by default.

For remote access VPNs, never choose PPTP unless you have no other option and are doing basic activities such as streaming Netflix, which doesn't require security or safety. Use L2TP/IPsec when you have to and keep in mind that SSTP is a good alternative for Windows devices that need stronger security. IKEv2 is the latest and greatest offering which is perfect because it won't drop a secure VPN connection when switching between a Wi-Fi network or cell connection. We will discuss the IKEv2 feature in our next section.

VPN Design

Let's discuss design considerations for site-to-site firewall termination points.

- **A Separate VPN Firewall**: You might have seen multiple scenarios for enterprise networks. Having a single firewall gives networks less flexibility and a single VPN termination point. However, most networks have at least a dual firewall layer from a security point of view. The first firewall is there to stop all unwanted data traffic and to control DMZ traffic, while the second firewall can be used to terminate a VPN connection, along with next generation firewall features such as URL filtering, and antivirus:

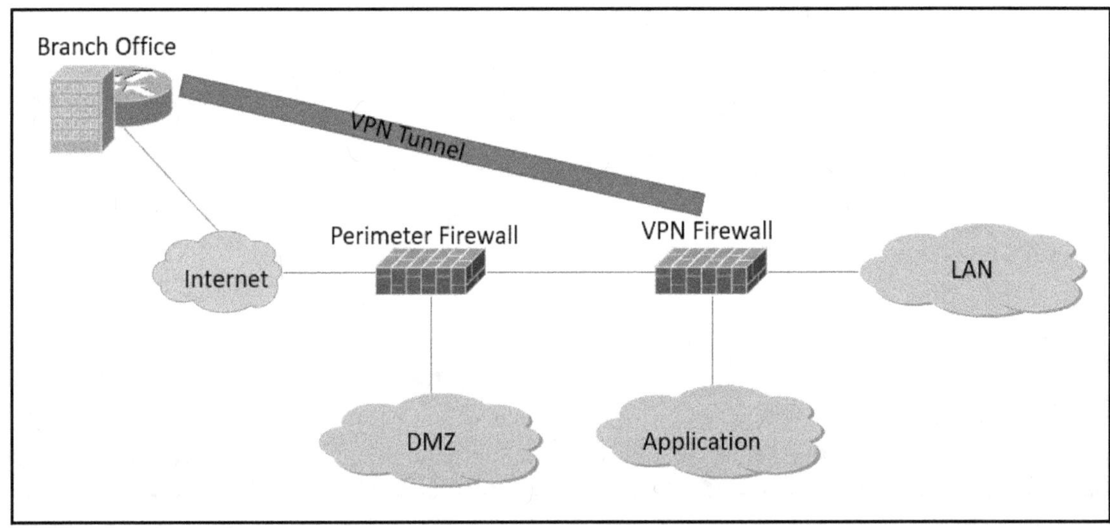

- **Remote Access VPN Tunnels—to split or not to split?**: Whenever an organization evaluates options to set up VPN for its remote workers and partners, one of the security considerations that arise is whether or not to support a split tunnel model. Let's explore the pros and cons of this. A full tunnel translates a secure connection when all your traffic goes through the VPN. A split tunnel means that only corporate traffic goes through the tunnel. For the rest of the traffic, a local internet connection would be used.

  The following diagram shows a split tunnel: Red traffic goes through a local internet gateway.

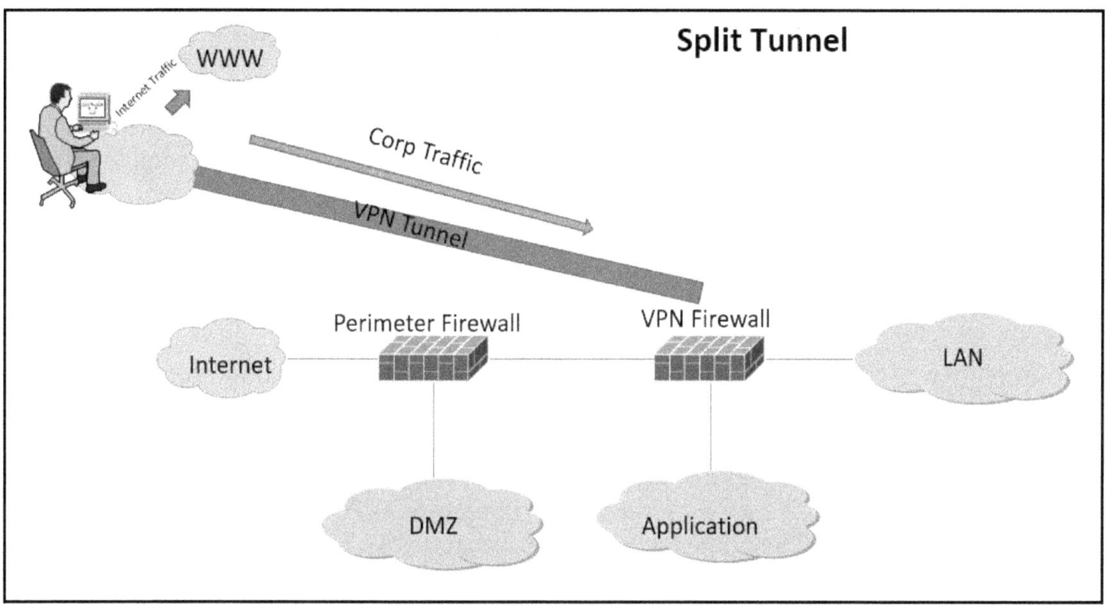

The following diagram shows a full tunnel: All traffic goes through the VPN.

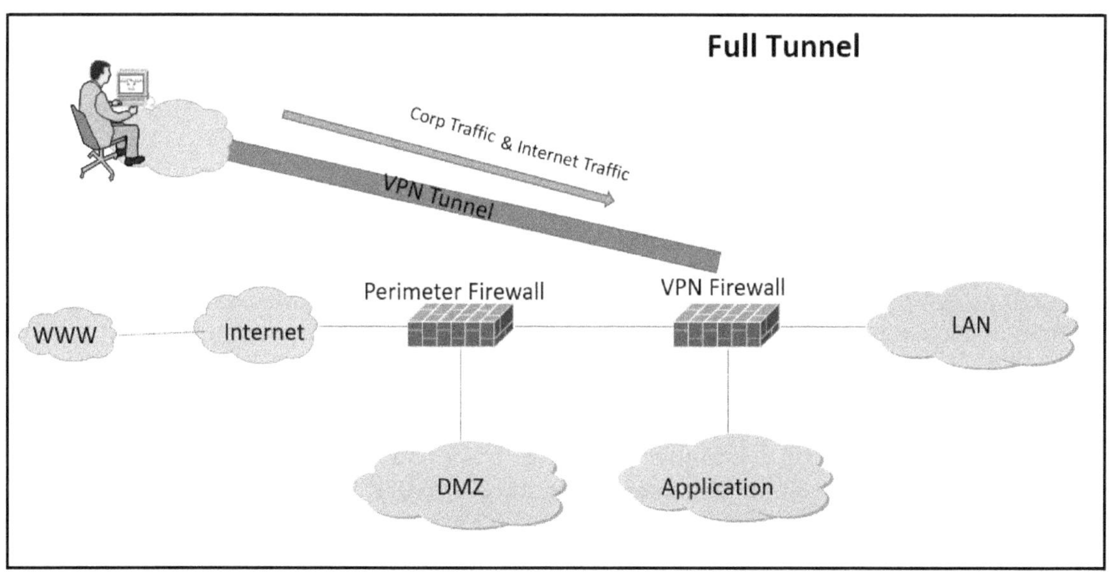

As we have seen, a split tunnel might make a faster internet connection via a local internet gateway, but direct connection bypasses all corporate control and security policies, such as URL filtering and malware protection. In a full tunnel, all traffic travels through a corporate gateway, providing great security. However, an extra hop to a network might cause slow network access. A full tunnel also helps you to hide your identity on the internet.

If your business has enough bandwidth to accommodate all remote users, then the network and security administrator must use a full tunnel. An organization with a large remote workforce can consume significant amounts of bandwidth.

A common practice followed by most network administrators is to choose pre-shared secrets for authentication, which is identical on both ends of the connection termination point. This would be done rather than setting up a **Certificate Authority** (**CA**) and issuing individual keys to each IPSec endpoint. Consequently, if one endpoint is compromised or physically stolen, the whole network becomes vulnerable. As IT staff keeps changing, the secrecy of that pre-shared key defeats the object over time. An SSL/TLS certificate based VPN works well, but that also brings device configuration overheads. However, if you still decide on using pre-shared keys then you should have a process in place for changing them after a certain amount of time, and you should use different pre-shared keys on different VPN connections. For approved and strong encryption, you must look at the **Federal Information Processing Standards** (**FIPS**), published by the National Institute of Standards and Technology.

IKE V1 versus IKE V2

In this section, we will go over what IKE is and what the differences are between IKEv1 and IKEv2.

IKE is a protocol that belongs to the IPsec protocols suite and is responsible for setting up a security association (an agreement between both parties) that enables two end IPsec enabled devices to send data securely:

- IKEv2 is faster and light on bandwidth, as a smaller number of messages are needed to establish a tunnel. With IKEv1, we had main mode (nine messages), and aggressive mode (six messages). In contrast, IKEv2 only has one mode that has only four messages.

- IKEv2 provides inbuilt NAT Traversal and, by default, IKEv1 does not provide this facility. It is a well-known fact that the IPSec protocol was not designed with **Network Address and Port Translation** (**NAPT**) in mind. The initial payload and, in particular, the headers are encrypted when using IPSec ESP mode. An intermediate NAT device cannot change these encrypted headers to its own address. During phase one negotiations, if NAT Traversal detection is on, one or both peers signify to each other that they are using NAT Traversal, then the IKE negotiations switch to using UDP port **4500**.
- IKEv2 has inbuilt tunnel liveness status checks. If a tunnel is broken down, it has the facilities to detect and re-establish the tunnel. However, IKEv1 does not have this functionality. There are several workarounds for IKEv1, but these are not standardized.
- IKEv1 supports authentication via pre-shared keys, digital signatures, and public key encryption. IKEv2 supports pre-shared keys, digital signatures and **Extensible Authentication Protocol** (**EAP**). IPSec peers in IKEv1 must use the same type of authentication - for example, both pre-shared keys or both digital signature. However, IKEv2 supports asymmetric authentication—one side can authenticate using pre-shared keys while the other side uses digital signatures.
- IKEv2 Mobility and Multihoming Protocol RFC 4555 (MOBIKE) supports a remote access VPN user in moving from one IP address to another without reestablishing all security associations with the VPN gateway. The ability to move between IP addresses without performing cryptographic calculations and without the overhead of reconnecting to the VPN gateway improves the user experience. IKEv1 does not support any mechanism to do this, whereas IKEv2 does.

WAN Encryption technique

In the internet and WAN connected environment of today, it is important to encrypt business-critical data in order to keep the data secure and reduce the risks of spying and snooping. Data breaches also include fiber tapping. With the continued increase of WAN bandwidth driven by video traffic, the online gaming industry and cloud services, we have seen the speed grow from 1 GB to 10 GB, to 40 GB, and now to 100 GB. With growing link speeds and a demand for bandwidth to continually increase, the traditional layer-3 encryption will not be enough to meet requirements.

The three most common methods for implementing encryption are as follows:

1. IPsec, or Layer-3 (L3) encryption
2. MACsec, or Layer-2 (L2) encryption
3. **Optical Network** (**OTN**) or Layer-1 (L1) encryption

IPsec Layer-3 encryption

We have already discussed IPsec in the previous section. Here, we will discuss how IPsec complements WAN technology. Layer-3 encryption is well-suited to environments where you have low-bandwidth connections and do not have the devices to support encryption at Layer-2 or Layer-1 levels. Organizations are running WAN technology in a different way, for example, with ATMs, Frame-Relay, Metro-Ethernet and MPLS-based solutions. The ultimate security question is: *Who do you trust with your business-critical data?* If your answer is the service provider, then you probably do not need to encrypt your data. However, if your answer is nobody, then you must transmit data to an encrypted service provider.

Let's look at the MPLS VPN provider, which is widely deployed in WAN technology. The primary benefit of this service provider is faster transport techniques with proper isolation between customers. The terminology includes VPN, but this does not mean that your data is being encrypted by default.

As the following diagram shows, two customers can use the same subnet and connect to the same router of services provided with proper isolation:

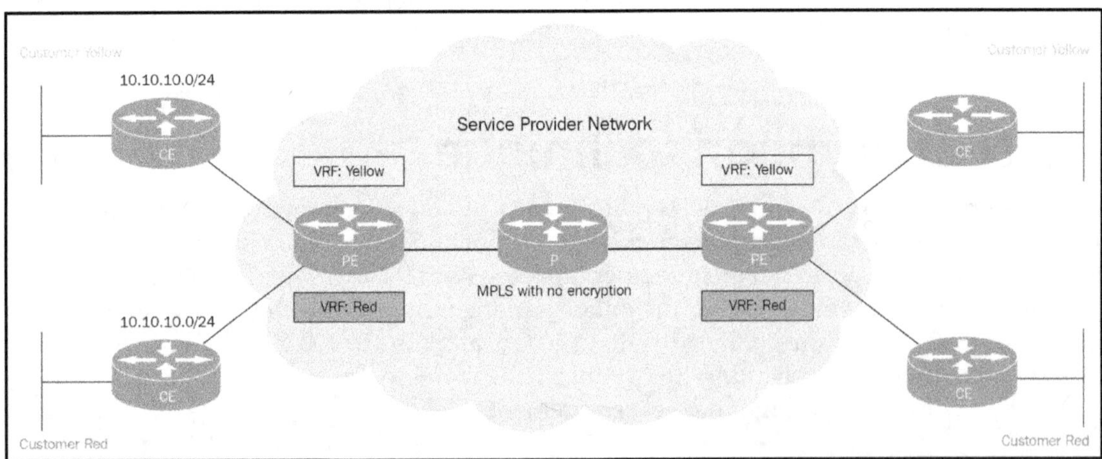

To secure data transmission over MPLS, you can take an IPsec approach from CE to CE for securing the VPN customer's traffic across an untrusted infrastructure. Introducing IPsec prevents the insertion of bogus CE into the VPN and the leakage of traffic from the secured VPN to a non-trusted VPN. This added a complexity and scalability issue for large-scale deployment.

The **Dynamic Multi-point VPN** (**DMVPN**) model works with the principle of the **Next Hop Resolution Protocol** (**NHRP**). Every IPsec node holds information about how to reach the next hop server, which returns the address of the target IPsec node to the originating node. This is a very scalable way to dynamically establish IPsec tunnels on demand. This is pretty much a scalable solution that is independent to underlying WAN infrastructures:

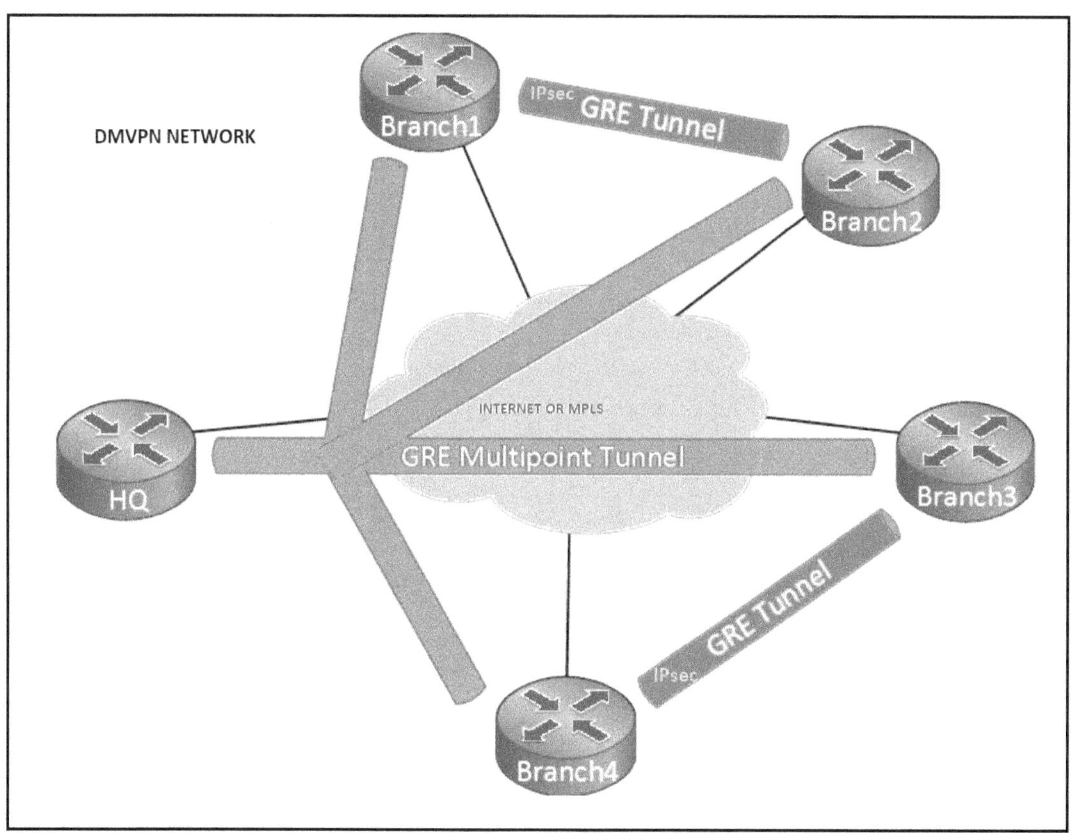

You must consider performance before leveraging IPSec for high-speed link encryption. The routers' throughput capabilities are restricted to the IPSec encryption engine limits, rather than using an encryption solution that can leverage the maximum aggregate throughput capabilities of the router. Using IPsec encryption adds 57 bytes of overhead to encapsulate the IP header of the original packet and to add an additional authentication header and trailer. Using IPsec along with GRE adds an extra overhead of 76 bytes. More overhead directly translates into less bandwidth throughput.

MACsec—Layer-2 Encryption

As the name implies, MACsec is a MAC layer or link layer encryption that offers a simplified, line-rate, per port encryption option for secure next-generation high bandwidth deployments. Organizations that comply with FIPS, HIPAA, and PCI DSS have to implement strong cryptography to protect sensitive data during transmission. MACsec provides great hop-by-hop deployment flexibility. Whenever you feel the public infrastructure is not safe, you can implement MACsec between transport nodes.

Use Cases: You can use MACsec encryption end-to-end using the following examples:

- Host-to-Switch
- Switch-to-Switch
- Router-to-Switch
- Router-to-Router Data center Interconnect

Let's look at the 802.1 AE (MACsec) format: The actual Ether-type + Payload is encrypted as follows:

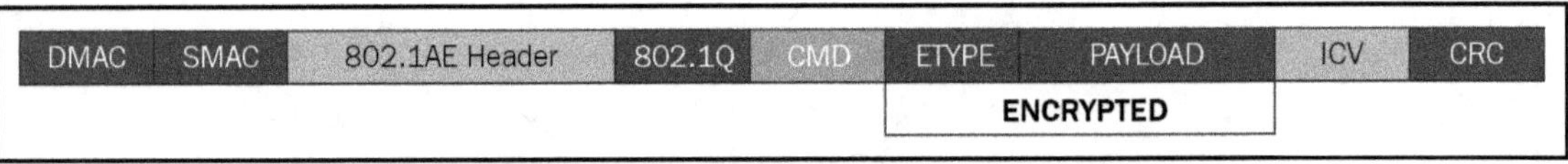

Now let's look at one Cisco example for data center interconnection using MACsec. Introducing Layer-2 devices between Layer-3 and any routing protocol can be run between Layer-3 devices. The DWDM WAN link would be encrypted; the main reason to encrypt this link is that it might be a shared infrastructure provided by a third party:

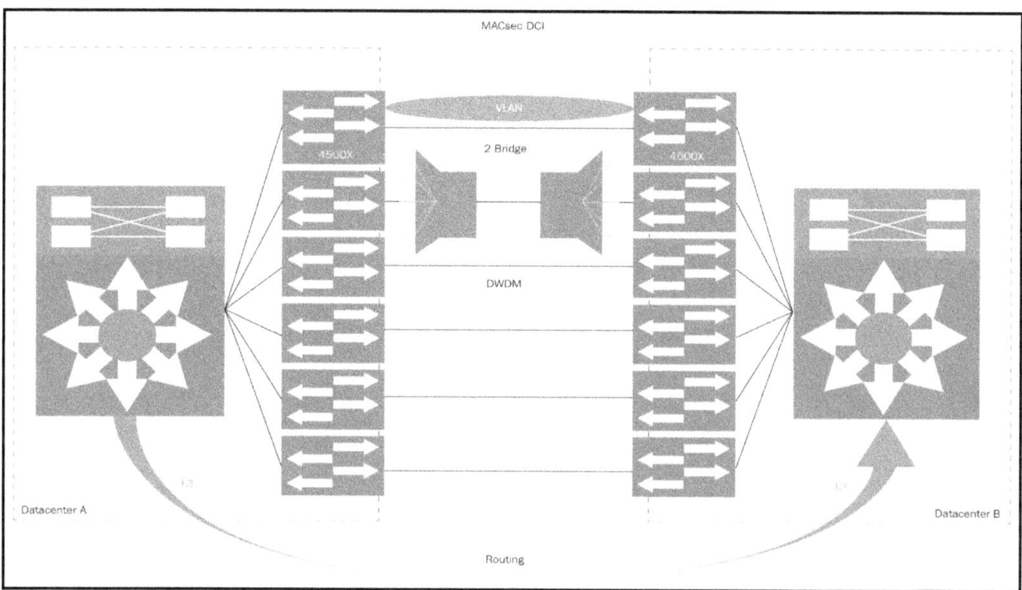

Optical Network—Layer-1 Encryption

There are multiple ways to access fiber. This includes:

- Tapping on street cabinet
- Fiber coupling devices
- Protocol analyzer and splice boxes.

A Layer-1 encryption solution supports applications such as secured data center connectivity for financial institutions, encrypted managed services for carriers, and secured networks for government institutions. Since it is done at the lowest layer possible in the OSI model, Layer 1 encryption technically provides the highest level of security. It also has fast speed and low latency, as well as 100% throughput with 0 bytes overhead:

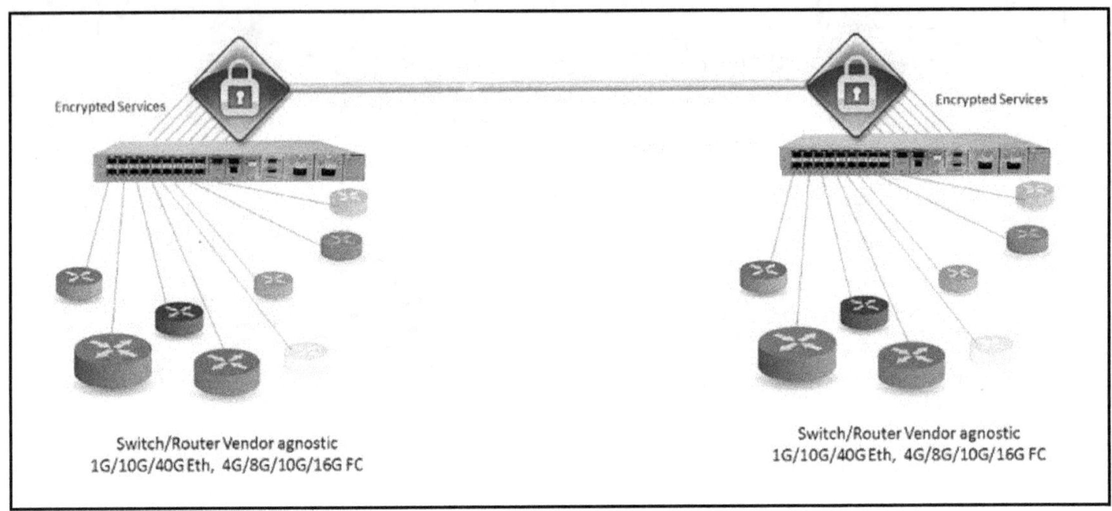

Summary

This chapter provides a very detailed overview of VPNs, with a focus on using IPSec as a VPN technology. It started by covering the various use cases for VPN and available options. It then covered the technicalities of different VPN protocols, such as PPTP, L2TP, SSTP, IPsec, and the components that make up IPSec.

The middle section of this chapter covered the design principle of corporate remote access VPNs by looking at full and split tunnel options and their benefits. The chapter finished by looking at WAN encryption techniques, from Enterprise to cloud services and financial organizations, in order to ensure security on different layers of the data communication model.

Now that you have a basic knowledge of all layers from network to application security, the next chapter will look at an overall approach to infrastructure security and future technology.

Questions

1. Which of the following may be used as a terminating point for a site-to-site VPN tunnel?
    1. Firewall
    2. Router
    3. Concentrator
    4. All of the above

2. Which of the following is not a Layer-2 tunneling protocol?
    1. PPTP
    2. IPsec
    3. L2TP
    4. .MPLS VPN

3. IKE creates SAs for:
    1. SSL
    2. PGP
    3. IPSec
    4. VP

4. IPSec defines two protocols: _______ and ________.
    1. AH; SSL
    2. PGP; ESP
    3. AH; ESP
    4. All of the above

5. ______ provides authentication at the IP level.
    1. AH
    2. ESP
    3. PGP
    4. SSL

Further Reading

For more information, visit the following links:

- https://tools.ietf.org/html/rfc2409
- https://tools.ietf.org/html/rfc5996
- https://tools.ietf.org/html/rfc3031
- https://www.sans.org/reading-room/whitepapers/vpns/

12
Summary and Scope of Security Technologies

In the previous chapter, we discussed the security aspect of WAN infrastructure as well as the ability of technologies such as IPSec and VPN design to build a secure network over a public internet infrastructure.

Almost 3 to 4 billion devices are currently connected to the internet and this number will be doubled with IOT devices. In this case, hackers won't be limited to one space. Instead, the area can be accommodated in almost every field from hospitals to traffic lights, as these will also be controlled and operated over some sort of WAN connectivity. The main question here is: What are the long-term implications for network security? One thing is for sure, it will be different from today. We will also talk about how Artificial Intelligence will help in cyber security space.

We are going to cover the following topics in this chapter:

- DDoS protection
- BGP FlowSpec
- AI in cyber security
- Next Gen SIEM
- SDN Firewall
- Bring-Your-Own-Identity (BYOI)

DDoS protection

DDoS, short for **distributed denial of service**, is a form of attack in which multiple compromised networks/hosts are used to target a single system. Organizations need to seriously consider the fact that even if they have sufficient protection against DDoS attacks, their business could be taken out of service or offline if their **Internet Service Provider** (**ISP**), hosting provider or **Domain Name Service** (**DNS**) provider does not have sufficient DDoS protection. In this section, we are going to discuss the old ISP mechanism and we will also focus on discussing the new automated mechanism.

Remotely triggered black hole routing (RTBH)

Do you recall days when network admins used to call internet service providers to mitigate DDoS attacks? **Remotely-Triggered Black Hole** (**RTBH**) routing is an interesting application of **Border Gateway Protocol** (**BGP**) as a security tool within service provider networks. One common use for RTBH is mitigation of DDoS attacks. RTBH provides two methods:

- Source-based
- Destination-based

The basic approach is to either drop all traffic from the source or to drop all traffic to the destination. This could be both wanted and unwanted traffic. At this point, we do understand that RTBH routing is a technique that can be used to protect from DDoS attacks. Let's discuss how it works to protect your network.

The following diagram shows an ISP with several provider edge routers and a customer network connected to the edge router for public internet access.

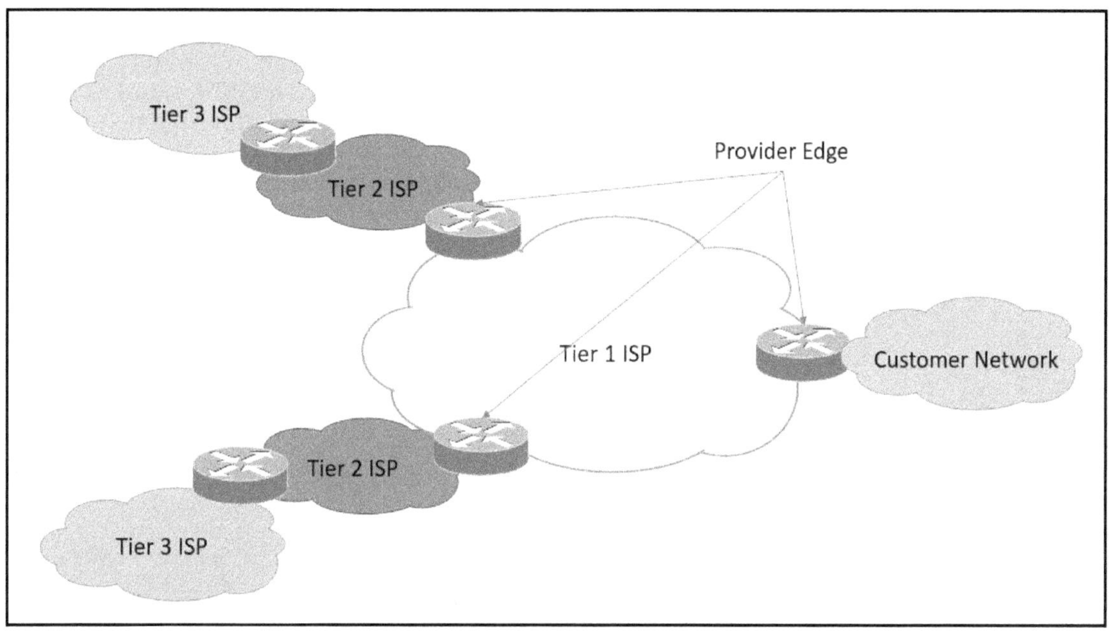

Keep in mind that RTBH routing works with BGP.

Let's assume that a DDoS attack is launched against a customer's application, such as a web server. In case an ISP does not have any protection to stop and this continues, this attack will cause a customer's application to become out of service as well as impacting other customers with degraded services. When I refer to a degraded service, this will depend on what kind of DDoS attack was launched that might congest the ISP links. The ISP router may not be able to process a number of packets during an attack.

In this diagram, you can see a customer network connected to Tier-1 ISP and Tier-1 ISP further connected to Tier-2 ISP. Once the attacker launches an attack, it can originate from anywhere on the internet in the direction of the customer network. The PC symbol marked in red represents the attacker's machines or comprised machines on the internet that belong to the **Botnet Army**.

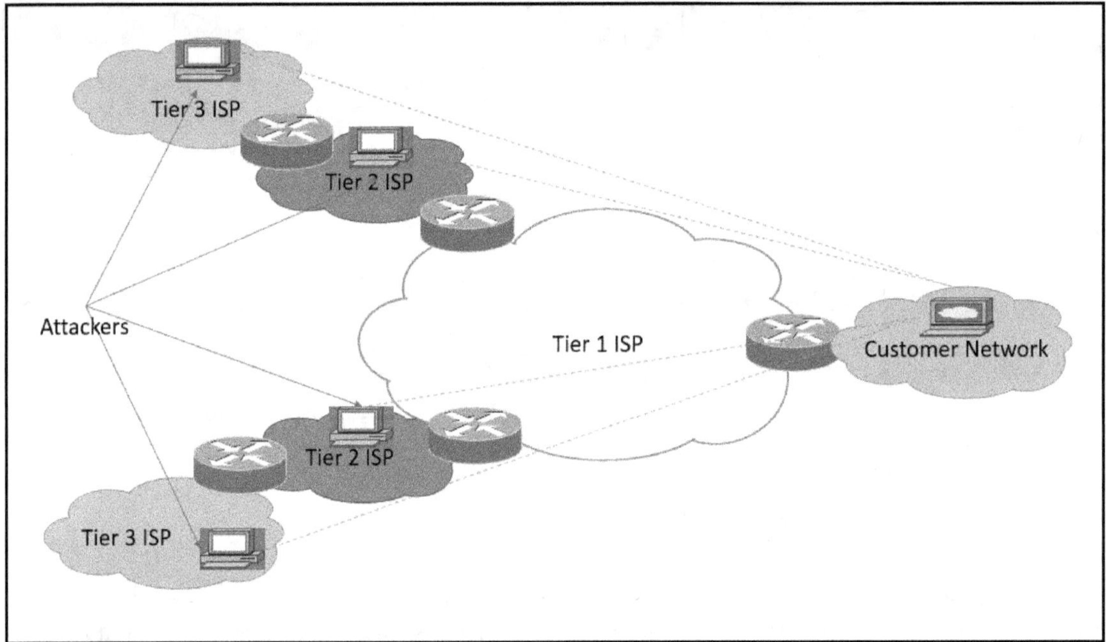

What can the ISP do during an attack?

- Black hole traffic from the source of the attack
- Black hole traffic to the destination of the attack

The big question is: which method of ISP should you opt for? Let's discuss both options in detail.

Black hole traffic from the source of the attack

A source-based method is the preferred method by ISP. This would drop all traffic coming from the attackers to the customer's web server while allowing other legitimate traffic to go through. This can be a pretty nice solution if the source IP address is fixed, but the problem comes when today's sophisticated attack comes with constantly changing origins.

Black hole traffic to the destination of the attack

Using a destination-based approach will drop all traffic (including legitimate traffic) to the customer's web server. This simply translates to helping attackers to achieve their goals to make customer services unavailable. The only good part of this method is that it won't impact other ISP customers or cause any kind of service degradation.

BGP FlowSpec

BGP FlowSpec is a new method defined in RFC 5575 that can be used to prevent DDoS attacks in an automated fashion by leveraging BGP. The BGP **flow specification** (**FlowSpec**) feature allows you to automatically propagate the filtering and policing functionality to service a provider's upstream BGP peer routers. This will mitigate the effects of a DDoS attack on your network. Most vendors still have this implementation in their roadmaps. For support, please check with ISP before implementing this solution.

BGP FlowSpec uses a more granular approach and provides you with the flexibility to effectively construct instructions to match a particular data flow with source, destination, L4 parameters, and packet specifics, such as length, and fragment. In this example, the customer router (which is the FlowSpec router) advertises these flows to the ISP edge routers. These edge routers then install the flows in the hardware. Once the flow is installed in the hardware, the transit routers are able to do a lookup to see if incoming traffic matches the defined flows and take appropriate action.

In the following diagram, a customer advertises the `1.1.1.1/32` host network with special community `100:100` to the service provider. Once this community is matched at the service provider end, all the traffic destined for the customer network will be dropped by all edge routers within service provider 1.

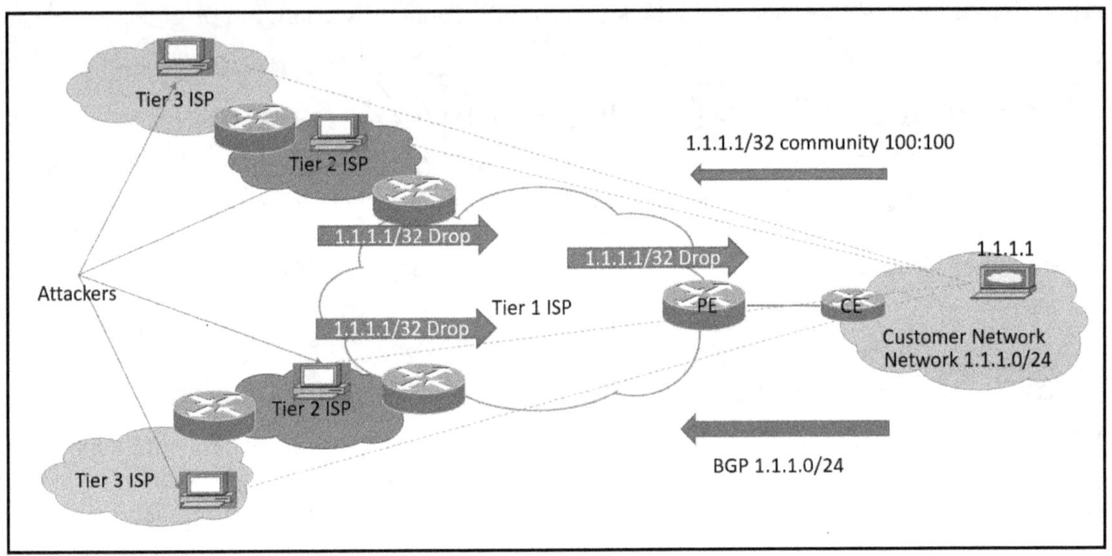

These are the specifications for BGP FlowSpec and the list of actions that can be taken.

BGP FlowSpec can include the following information:

- Type 1–Destination Prefix
- Type 2–Source Prefix
- Type 3–IP Protocol
- Type 4–Source or Destination Port
- Type 5–Destination Port
- Type 6–Source Port
- Type 7–ICMP Type
- Type 8–ICMP Code
- Type 9–TCP flags
- Type 10–Packet length
- Type 11–DSCP
- Type 12–Fragment Encoding

Actions are defined using BGP Extended Communities:

- Traffic-Rate (drop/police)
- Next-hop Redirect
- VRF Redirect
- DHCP Marking

Please check hardware specifications and support before configuring BGP FlowSpec.

DDoS scrubbing

Organizations have only two options for handling DDoS attacks: **black-holing** or **scrubbing.** As we have already discussed, black-holing does not scale well and could shut down the designated target to protect everyone else. The other solution is scrubbing, which uses separate DDoS cleaning engines. The tricky part is the BGP announcement, which diverts all network layer packets from the targeted IP address to your mitigation provider's scrubbing servers. The malicious packets are filtered out and clean traffic or non-DDoS is forwarded to actual services.

Cloud service providers, or internet service providers, often provision these scrubbers to a local data center. Industry has seen that DDoS attacks have scaled to > 1 Tbps traffic and having that much network capacity is a major task. Deploying that amount of bandwidth for DDoS mitigation is expensive and complicated to manage. Scrubbers are dumb pieces of equipment that have to be configured by experts. This means that you also have to build competency at all levels for all protocols. Scrubbing centers operate in an offline mode and are only activated when DDoS occurs. This simply means that an internet application will succumb to DDoS before traffic is redirected to a scrubbing center.

Blockchain Technology for Fighting DDoS Attacks

An increase in DDoS attacks has led to discovering newer and better ways to protect our systems. The basic idea is to create a system that would allow people to rent out their unused bandwidth, so that it can be used to absorb malicious DDoS traffic and mitigate attacks. ISP charges the customer a minimum amount and the customer loses this money by not utilizing the bandwidth.

For more information on this project visit `https://gladius.io/`.

AI in cyber security

In the future, AI could be a cyber security game-changer. Cyber security vendors are innovating to bring AI-based cyber security products to market in a big way. The deployment of such technology will gain momentum in the coming years. **Machine learning** (**ML**) is a sub-branch of **artificial intelligence** (**AI**) that refers to technologies that enable computers to learn and adapt through experience. ML can be used to identify malicious behavior or malicious entities, hackers, attackers, malware, unwanted behavior, and so on. The biggest challenge would be to define what normal behavior is for an application.

For example, you can see when the maximum number of users are online on an online shopping company, as well as being able to view the number of connections with a data pattern. When it comes to a big sale, the number of users is expected to be high, so you could add another pattern to accommodate this. By using ML, you can record the pattern of users and data traffic on that portal. Anything that is not expected, such as a connection surge in the night, can be treated as an attack. Another example would be if you have a network printer installed on your network. What would the expected behavior be here? It will print the document correctly but what if your network printer starts sending documents outside of the network to someone else?

So the basic point is to deploy a solution that scans everything on your network. This includes the employee logon host, printer, web services, network devices and firewall. You should also learn the behavioral pattern to identify what is normal and what is abnormal. Tools such as Datatrace and Splunk are good examples of network behavioral analytics.

AI can solve the following problems in cyber security space:

- Malicious external and internal threats
- DDoS and large-scale attacks
- Data loss
- User behavioral analytics

Next Gen SIEM

Security operation centers always struggle with alert floods coming from the legacy SIEM systems and false positives continue to haunt the network with data breaches. With the evolution of the computer landscape, cyber security has also changed. Let's talk about the days when employees used office desktops to access corporate applications. Things were rapidly replaced with laptops and smart devices, which has secure access to corporate applications from anywhere in the world. Traditional methods for detecting and responding to security threats are no longer effective when it comes to addressing today's security challenges. Today, organizations need a SIEM solution that can scale to support large data volumes coming from various IT resources, as well as analyzing data at a faster speed in order to detect security threats in real time. At the same time, it should fit into the organization's budget.

In this section, we will discuss the key capabilities that a next generation SIEM platform should have.

- **Big-Data Storage Capabilities**: Network-connected devices' methods for data amount growth is expanding. It's not all about simply collecting huge amounts of data; it also has to be maintained for threat analysis and forensic and regulatory compliance. You must have the capability to store data in a different way, and that different way comes in the form of a big data model. Big data can consume and analyze terabytes of data in real time. Query-based data can be further used for analysis and reporting.

The following diagram shows a **SIEM MODEL** that has the capabilities discussed previously in this section:

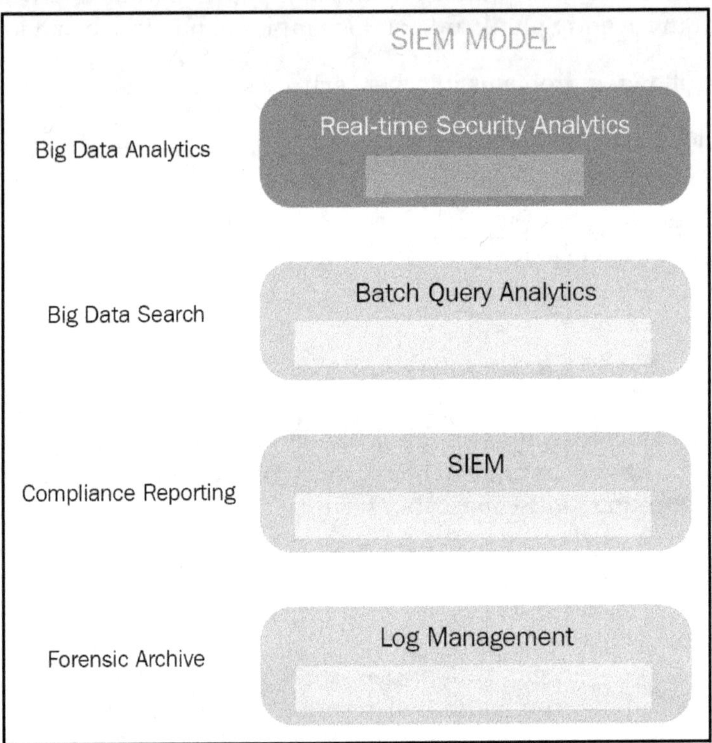

- **Real-Time Analytics**: Cyber threats and cyber attacks have become highly sophisticated. With an increasing number of surface attacks, attackers are now targeting organizations with ease. Legacy SIEM solutions are rule-based and dependent to know threat patterns. A next generation SIEM should be sufficiently capable of detecting threats in real time for any dynamic environment. This is done by using ML and behavior analytics in order to find highly advanced threats in today's environment.

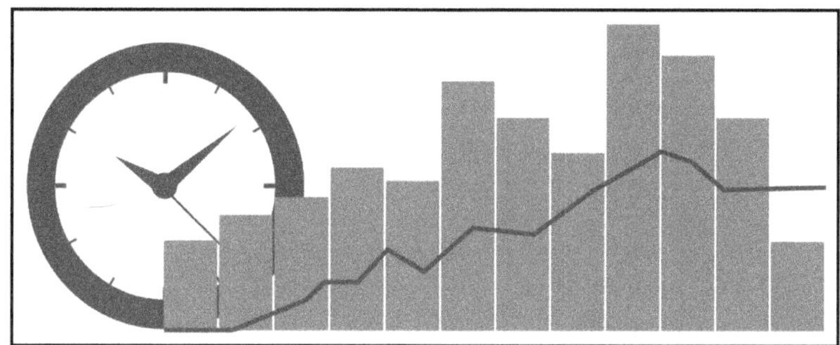

- **Accuracy**: Threat intelligence can help you to stay one step ahead of cyber threats by providing you with a rich, external context. Without the proper context, a security alert may likely get lost during an alert flood or may be confused with a **security operations center** (**SOC**) analyst. As SOC professionals, how might we react to such alerts? Next generation SIEM should send alerts with a meaningful context. A meaningful context can include an IP address, location, vulnerability type, action required, and, of course, alert priority or severity.
- **Automated Incident Response**: Detecting cyber security threats is just one part of SIEM, but responding to threats faster is considered the most critical part of SIEM. Every alert generated by SIEM always has a recommended action associated with it. Next generation SIEM should follow best practice by having APIs interact with network and system vendor devices such as firewalls, routers, switches, and endpoint protection devices.The basic idea of this is to take an appropriate, well-defined and automated set of actions once an incident is detected.
- **Easy Deployment**: For any business and IT process, the deployment of SIEM systems begins with thoroughly planning and reviewing impact and policies. You should also review your security policies and the best practices available in the industry. The deployment model should correspond to the overall IT strategy of organization. The SIEM solution should offer virtual, cloud-based and hardware- based appliances to the customer.
- **Low Cost**: Security analytics work well with large amounts of data. With a growing number of devices, a large volume of logging data and storage might escalate the cost of the solution. A pricing model should not be based on the volume of data that is collected because this may cause unpredictability in the costing model. Next Generation SIEM costing can be based on the number of users and devices, which is a predictable number. The use of commodity hardware may reduce this cost further.

Software Defined Networking Firewall

Over the past few years, continuous innovation and the need to adapt to the constraints of conventional networking has made **software defined networking** (**SDN**) pretty popular. Let's discuss what is so special about SDN that legacy technology is not able to deliver.

The current design of network infrastructure does not support dynamic scalability, central control and management, end-to-end visibility and dynamic traffic load distribution. It is an approach that physically separates the network's control plane from the data plane. This allows network administrators to program directly without having to worry about the commodity hardware specifications.

The following diagram shows SDN architecture. The SDN architecture can be divided into three layers: **Application Layer**, **Control Plane**, and **Forwarding Plane**.

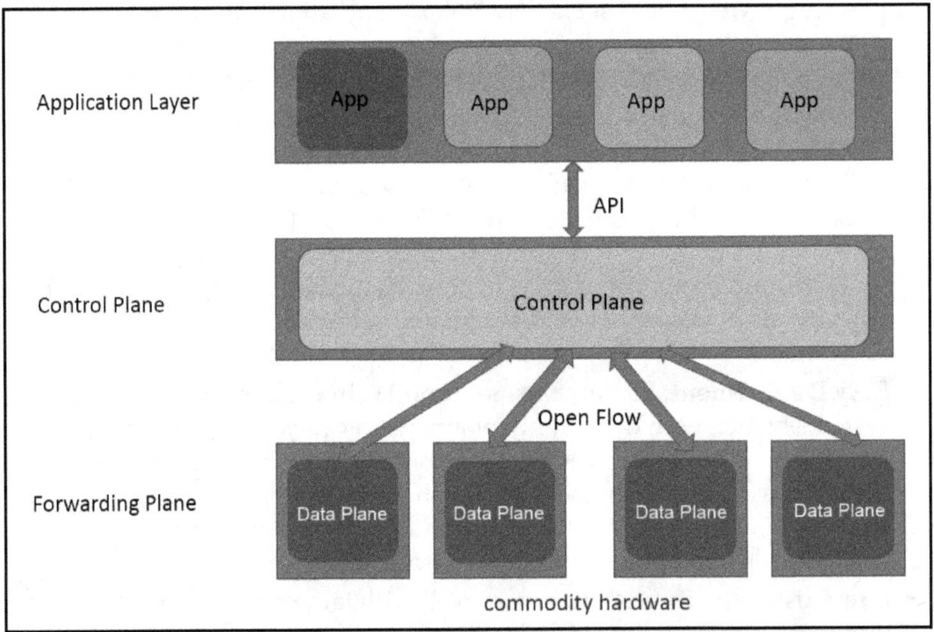

In this section, we will discuss how we can use SDN functionality for firewalls. A firewall is a device that filters incoming and outgoing traffic in the network that has passed through network devices based on firewall rules. A traditional firewall is placed between a public and private network. The rule configuration is defined by the network administrator and, with every new rule, firewalls have to be configured. Hardware firewalls are expensive and vendor locked-in, which means that only vendors can modify the behavior of the firewall. As discussed, software defined networking is a new approach to networking. SDN offers the flexibility to convert commodity-based OpenFlow supported hardware into firewalls, which is software managed.

Control Plane is used for management tasks and has a global view of network topology. All decisions regarding forwarding the packets are made by the Control Plane. The controller uses an OpenFlow protocol to communicate with commodity switches and it also has the capability to change the flow of entries directly into a TCAM table of switches. Similar to the firewall rule, the flow entry is used for matching purposes and has actions associated with the flow.

A typical flow table looks like the following diagram. Header fields are fields that should be matched to IP packets and the actions would be defined by the administrator.

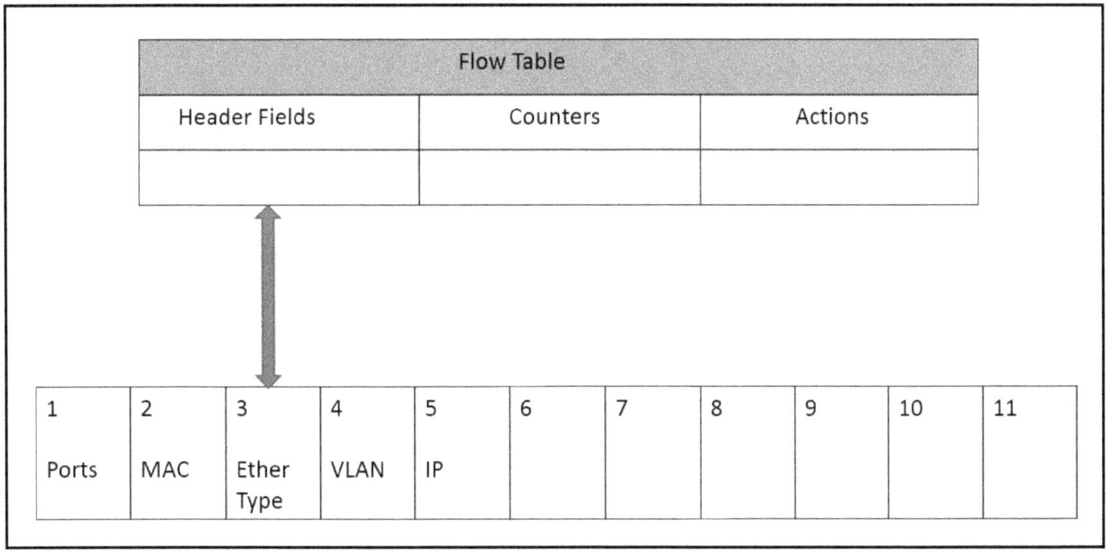

Overall, this approach creates a distributed firewall architecture and rules are pushed across all the devices or specified groups of device. In this diagram, you can see three layers: **Firewall Application**, **Control Plane**, and **Forwarding Plane**.

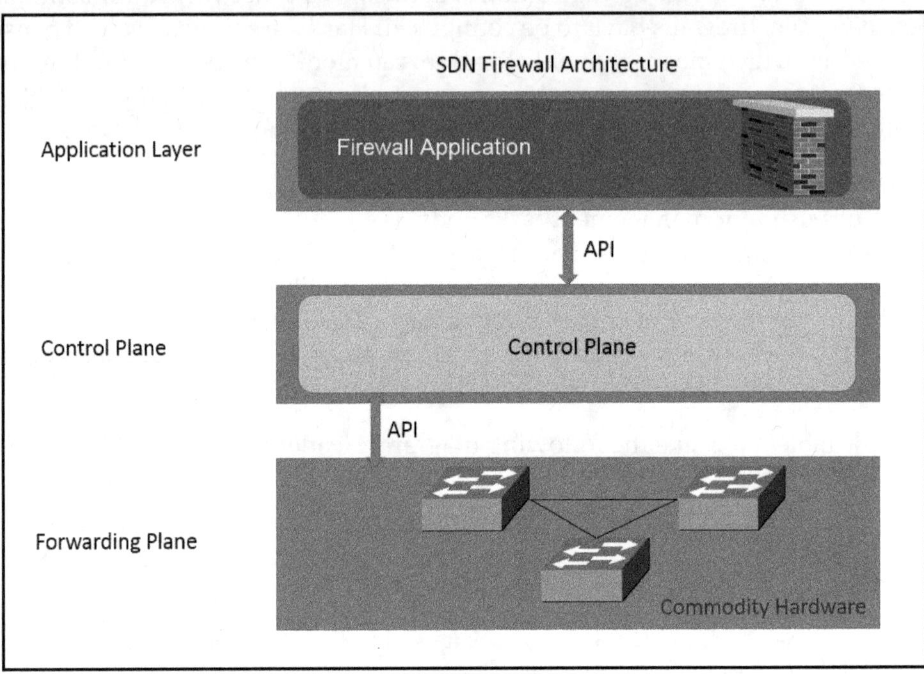

The following table demonstrates a firewall flow and rule:

RULE NO	SRC MAC	DST MAC	SRC IP	DST IP	PROTOCOL	DST PORT	ACTION
1	00:00:00:00:00:01	00:00:00:00:00:02	---	---	---	---	Drop

Bring-Your-Own-Identity (BYOI)

Bring-Your-Own-Identity (**BYOI**) is an authentication mechanism that offers a better user experience and is more secure than having multiple passwords for multiple services. BYOI simply refers to integrating with social networking sites (for example, Facebook, Google, and Yahoo). In practice, an example of BYOI is demonstrated by having an option to sign up to a website using Facebook, as demonstrated in the following screenshot:

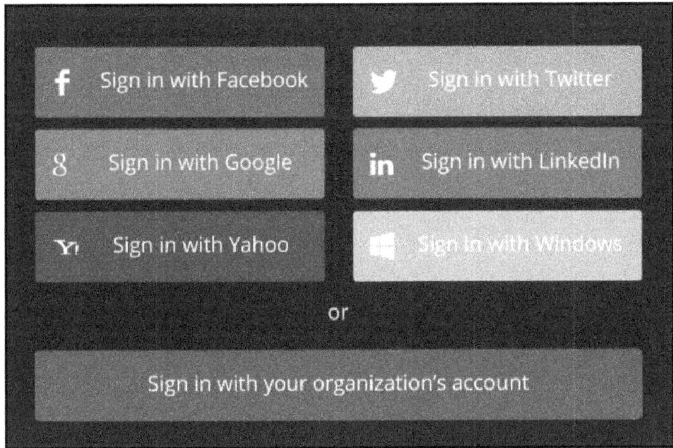

You are probably familiar with users in a typical organization complaining about having to use different passwords, applications and authentication methods. Wouldn't it be nice to have one unified solution and the same identity for all your Cloud, SaaS, Web Apps, or on-premises applications? Citrix work space experience is a cool solution that provides a better user experience.

Many websites attract more users just because they do not have to manage separate passwords, which is a headache for most of us, especially along with tackling security issues. This increases security by enabling users to use two-factor authentication with a single trusted provider. Single identity providers bring some privacy concerns, which makes it possible to track and profile user activity over multiple services.

Summary

In this chapter, we discussed how the security landscape is changing, keeping in mind that cyber attacks have evolved from worms and viruses to sophisticated attacks in cyberspace. It is high time that we shift our focus from protection to prevention. It has been proven by recent data breaches that the old legacy system is not enough to protect assets from advanced security threats. In this chapter, we discussed old methods and new, enhanced methods to combat DDoS protection by using BGP Flowspec.

Furthermore, we learned how DDoS scrubbing works and how Blackchain technology is going to change the security landscape. We also discussed the need for Artificial Intelligence in cyber space, and how this would help to build an intelligent next generation SIEM solution. Finally, we discussed the concept of a firewall built on top of software defined networking, as well as Bring-Your-Own-Identity, a new approach that introduces better security and a better user experience.

Further reading

For more information, please refer to the following links:

- `https://www.nanog.org/sites/default/files/tuesday_general_ddos_ryburn_63.16.pdf`
- `https://conference.apnic.net/data/37/apricot-2014-wei-yin-scalable-ddos-mitigation-using-bgp-flowspec_1393312254.pdf`
- `https://tools.ietf.org/html/rfc5575`
- `https://www.opennetworking.org/sdn-definition/`
- `https://www.sdxcentral.com`

Assessment

Chapter 1

1. Answer: 5
2. Answer: 1,2,3
3. Answer: 4
4. Answer: 3
5. Answer: 1

Chapter 2

1. Answer: 2, 4, 6
2. Answer: 2 and 3
3. Answer : 1
4. Answer: 2

Chapter 3

1. Answer: 4
2. Answer: 4
3. Answer: 2
4. Answer: 2
5. Answer: 4

Chapter 4

1. Answer: 3
2. Answer: 1
3. Answer: 1
4. Answer: 2 and 3
5. Answer: 3 and 4

Chapter 5

1. Answer: 4
2. Answer: 1
3. Answer: 1
4. Answer: 3
5. Answer: 4

Chapter 6

1. Answer: 4
2. Answer: 2
3. Answer: 3
4. Answer: 4
5. Answer: 3

Chapter 7

1. Answer: 3
2. Answer: 2 and 4
3. Answer: 4
4. Answer: 4
5. Answer: 4

Chapter 8

1. Answer: 2
2. Answer: 4
3. Answer: 1

Chapter 9

1. Answer: 2
2. Answer: 4
3. Answer: 3
4. Answer :2 and 4

Chapter 10

1. Answer: 1 and 2
2. Answer: 4
3. Answer: 2

Chapter 11

1. Answer: 4
2. Answer: 3
3. Answer: 3
4. Answer: 3
5. Answer: 1

Other Books you may enjoy

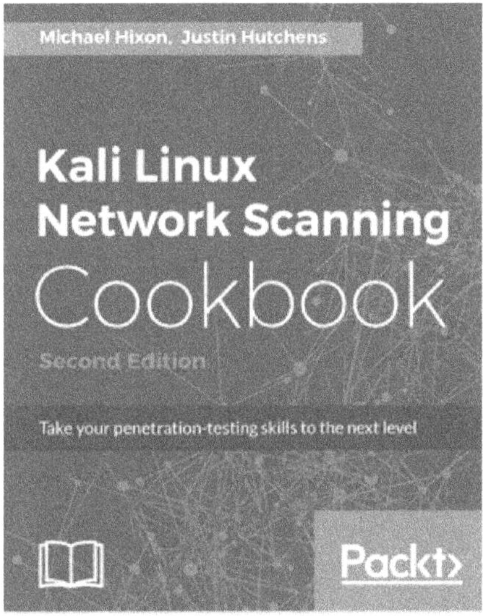

Kali Linux Network Scanning Cookbook - Second Edition

Michael Nixon, Justin Hutchens

ISBN: 978-1-78728-790-7

- Develop a network-testing environment to test scanning tools and techniques
- Understand the principles of network-scanning tools by building scripts and tools
- Identify distinct vulnerabilities in web apps and remote services and learn how they are exploited
- Perform comprehensive scans to identify listening on TCP and UDP sockets
- Get started with different Kali desktop environments--KDE, MATE, LXDE, and Xfce
- Use Sparta for information gathering, port scanning, fingerprinting, vulnerability scanning, and more
- Evaluate DoS threats and learn how common DoS attacks are performed
- Learn how to use Burp Suite to evaluate web applications

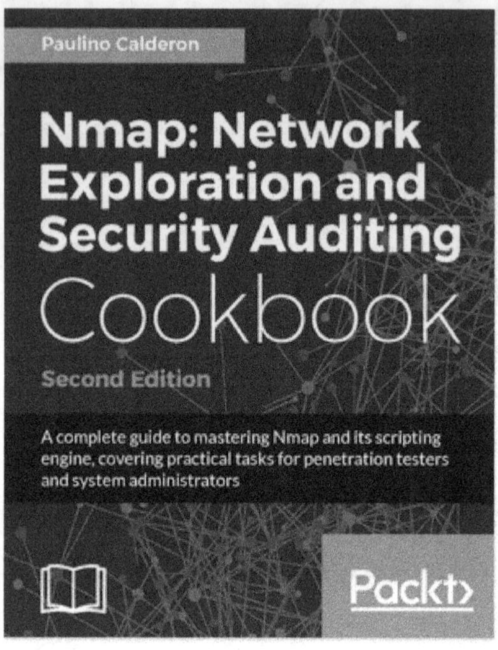

Nmap: Network Exploration and Security Auditing Cookbook - Second Edition
Paulino Calderon

ISBN: 978-1-78646-745-4

- Learn about Nmap and related tools, such as Ncat, Ncrack, Ndiff, Zenmap and the Nmap Scripting Engine
- Master basic and advanced techniques to perform port scanning and host discovery
- Detect insecure configurations and vulnerabilities in web servers, databases, and mail servers
- Learn how to detect insecure Microsoft Windows workstations and scan networks using the Active Directory technology
- Learn how to safely identify and scan critical ICS/SCADA systems
- Learn how to optimize the performance and behavior of your scans
- Learn about advanced reporting
- Learn the fundamentals of Lua programming
- Become familiar with the development libraries shipped with the NSE
- Write your own Nmap Scripting Engine scripts

Leave a review - let other readers know what you think

Please share your thoughts on this book with others by leaving a review on the site that you bought it from. If you purchased the book from Amazon, please leave us an honest review on this book's Amazon page. This is vital so that other potential readers can see and use your unbiased opinion to make purchasing decisions, we can understand what our customers think about our products, and our authors can see your feedback on the title that they have worked with Packt to create. It will only take a few minutes of your time, but is valuable to other potential customers, our authors, and Packt. Thank you!

Index

D

E

K

L

M

N

O

P

R

S

T

U

V

W

www.ingramcontent.com/pod-product-compliance
Lightning Source LLC
LaVergne TN
LVHW081515050326
832903LV00025B/1507

* 9 7 8 1 7 8 8 8 3 9 2 3 5 *